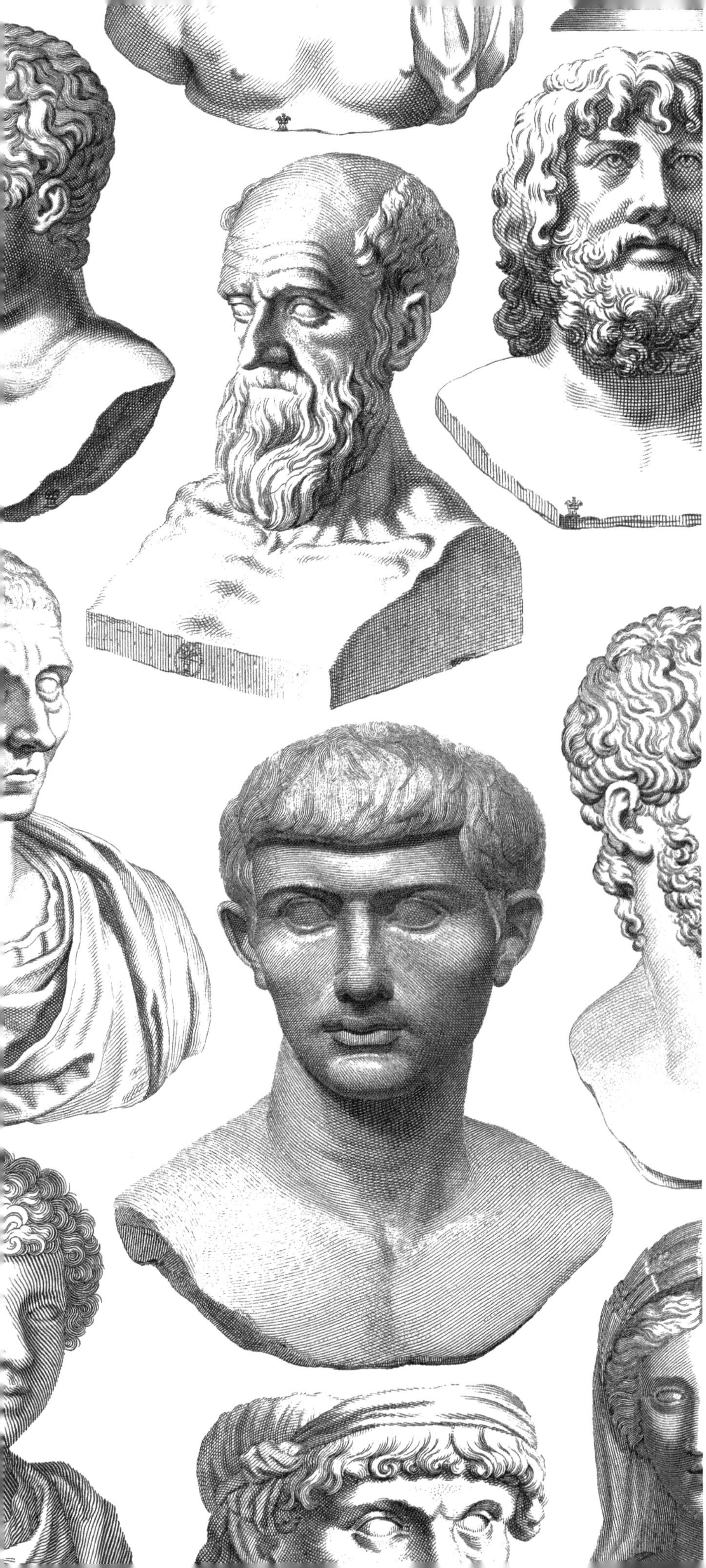

GREEK & ROMAN SCULPTURE

AN IMAGE ARCHIVE FOR ARTISTS *And* DESIGNERS

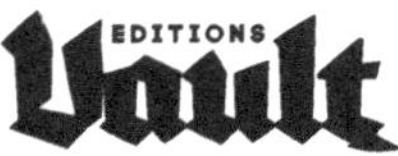

INTRODUCTION

Greek and Roman Sculpture: An Image Archive for Artists and Designers by Vault Editions is a brilliantly curated pictorial archive highlighting the incredibly detailed work of ancient Greek and Roman sculptors and the faithful depictions by 17th and 18th-century engravers.

This book features an extensive range of etchings and engravings. It depicts statues of prominent subjects including Bacchus, Minerva, Hercules, Venus, Apollo, Medusa, Plato, Julius Caesar, emperors, empresses, gladiators, athletes, heroes, and much more.

Features:
Each book comes with a unique download link providing instant access to high-resolution files of all 235 images featured. These images can be used in art and graphic design projects or printed and framed to make stunning decorative artworks. We promise you will be impressed with this pictorial archive.

About the author:
This book was curated and authored by the creative director of Vault Editions, Kale James. Kale has published over 30 acclaimed books within the art design space and has worked with brands including Nike, Samsung, Adidas and Rolling Stone. Kale's artwork is published in numerous titles, including No Cure, Semi-Permanent, Vogue and more.

This collection of vintage illustrations is an essential resource for all artists, collage artists, graphic designers, tattooists and fantasy artists looking to take their artwork to the next level.

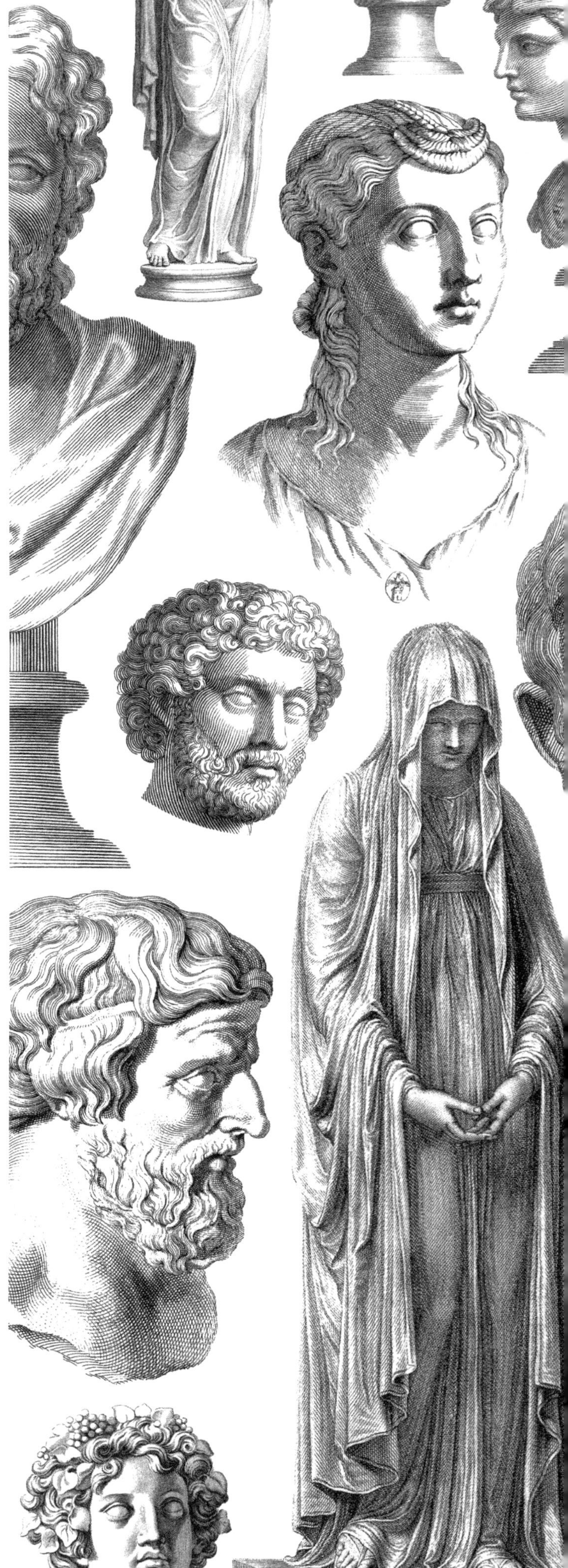

PREFACE

The ancient Greeks learned the art of sculpture from the Egyptians. Initially, they worked in the Egyptian style, creating figures that copied their rigid poses and forward-facing gaze. The distinctive classical Greek aesthetic emerged over centuries and celebrated freedom of movement, idealised proportions and a sense of harmony and balance.

Ancient Greek sculptors worked using limestone, marble, bronze, wood, terracotta and a combination of gold and ivory known as chryselephantine. Most of the statues that survive today are made of marble. You may think that Greek statues are designed to be unadorned and monochromatic, as we see them presented in museums and galleries today, but this is far from what the ancient Greeks conceptualised.

Statues were painted and decorated with life-like accessories, such as hair and eyelashes made of a metal such as copper. Looking at an ancient Greek statue today, you may wonder why it doesn't have any carved eye details, but at the time, eyes would be painted or created using ivory and glass stones. Clothing was painted using bright colours and decorated with patterns. Some statues still bear fragments of the ancient pigments, allowing today's audiences to enjoy an authentic reproduction of the original work. Once painted, it was ready to be adorned with relevant accessories, like swords and shields for a soldier's statue or a victor's wreath for an athlete.

GREEK & ROMAN SCULPTURE

VAULT EDITIONS

DOWNLOAD YOUR FILES

Downloading your files is simple. To access your digital files, please go to the last page of this book and follow the instructions.

For technical assistance, please email:
info@vaulteditions.com

Copyright
Copyright © Vault Editions Ltd 2022.

Bibliographical Note

This book is a new work created by Vault Editions Ltd.

ISBN: 978-1-925968-87-3

01

02

03

04

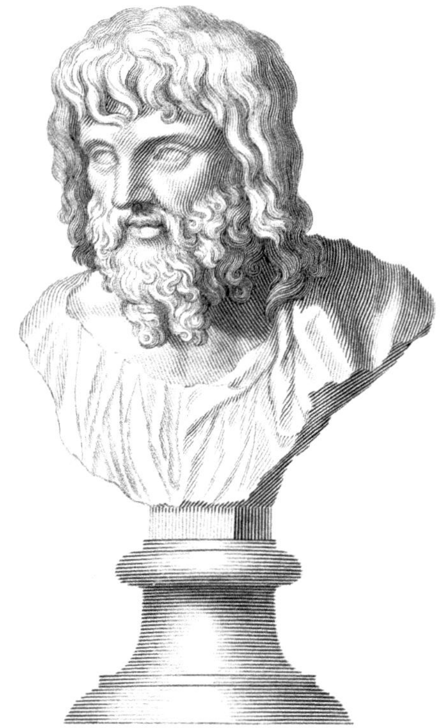

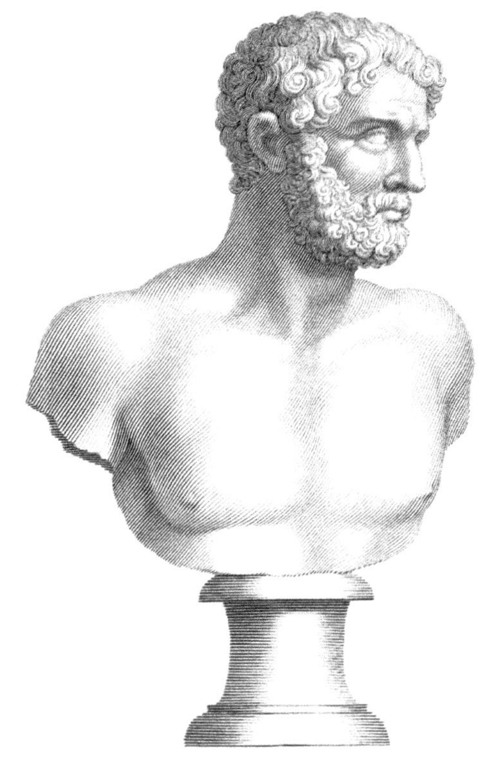

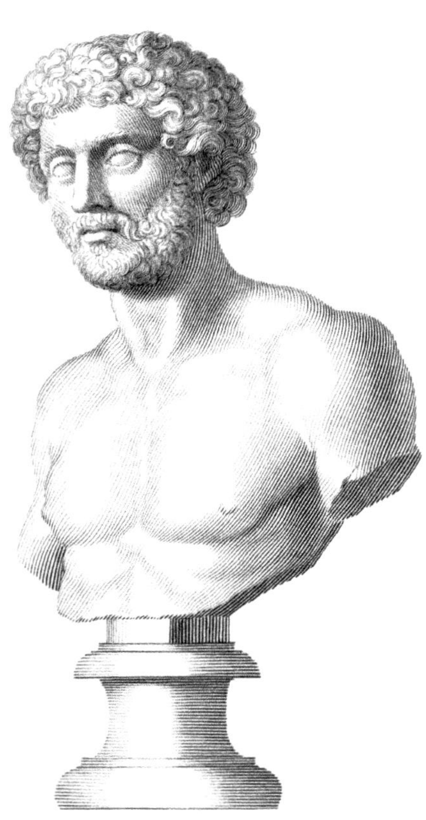

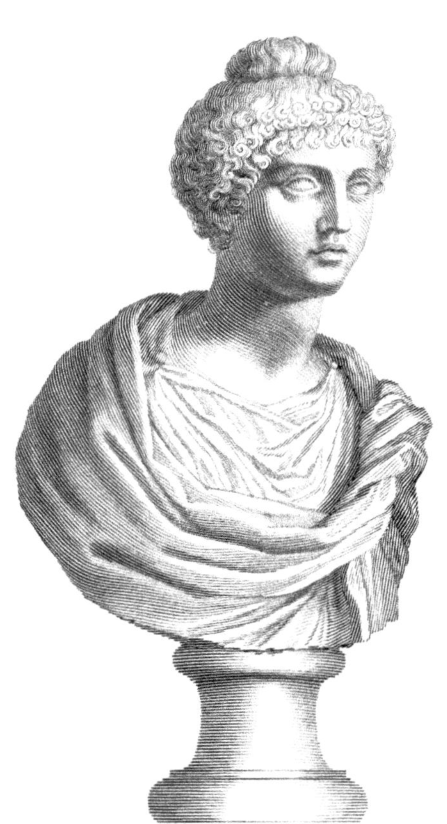

01. Antique bust of a bearded man, Etienne Baudet, 1678.

02. Antique bust of a bearded man, Etienne Baudet, 1679.

03. Antique bust of a bearded man, Etienne Baudet, 1681.

04. Antique bust of a Greek woman, Etienne Baudet, 1679.

05

06

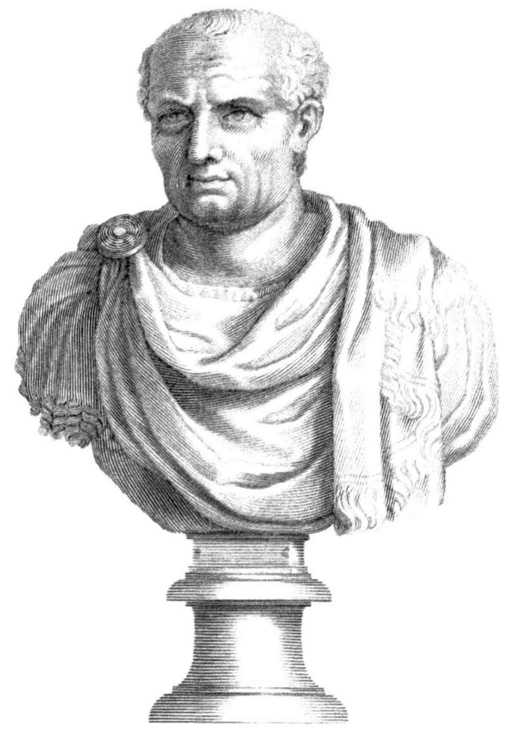

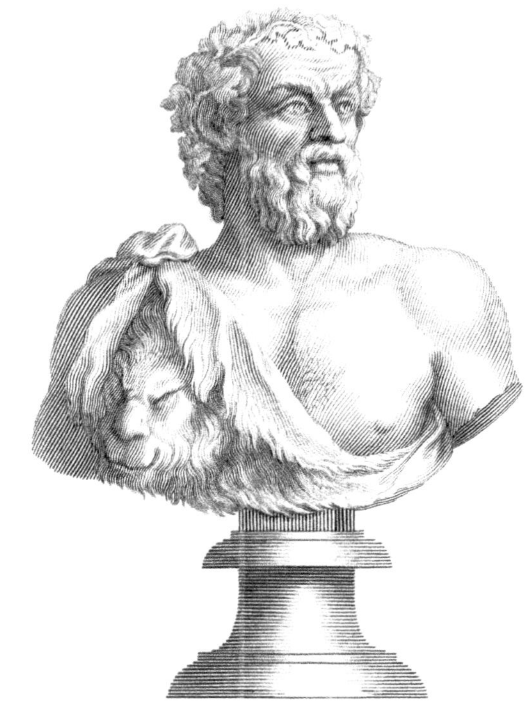

07

08

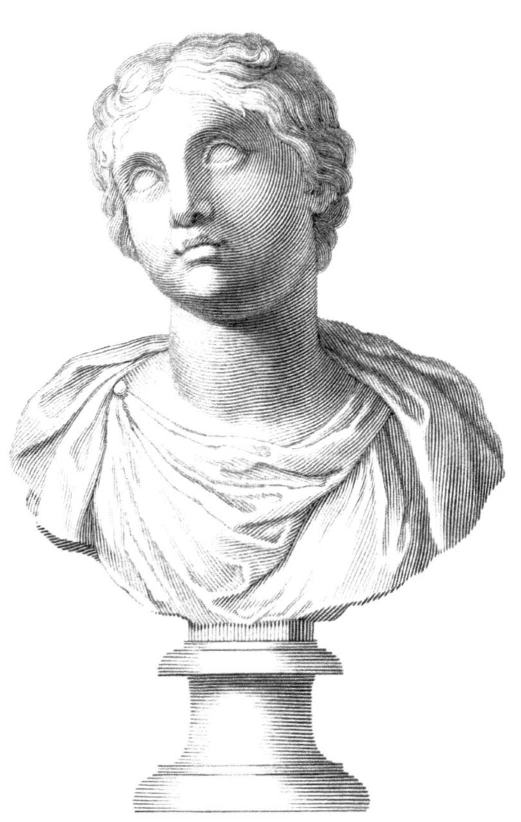

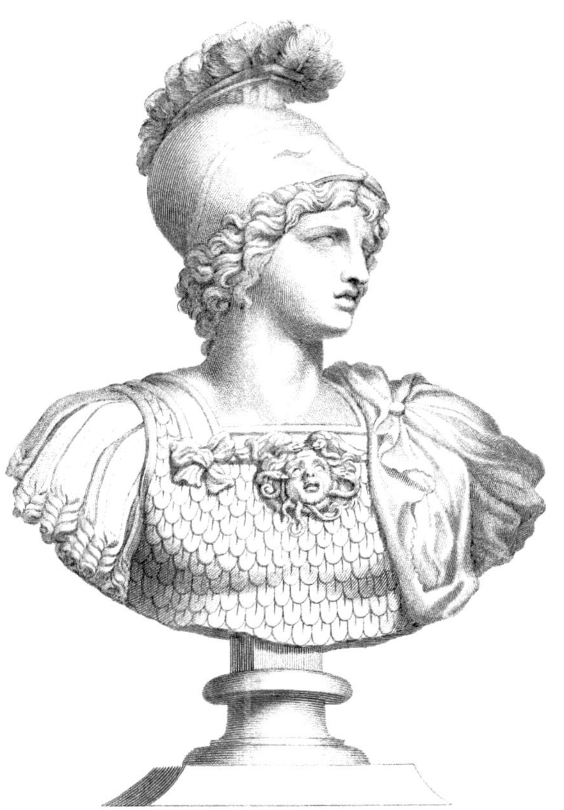

05. Antique bust of a Roman consul, Etienne Baudet, 1679.

06. Antique bust of a faun, Etienne Baudet, 1678.

07. Antique bust of a Roman woman, Etienne Baudet, 1680.

08. Antique bust of Alexander the Great, Etienne Baudet, 1677.

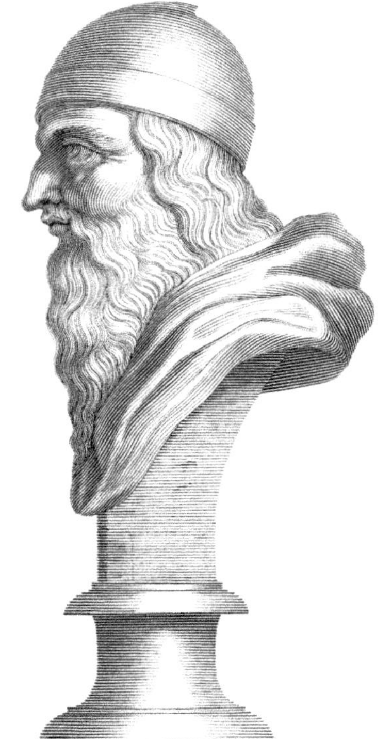

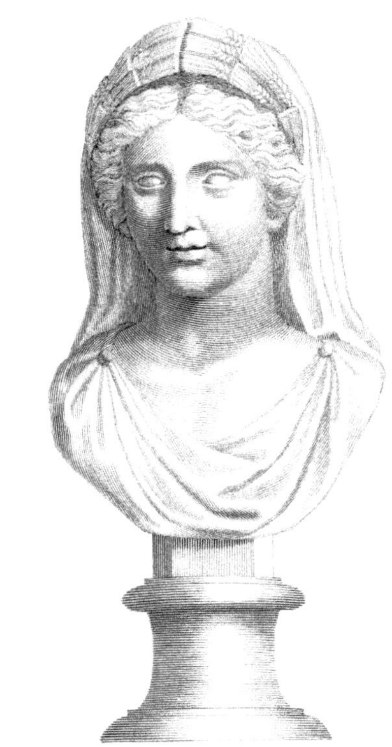

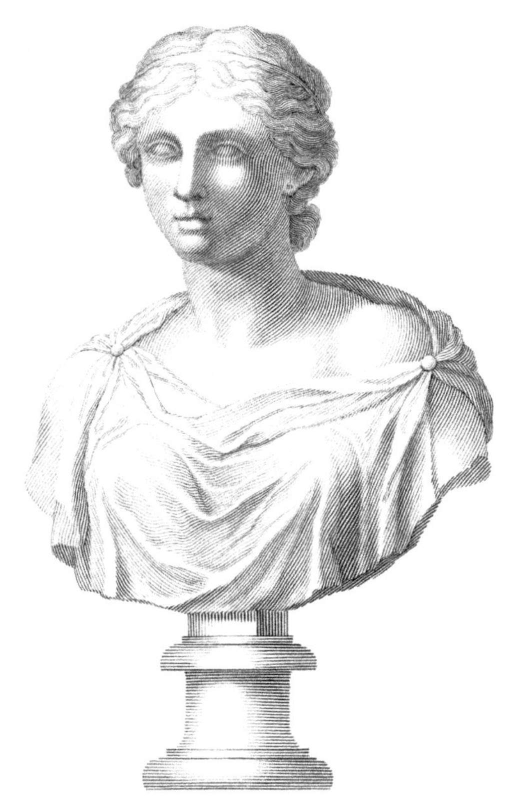

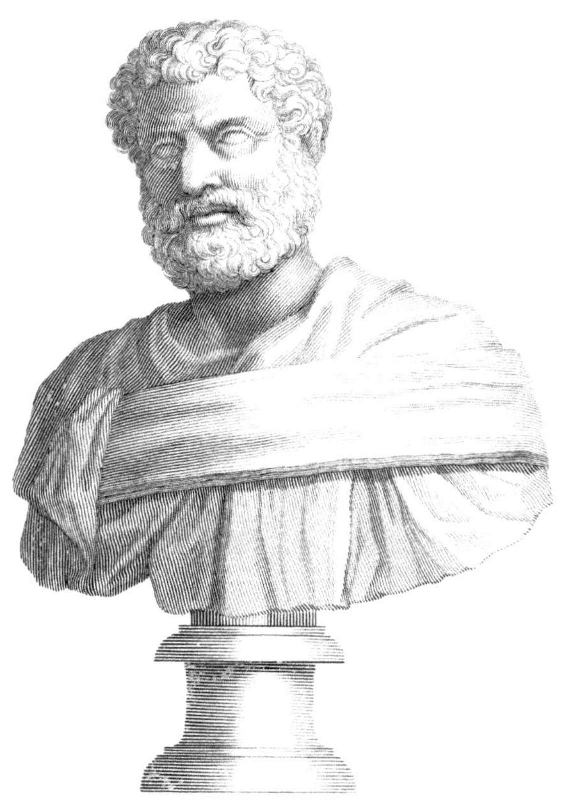

09. Antique bust of Aristotle, Etienne Baudet, 1678.

10. Antique bust of Ceres, Etienne Baudet, 1677.

11. Antique bust of Cleopatra, Etienne Baudet, 1680.

12. Antique bust of Clodius Albinus, Etienne Baudet, 1681.

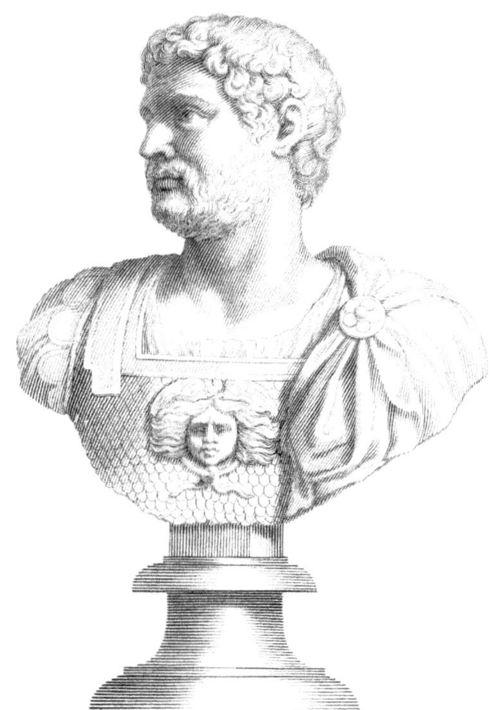

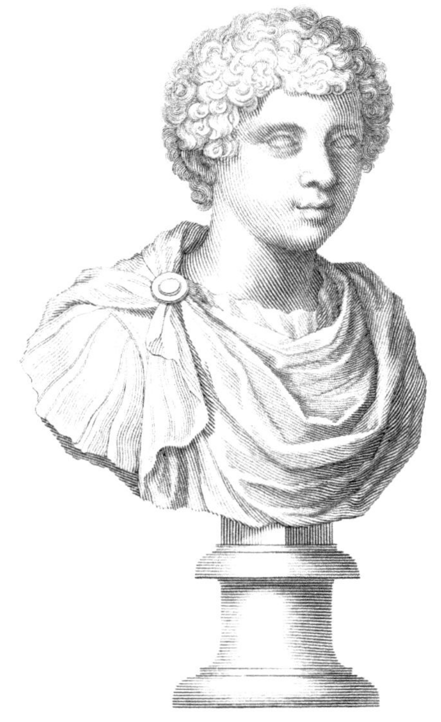

15

16

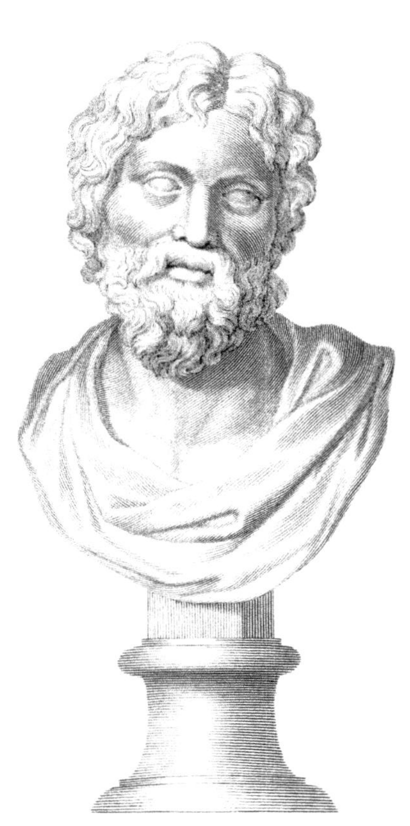

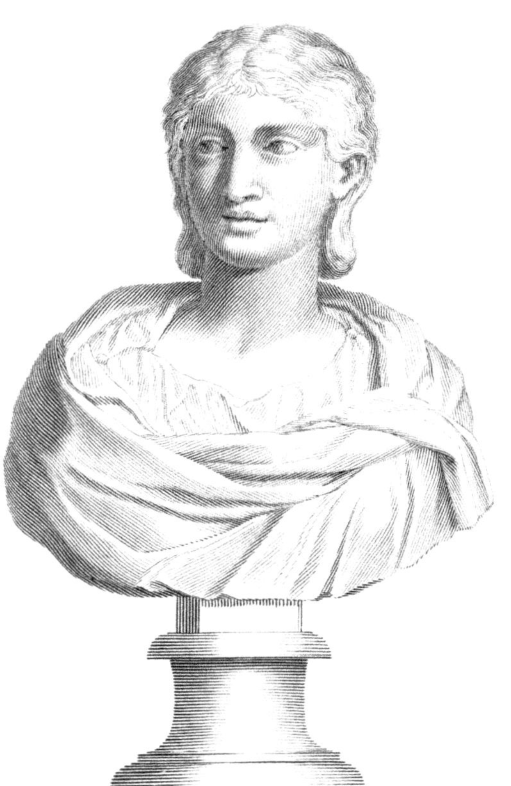

13. Antique bust of Emperor Hadrian, Etienne Baudet, 1678.

14. Antique bust of Geta, Etienne Baudet, 1680.

15. Antique bust of Isocrates, Etienne Baudet, 1677.

16. Antique bust of Julia Soaemias, Etienne Baudet, 1679.

17

18

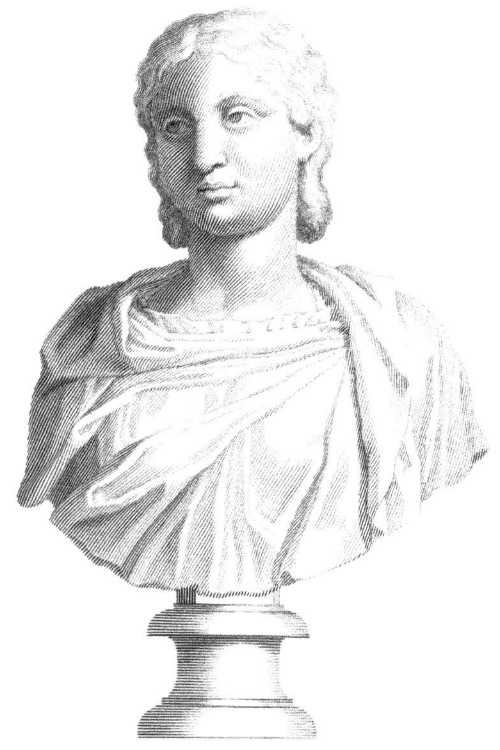

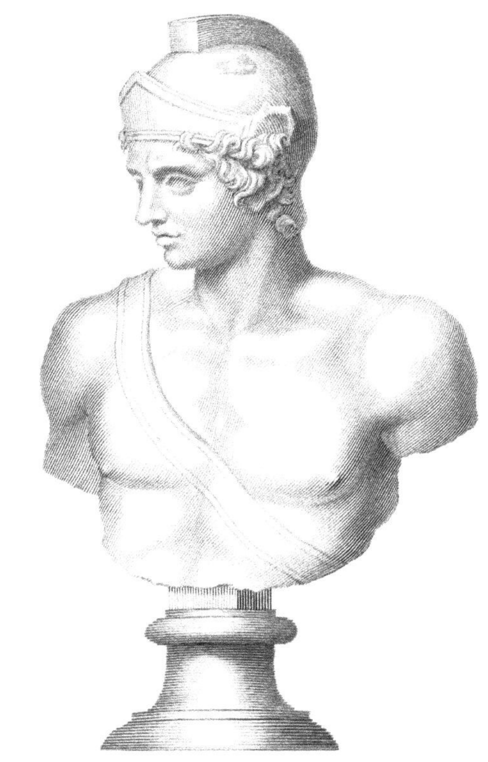

19

20

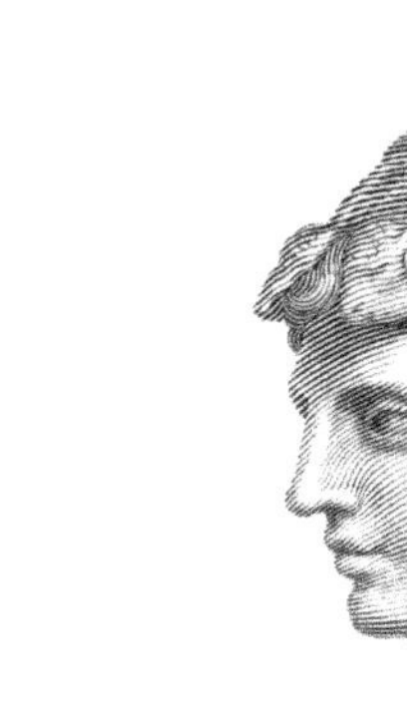

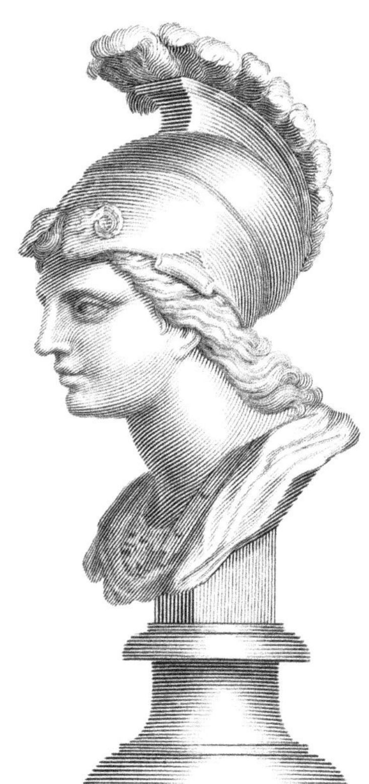

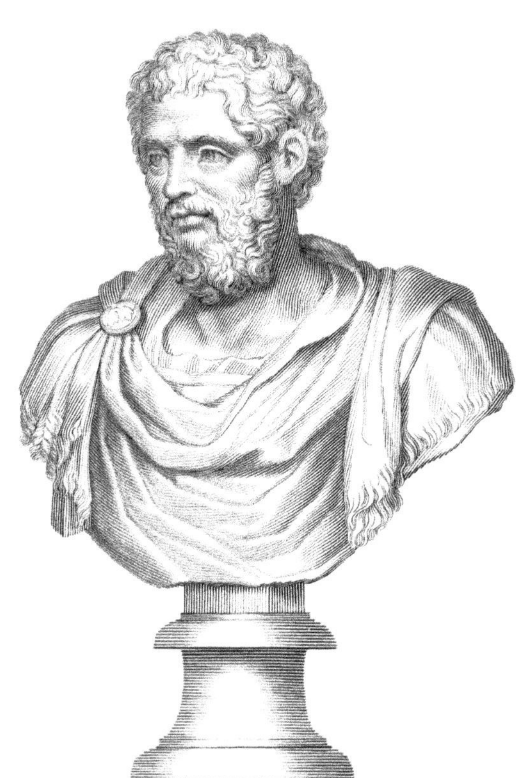

17. Antique bust of Livia, Etienne Baudet, 1681.

18. Antique bust of Mars, Etienne Baudet, 1677.

19. Antique bust of Minerva, Etienne Baudet, 1678.

20. Antique bust of Severus, Etienne Baudet, 1678.

21

22

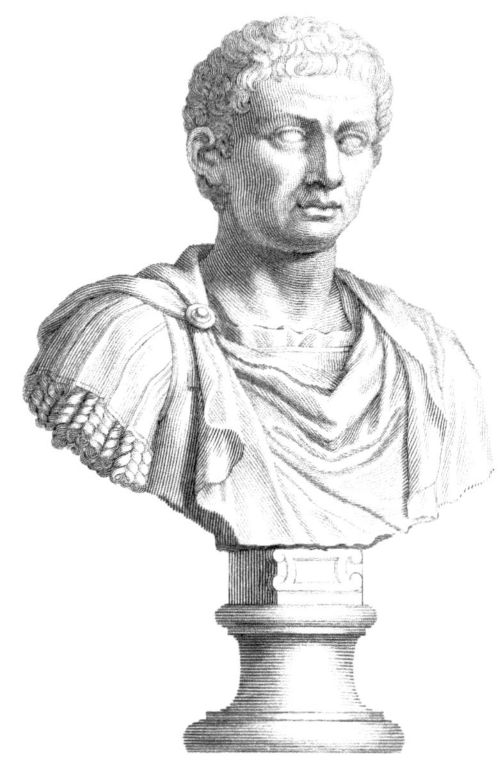

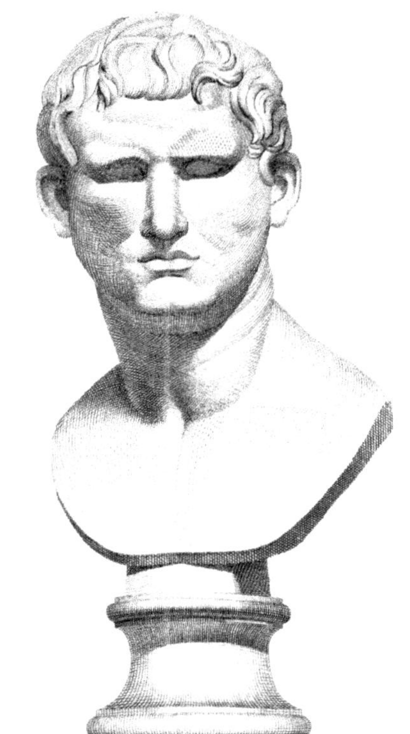

23

24

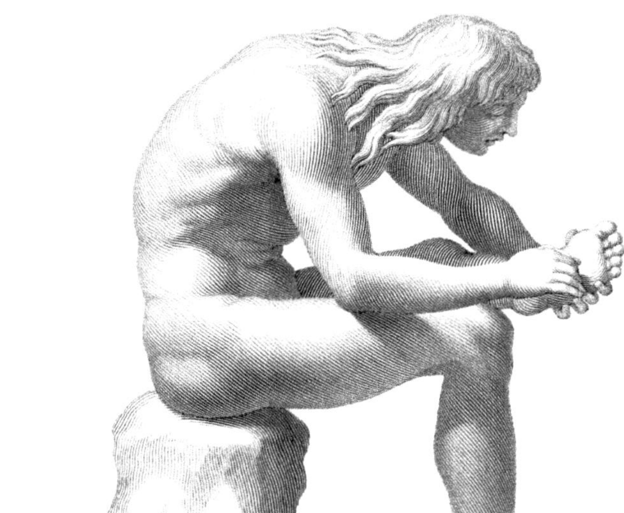

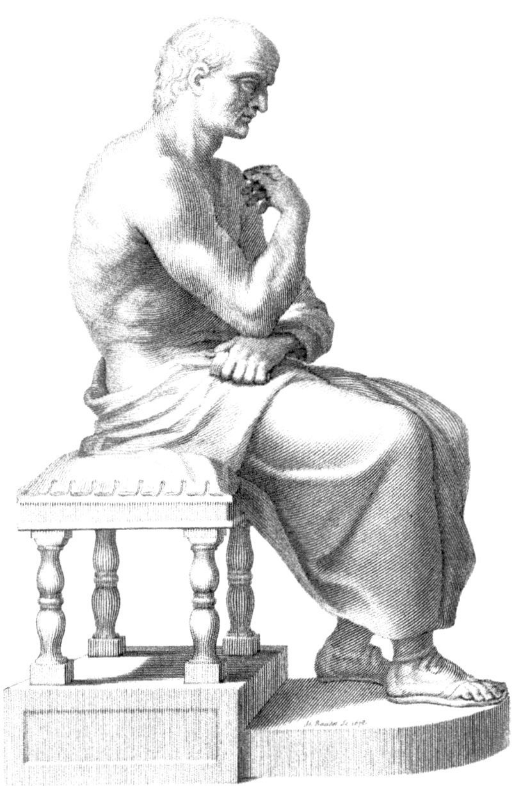

21. Antique bust of Trajan, Etienne Baudet, 1680.

22. Antique bust, Jean Théodore Joseph Linnig, 1825 – 1891.

23. Antique statue of a boy with a thorn in the foot (Spinario), Etienne Baudet, 1678.

24. Antique statue of a Roman senator after bathing, Etienne Baudet, 1678.

25

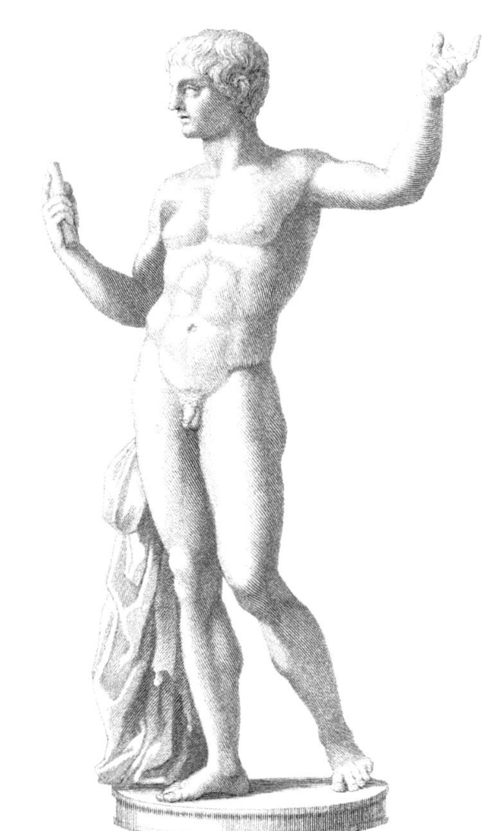

26

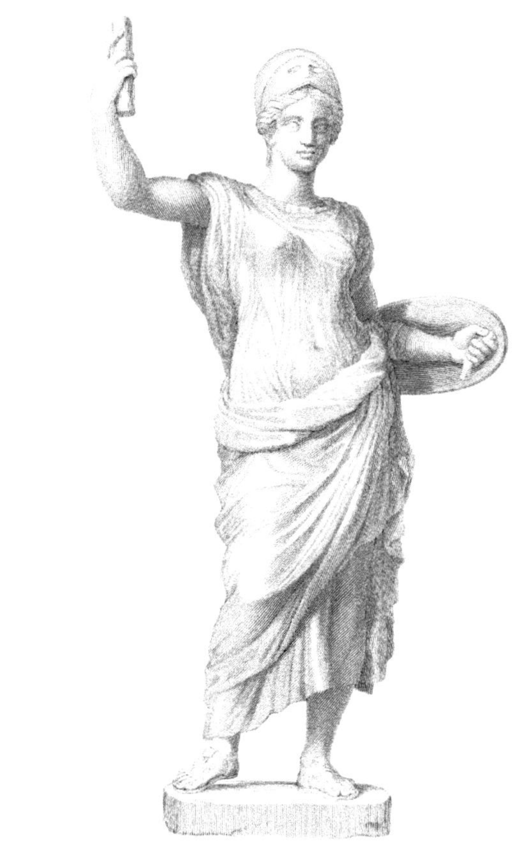

27

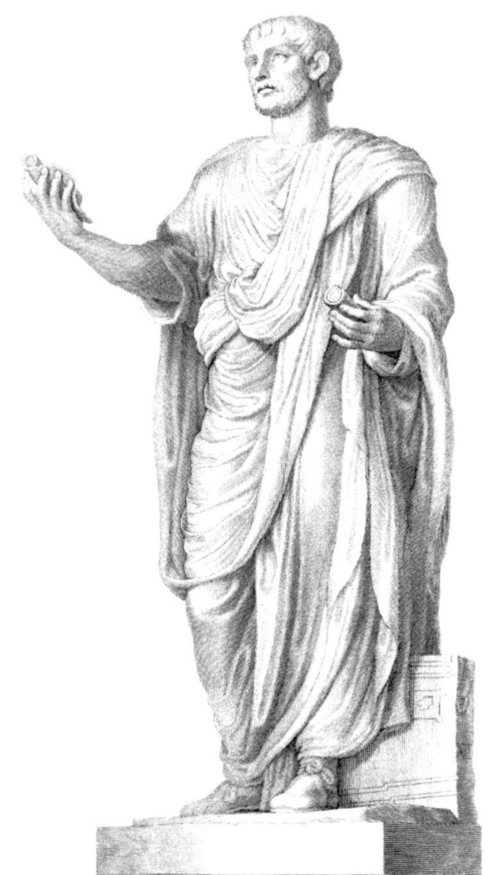

28

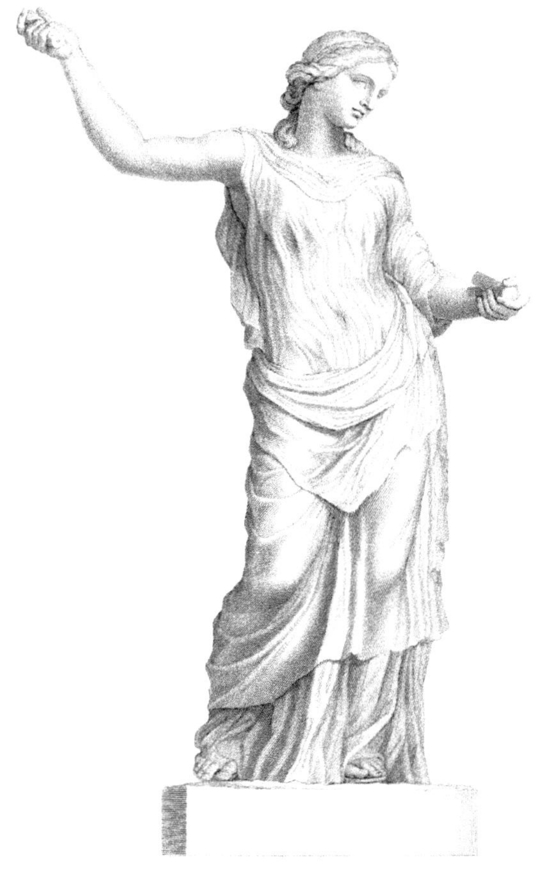

25. Antique statue of a young man, Etienne Baudet, 1680.

26. Antique statue of Pallas Athene, Etienne Baudet, 1680.

27. Antique Statue of a Roman Senator, Etienne Baudet, 1677.

28. Antique statue of a woman, Etienne Baudet, 1677.

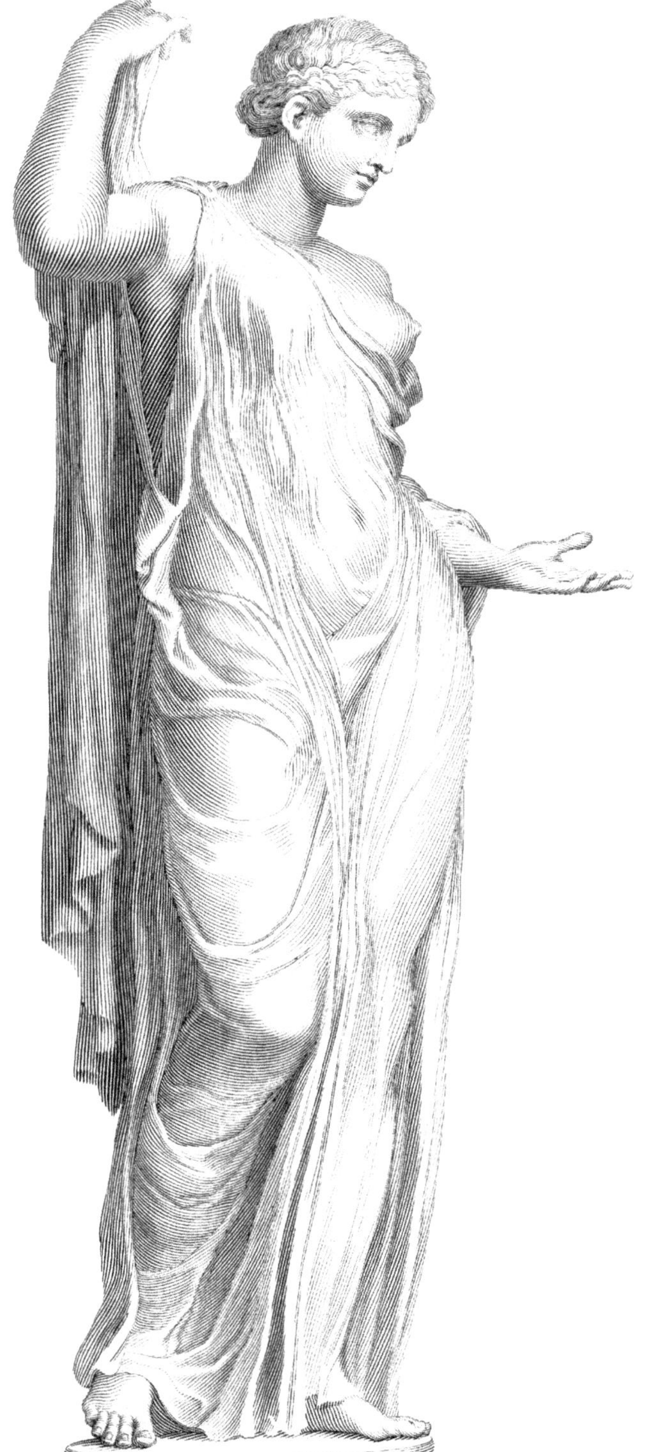

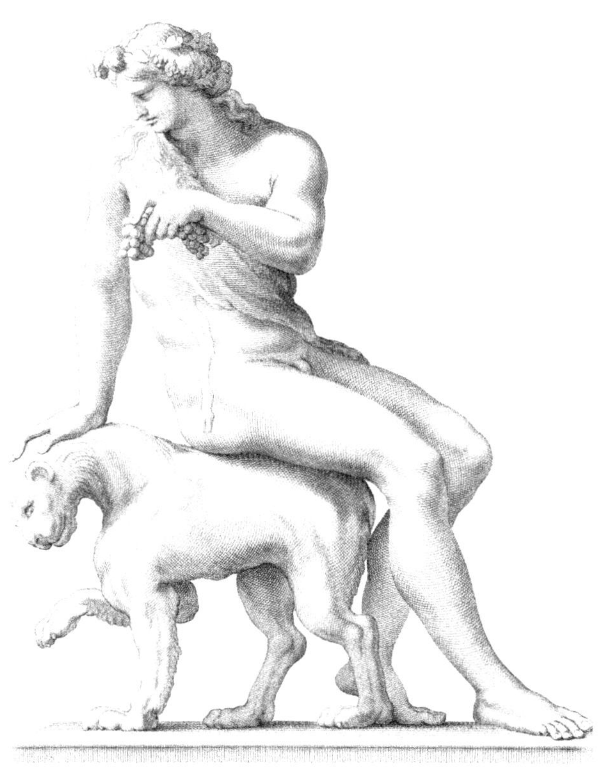

31

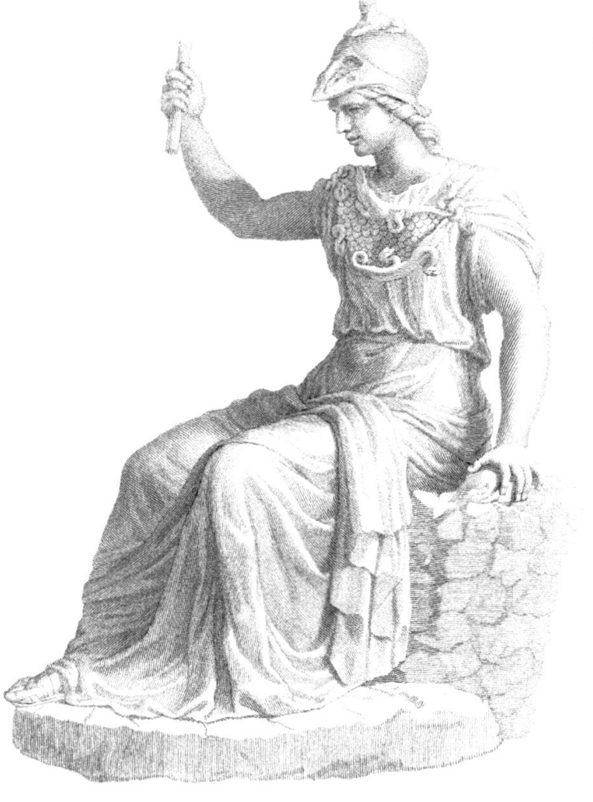

29. Antique Statue of a Woman, Etienne Baudet, 1678.

30. Bacchus Sitting on a Tiger, Cornelis Bloemaert (II), after Francois Perrier, c. 1636.

31. Antique statue of Minerva, Etienne Baudet, 1681.

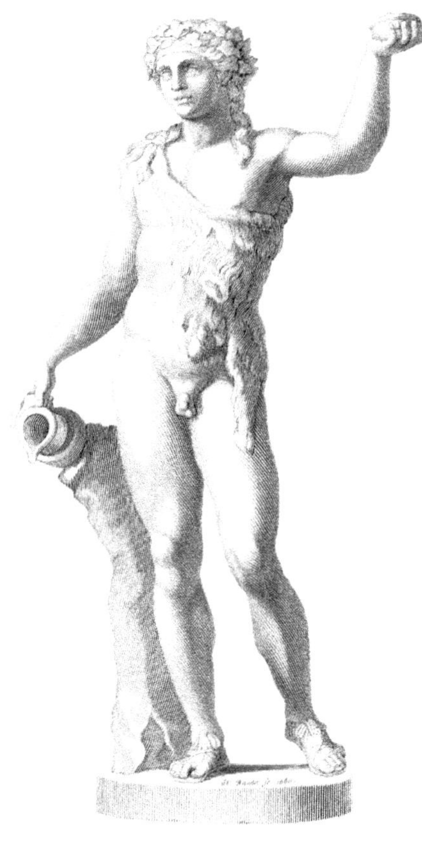

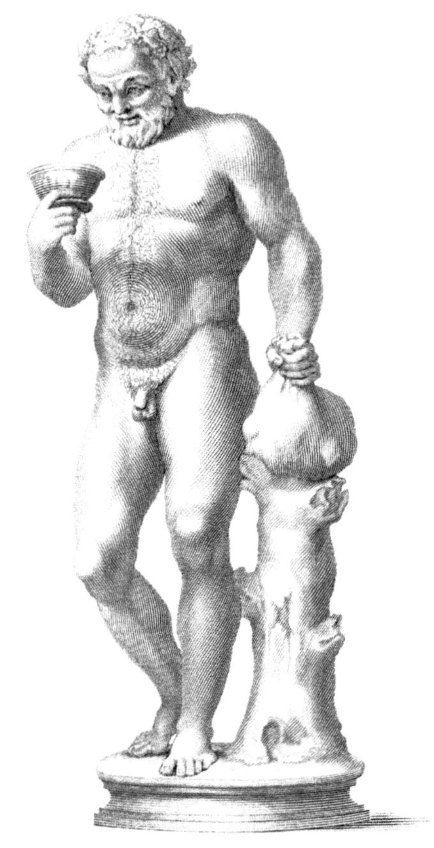

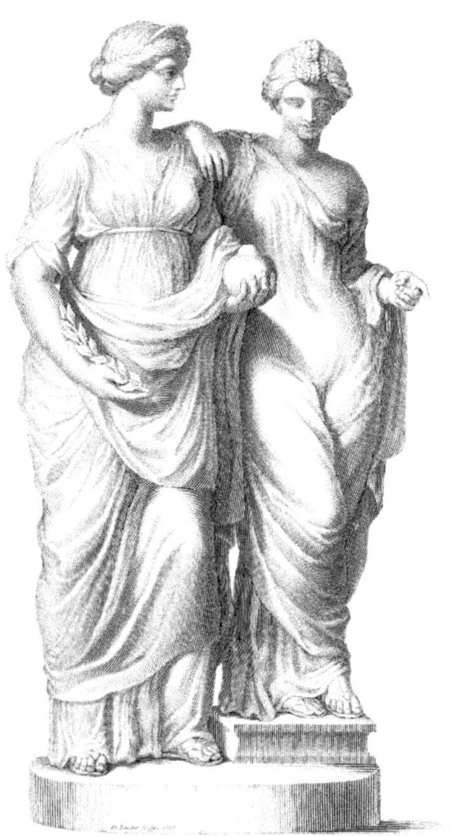

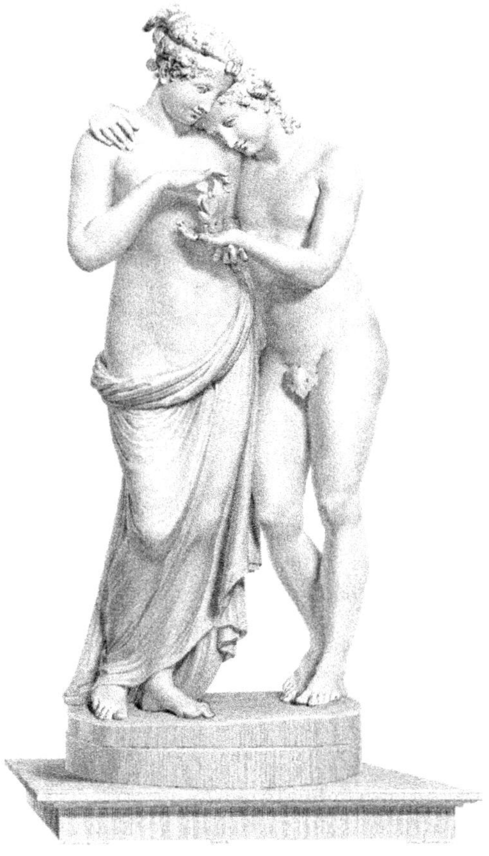

32. Antique statue of Bacchus, Etienne Baudet, 1680.

33. Antique Statue of Silenus, Etienne Baudet, 1678.

34. Antique statue of two Hesperides, Etienne Baudet, 1678.

35. Amor and Psyche, Domenico Marchetti, after Giovanni Tognolli, after Antonio Canova, 1814.

36

37

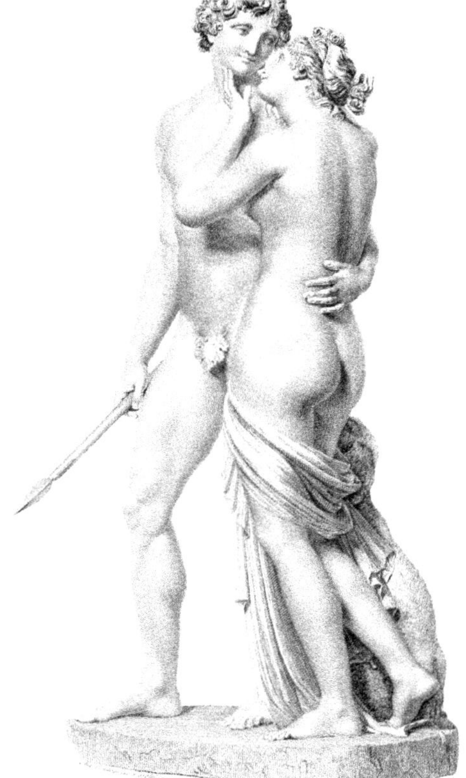

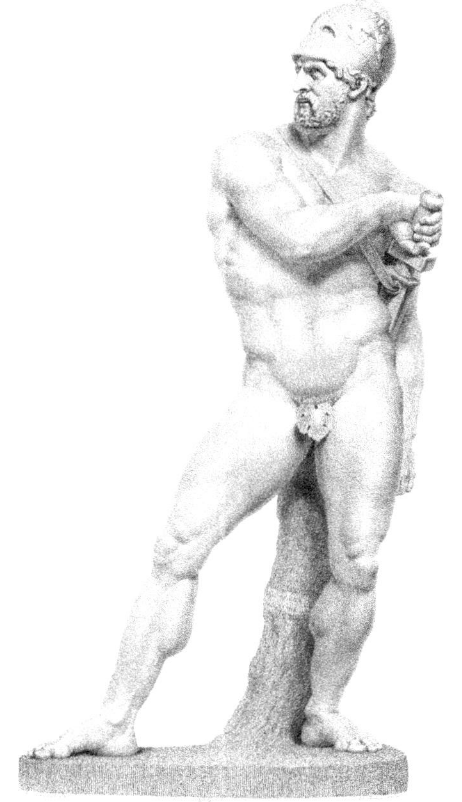

38

39

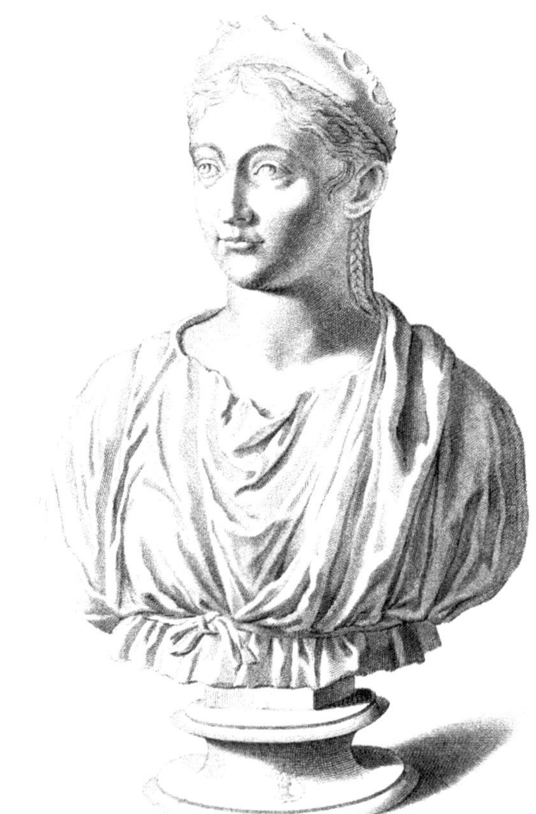

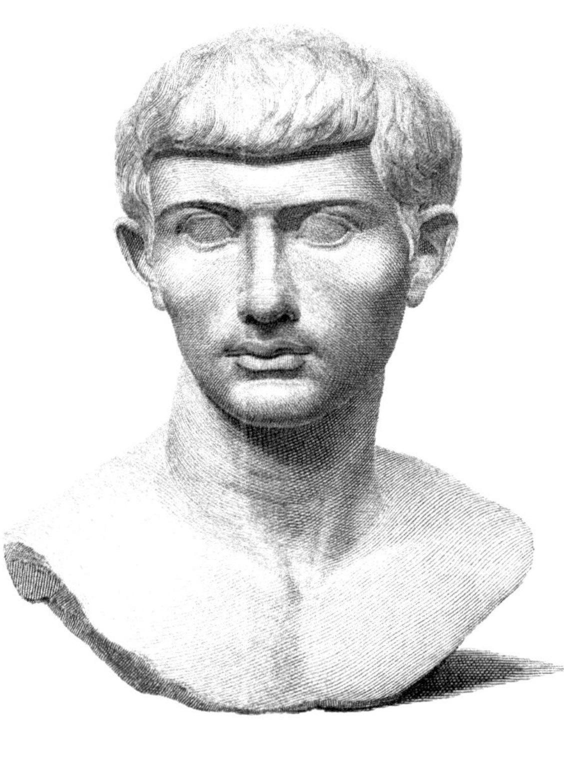

36. Adonis Says Goodbye to Venus Before the Hunt, Giovanni Tognolli, 1793 – 1838.

37. Ajax, Pietro Fontana, after Giovanni Tognolli, after Antonio Canova, 1772 – 1837.

38. Bust of a young woman with a diadem, Theodor Matham, 1640.

39. Bust of a sculpture of a man, Lubertus Teunis van Deth, 1824 – 1875.

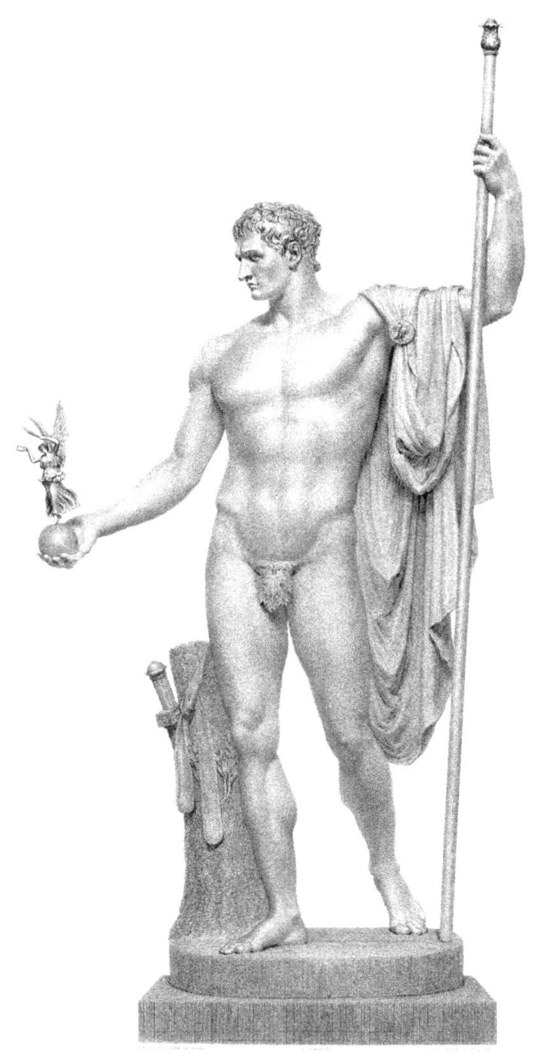

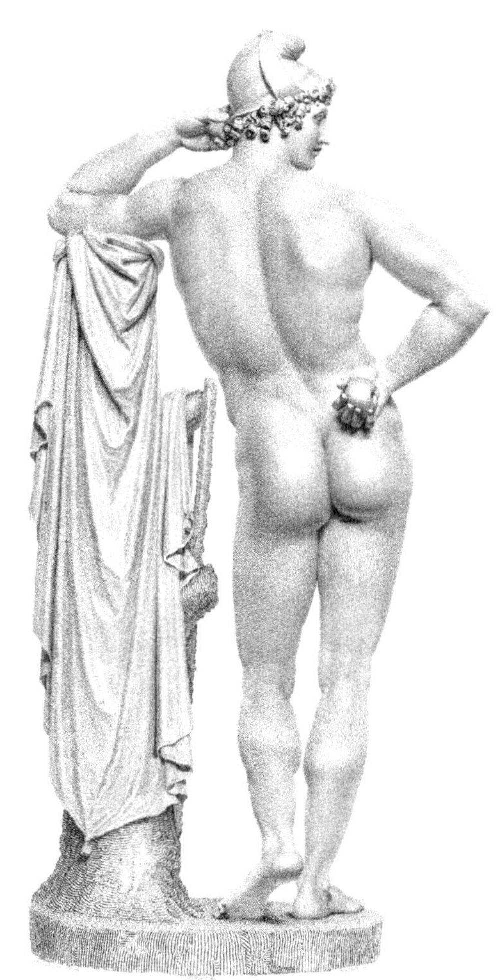

42

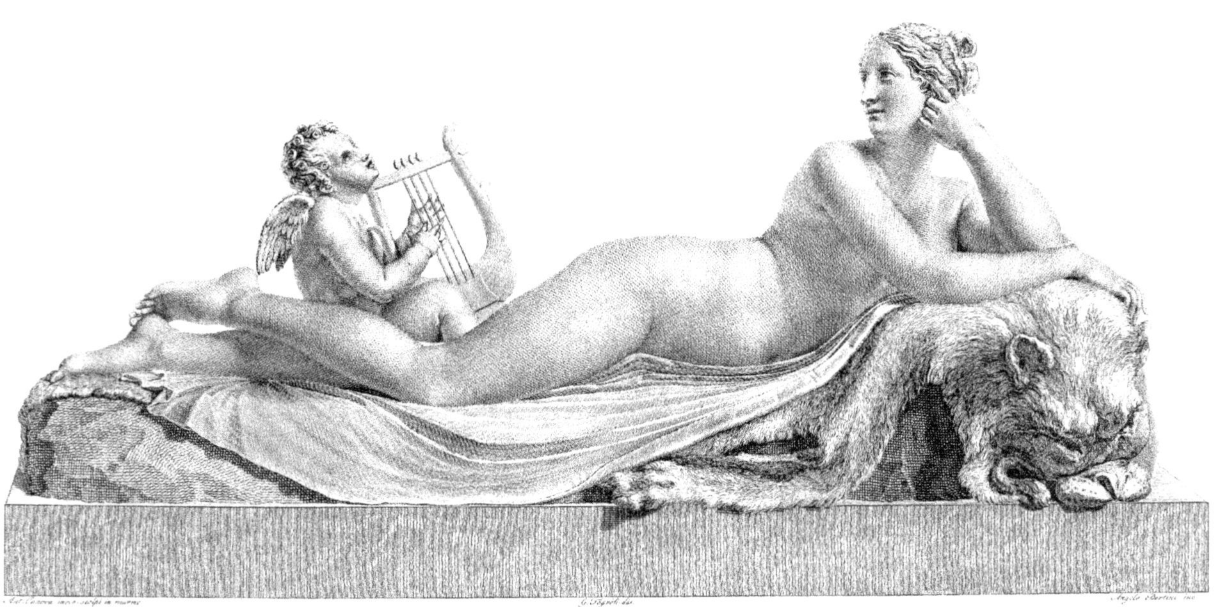

40. Napoleon as Peacemaking March, Antonio Ricciani, after Giovanni Tognolli, 1785 – 1836.

41. Paris, Angelo Testa, after Giovanni Tognolli, after Antonio Canova, in or after 1785.

42. Naiade, Angelo Bertini, after Antonio Canova, after Giovanni Tognolli, 1793 – 1838.

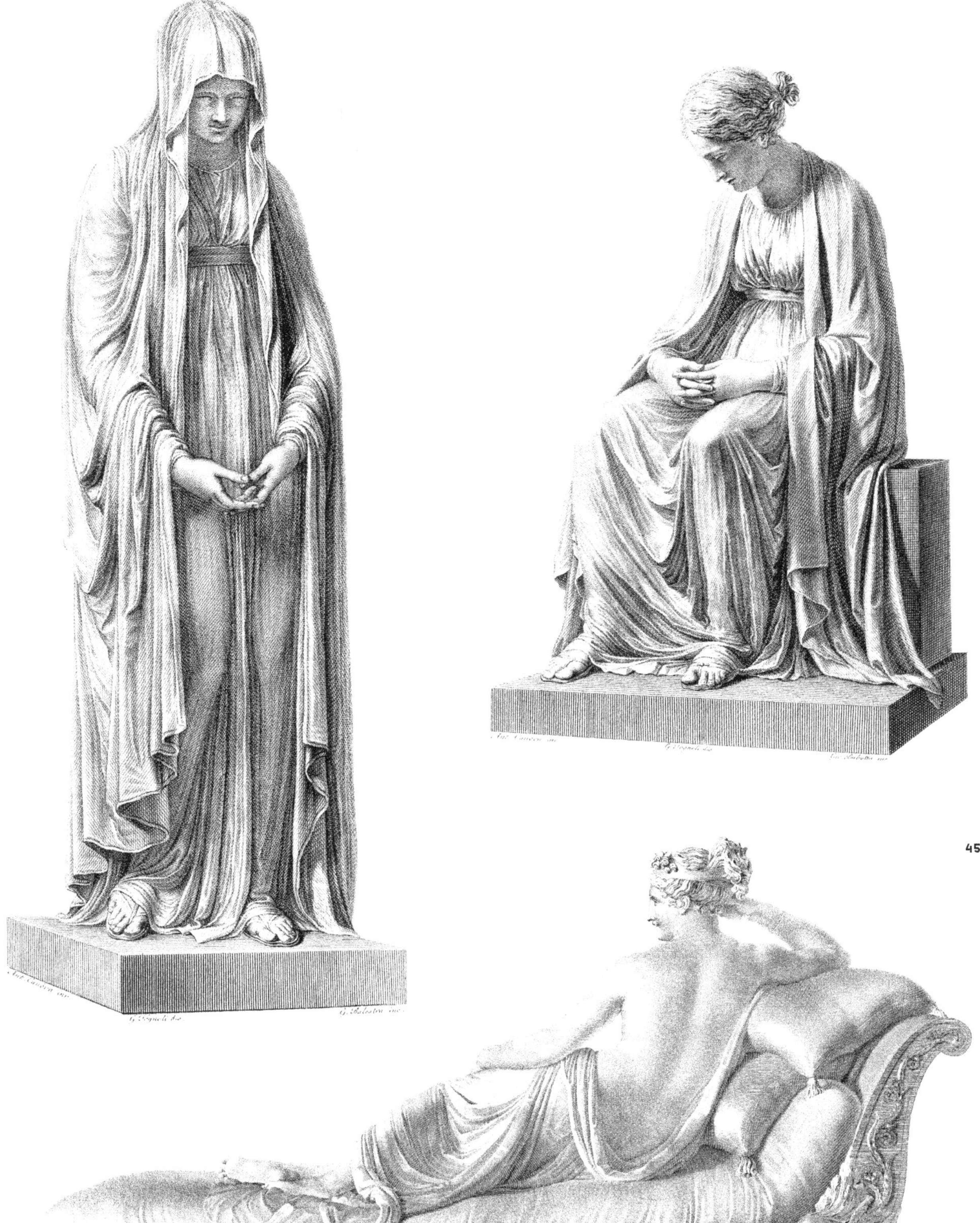

45

43. Pietas, Giovanni Balestra, after Antonio Canova, after Giovanni Tognolli, 1784 – 1842.

44. Mansuetudine, Giovanni Balestra, after Giovanni Tognolli, 1784 – 1842.

45. Pauline Borghese Bonaparte as Venus Victrix, Angelo Bertini, after Luigi Durantini, 1816.

46

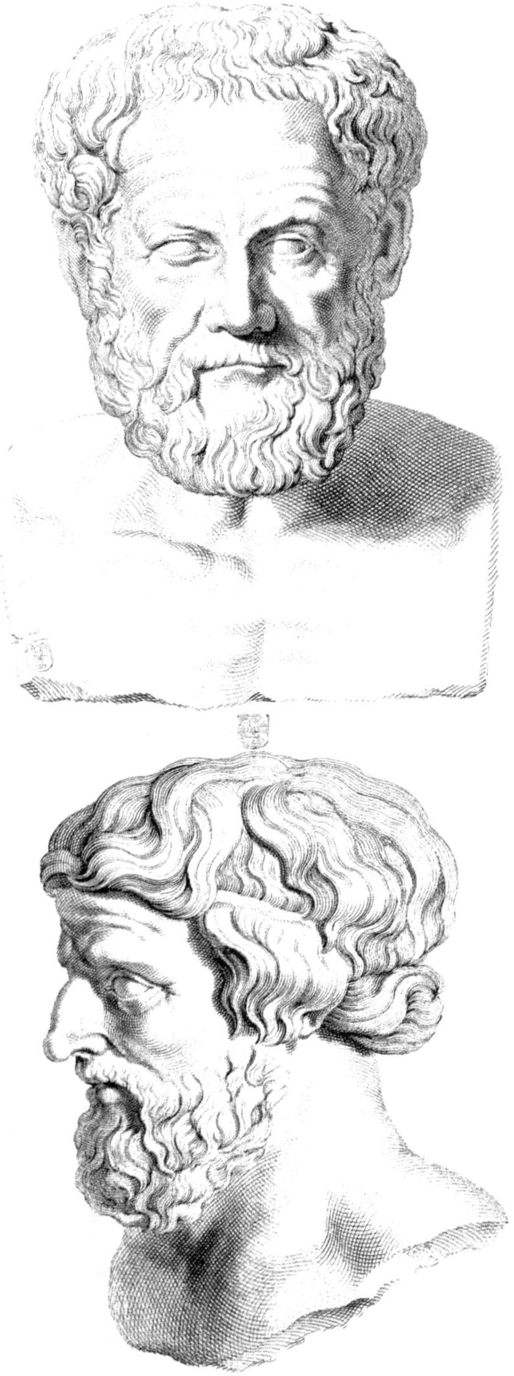

47

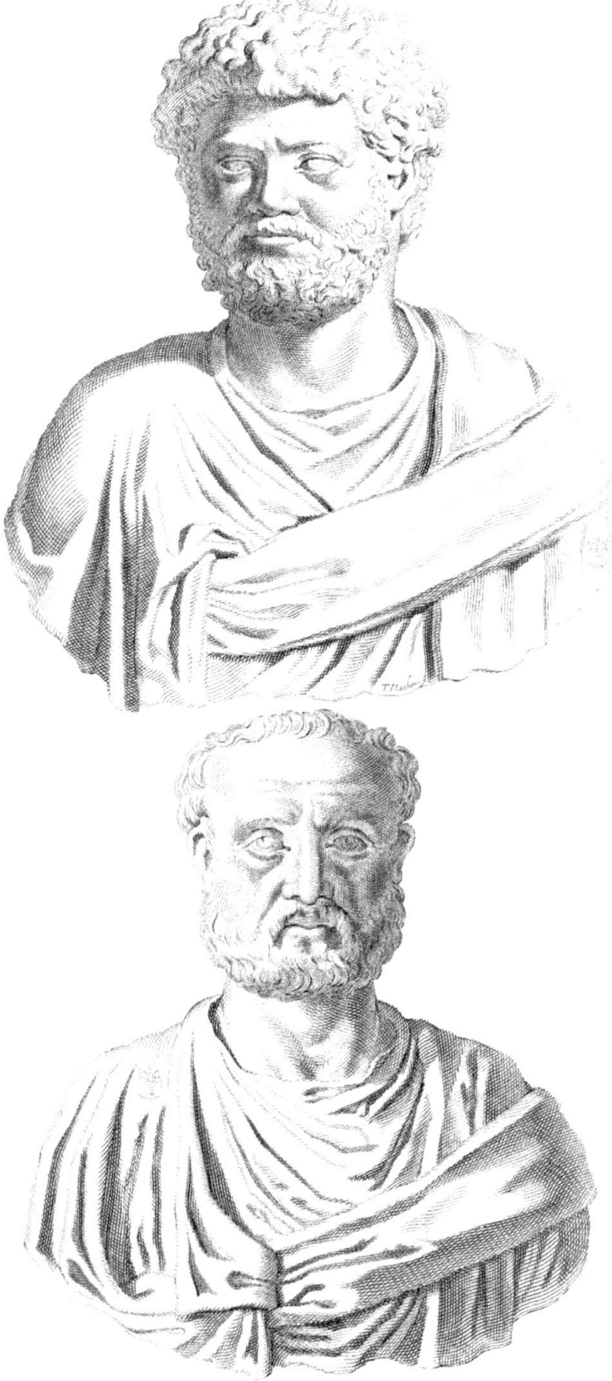

46. Busts of two bearded men, Theodor Matham, 1640.

47. Busts of Seianus and an Unknown Man, Theodor Matham, 1640.

48

49

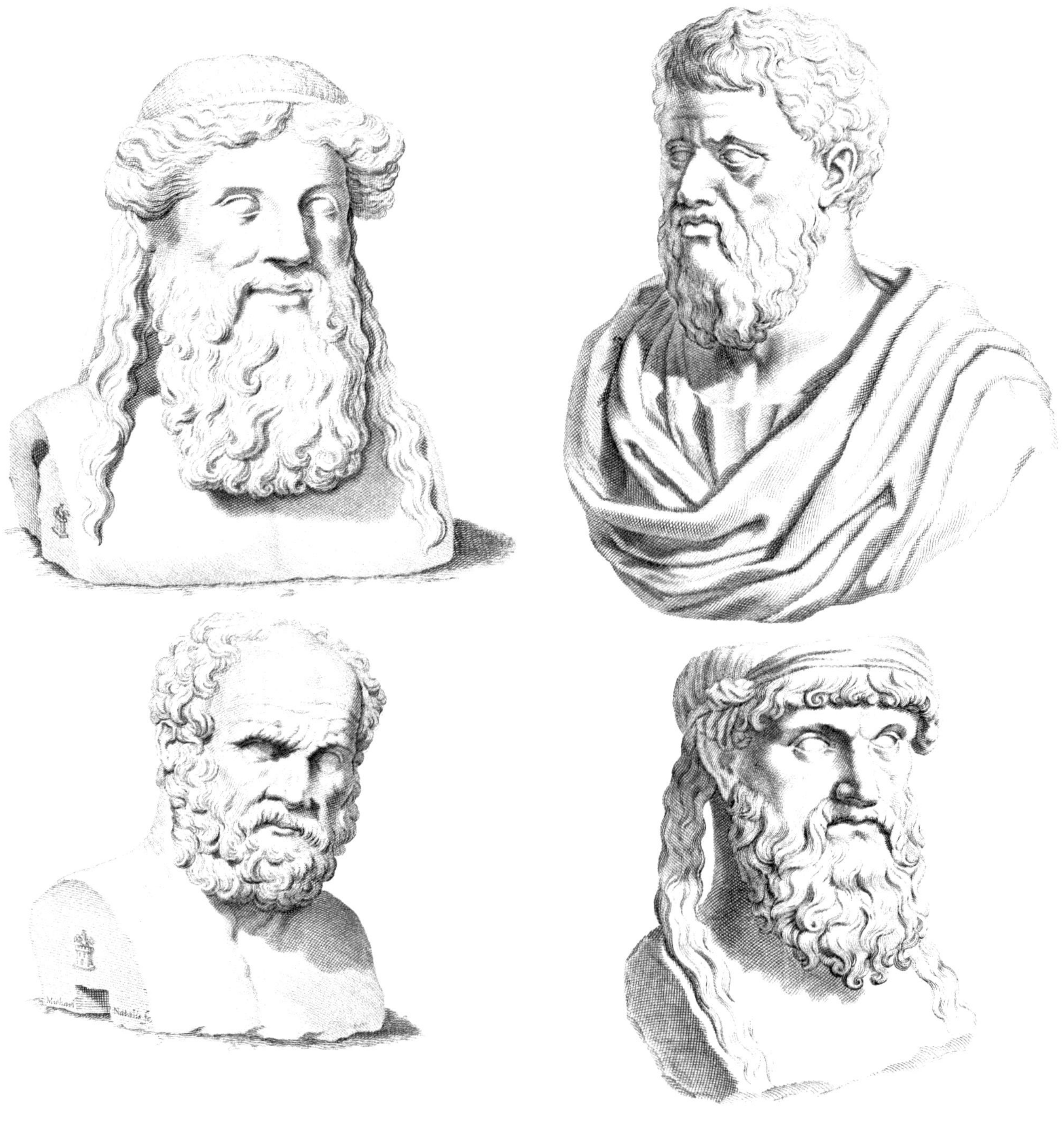

48. Busts of Plato and Diogenes, Michel Natalis, 1640.

49. Busts of Plato and an unknown philosopher, Theodor Matham, 1640.

GREEK AND ROMAN SCULPTURE

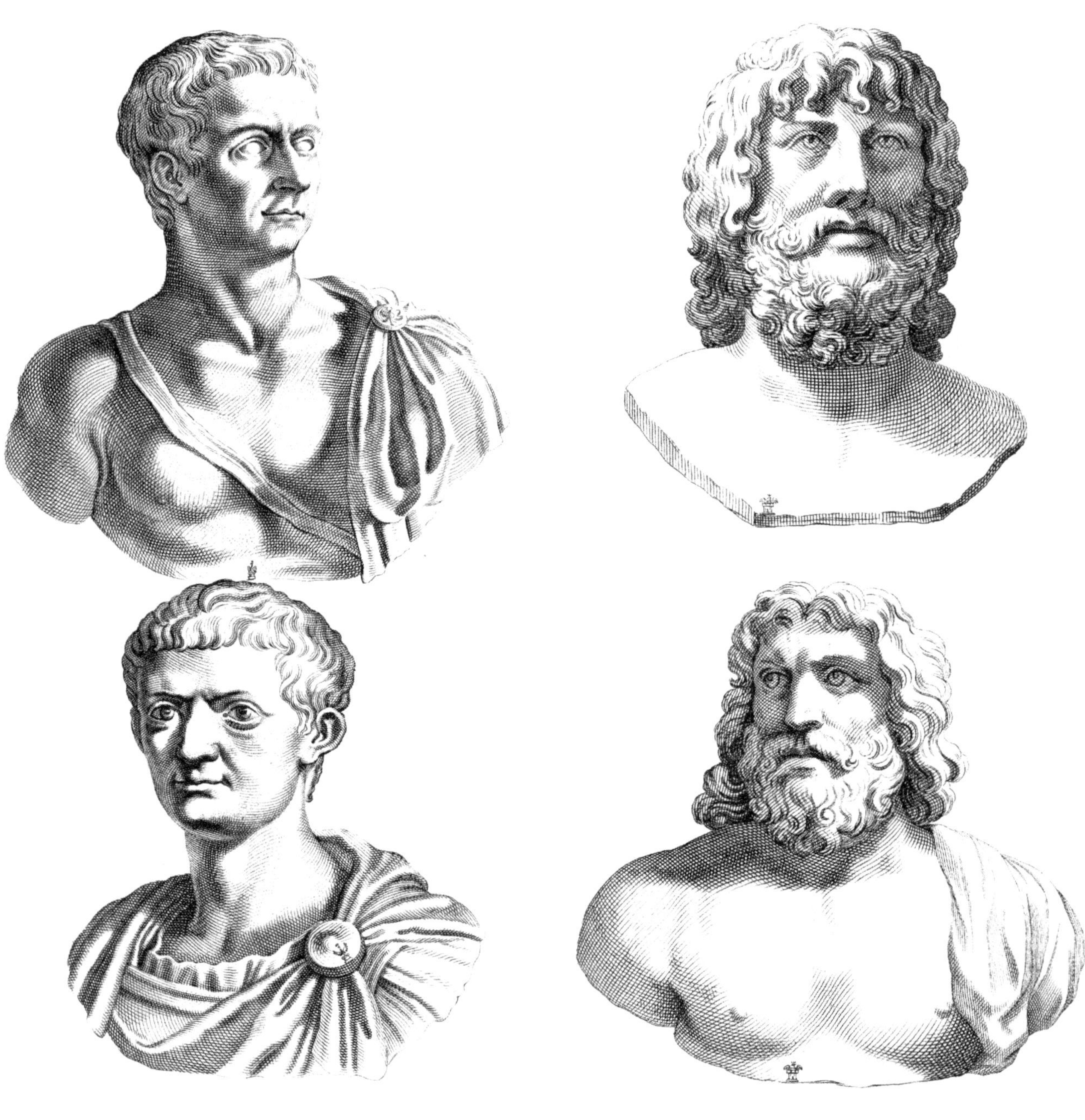

50. Busts of Pindar and Antoninus Pius, Theodor
Matham, 1636 – 1647.

51. Busts of two men, Anna Maria Valani, 1636
– 1647.

52

53

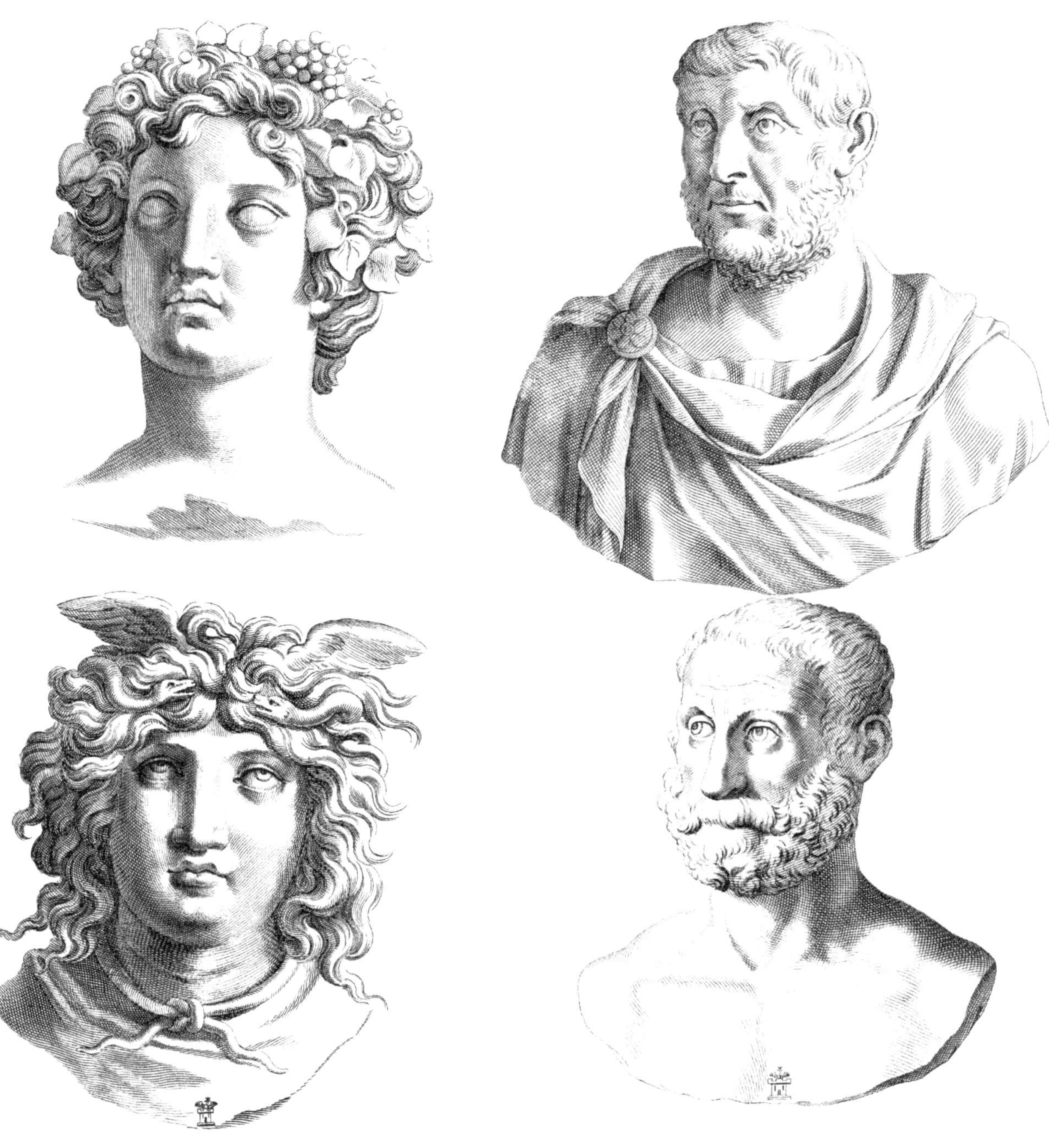

52. Busts of Agrippina and Livia, Theodor
Matham, 1636 – 1647.

53. Busts of Hercules and an Unknown Man,
Joan Comin, 1636 – 1647.

54

55

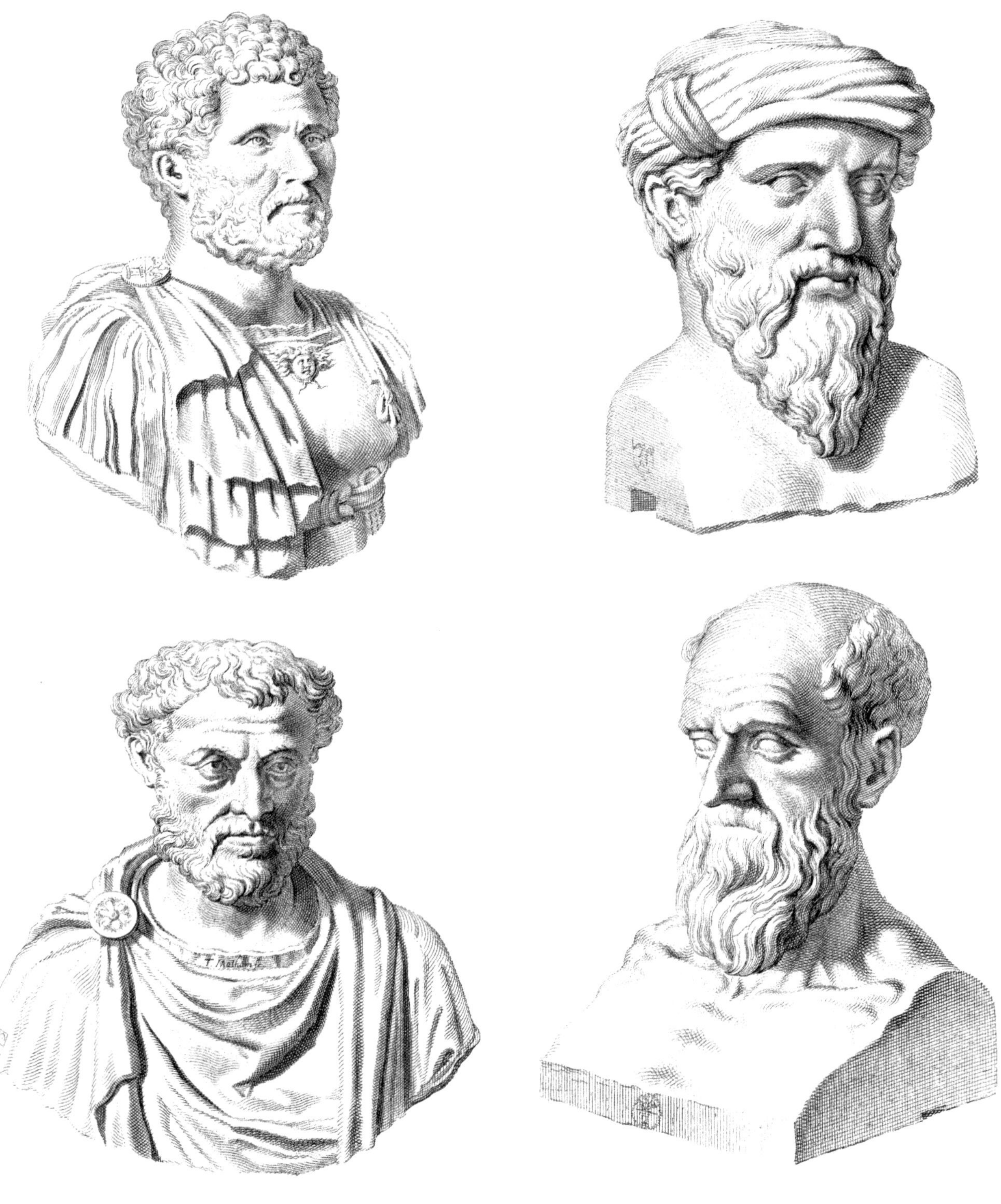

54. Bustes van Pupienus en Balbinus, Theodor
Matham, 1640.

55. Busts of Apollo, Michel Natalis, after Giovanni
Citosiblo Guidi, 1636 – 1647.

56

57

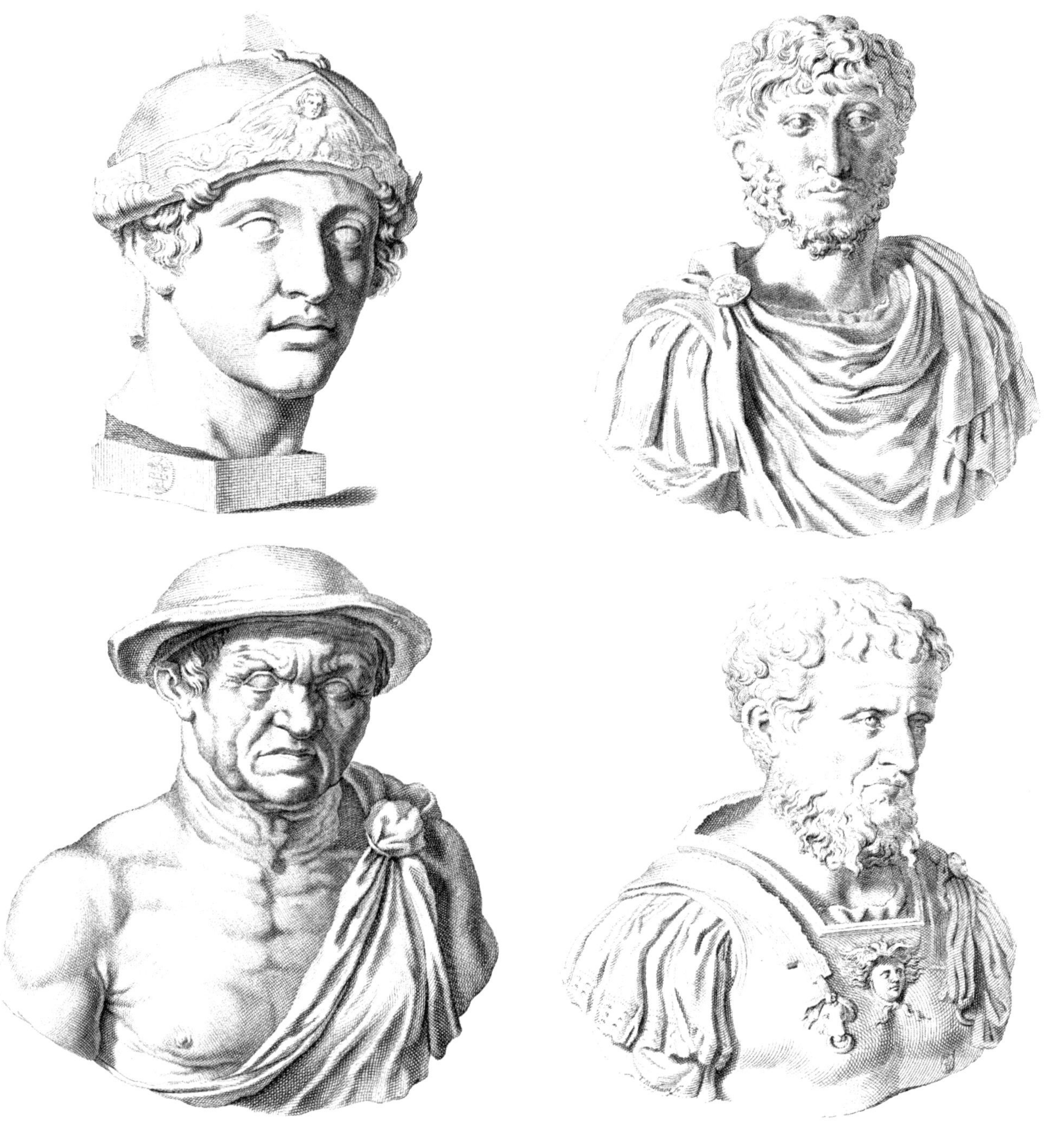

56. Portrait of a Gladiator with Helmet and
Portrait of an Old Man, Michel Natalis, 1640.

57. Busts of Gallienus and Macrinus, Theodor
Matham, 1640.

58

59

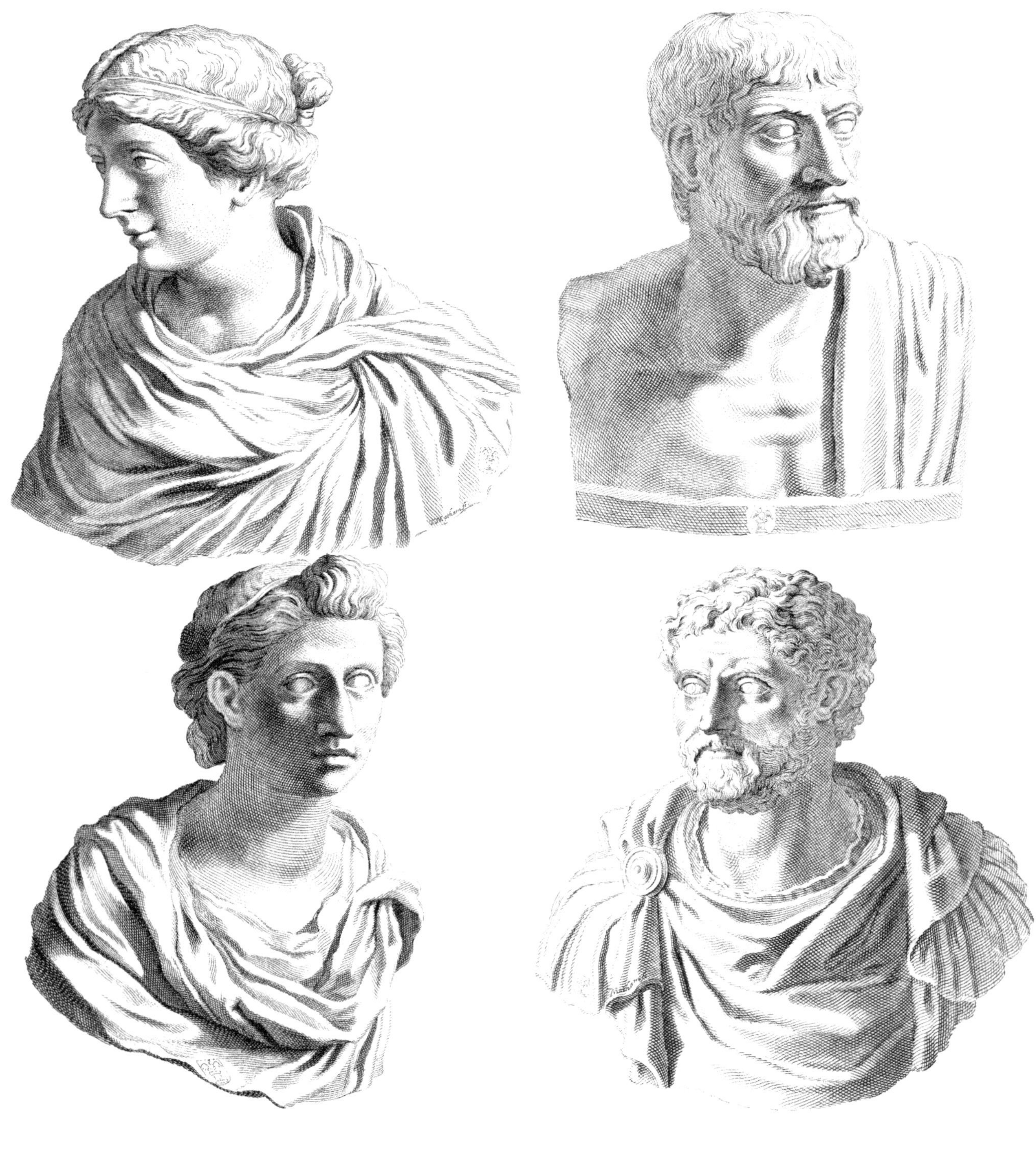

58. Busts of Crispina and Lucilla, Theodor Matham, 1640.

59. Busts of Pindar and Antoninus Pius, Theodor Matham, 1640.

60

61

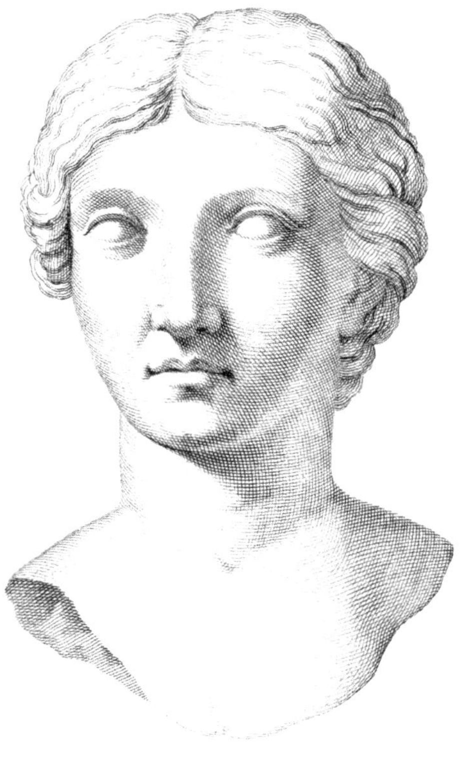

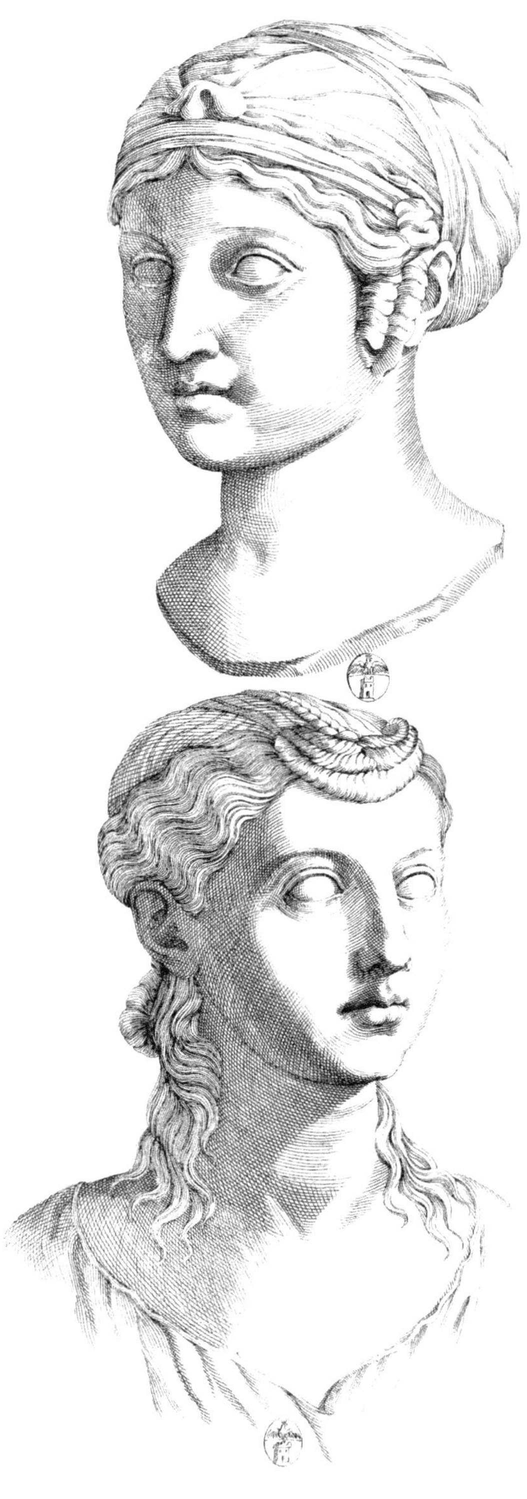

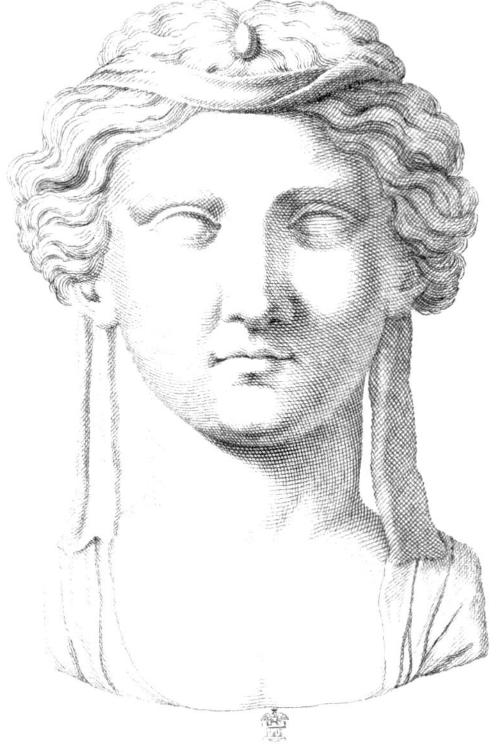

60. Busts of Faustina the Younger and an
unknown woman, Michel Natalis, 1640.

61. Busts of Empress Julia Titi, Luca Ciamberlano,
1636 – 1647.

62

63

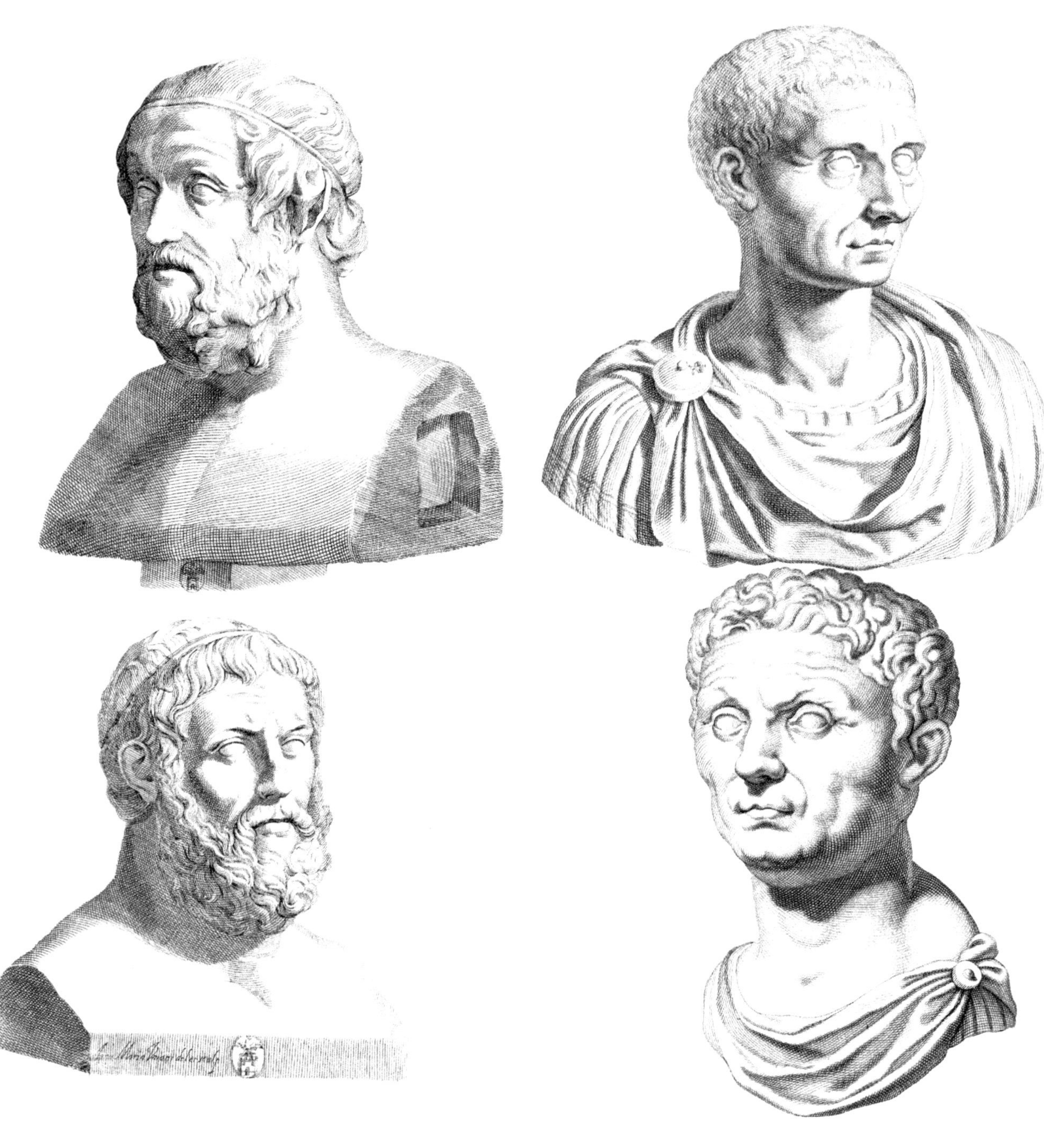

62. Bust of Plato and bust of an unknown
philosopher, Theodor Matham, 1636 – 1647.

63. Bust of Julius Caesar and Bust of Pompey,
Michel Natalis, 1640.

64

65

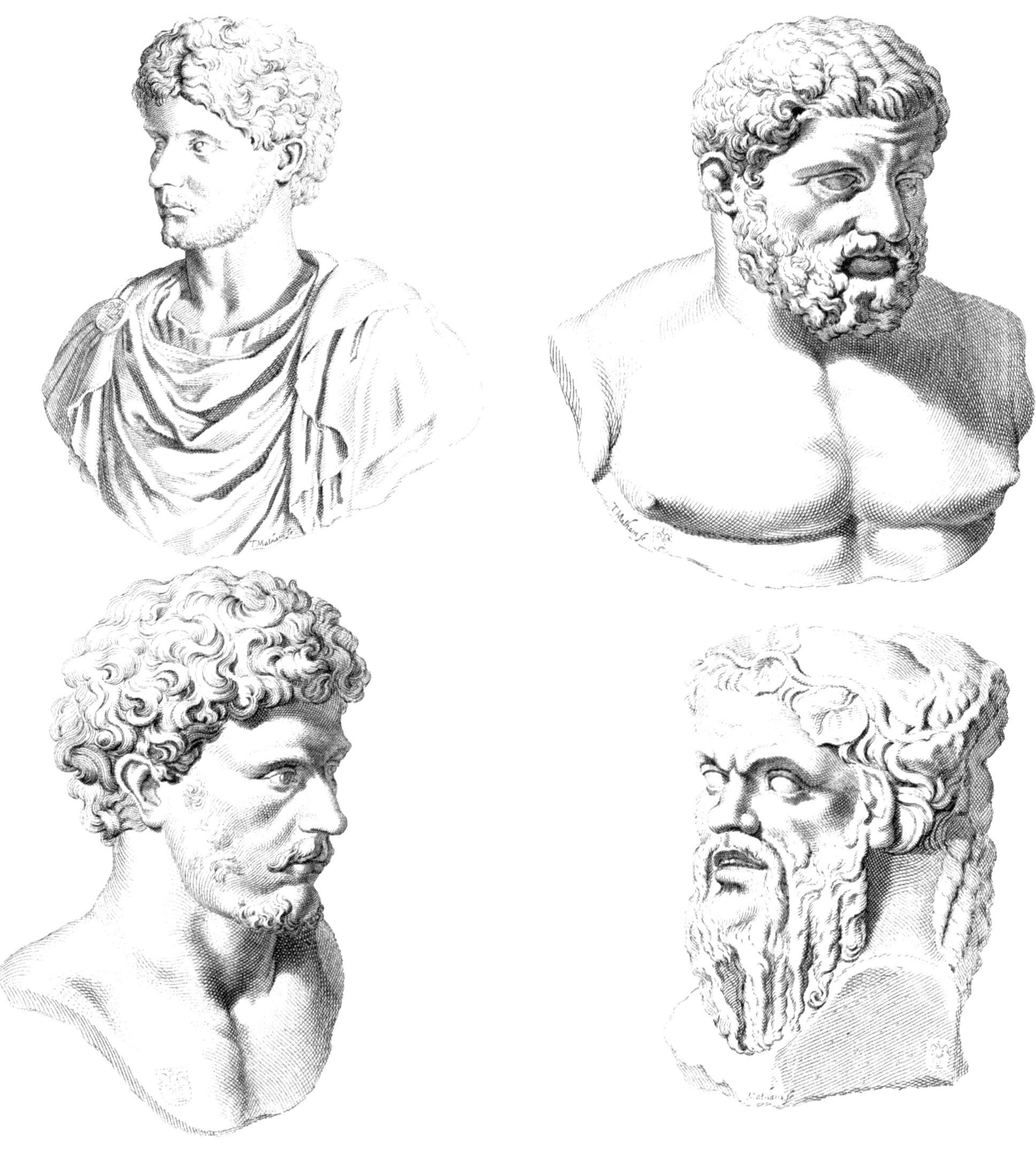

64. Busts of Lucius Verus, Theodor Matham,
1640.

65. Busts of Hercules and a Satyr, Theodor
Matham, 1640.

GREEK AND ROMAN SCULPTURE

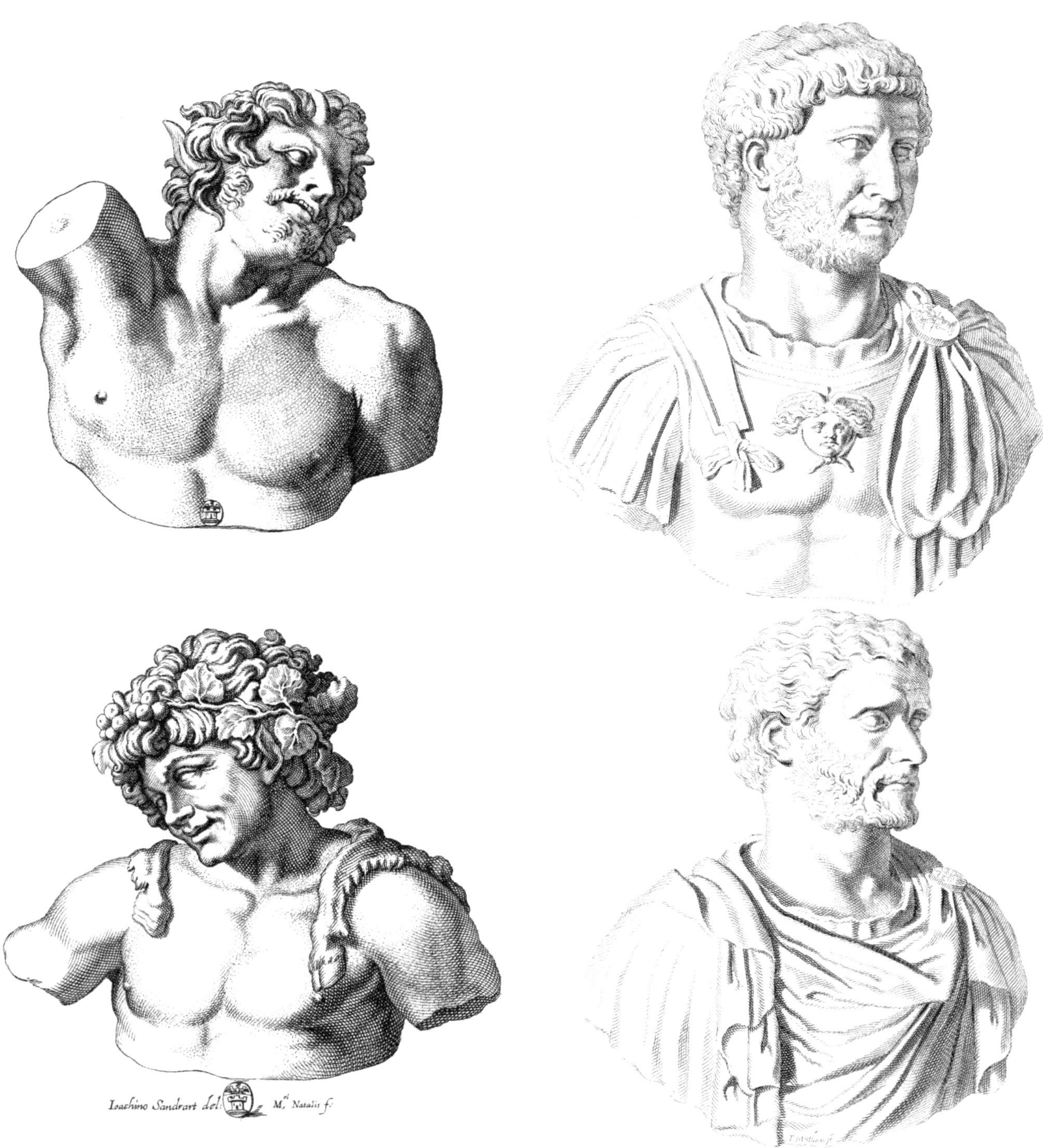

66. Two busts of Medusa, Michel Natalis
(attributed to), 1636 – 1647.

67. Busts of Hadrian and Antoninus Pius,
Theodor Matham, 1640.

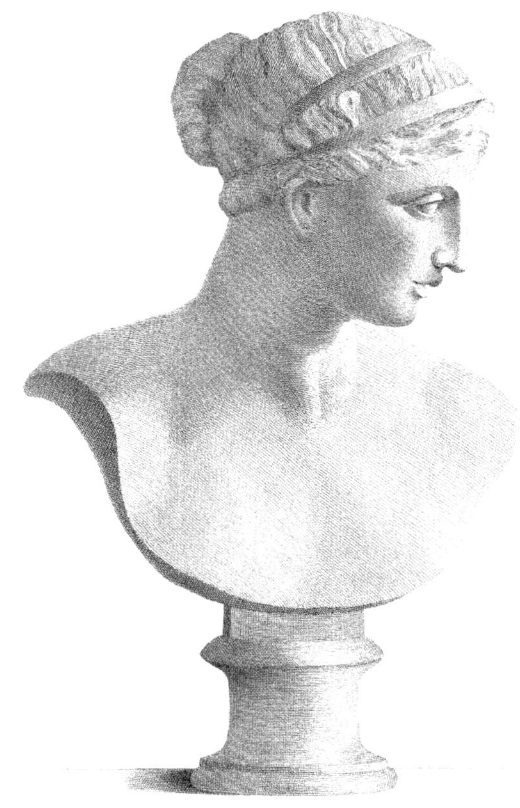

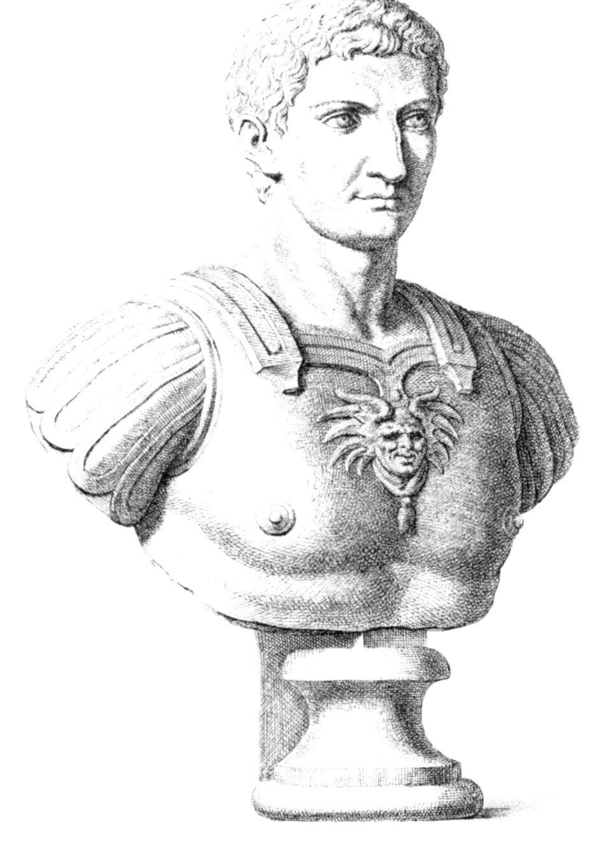

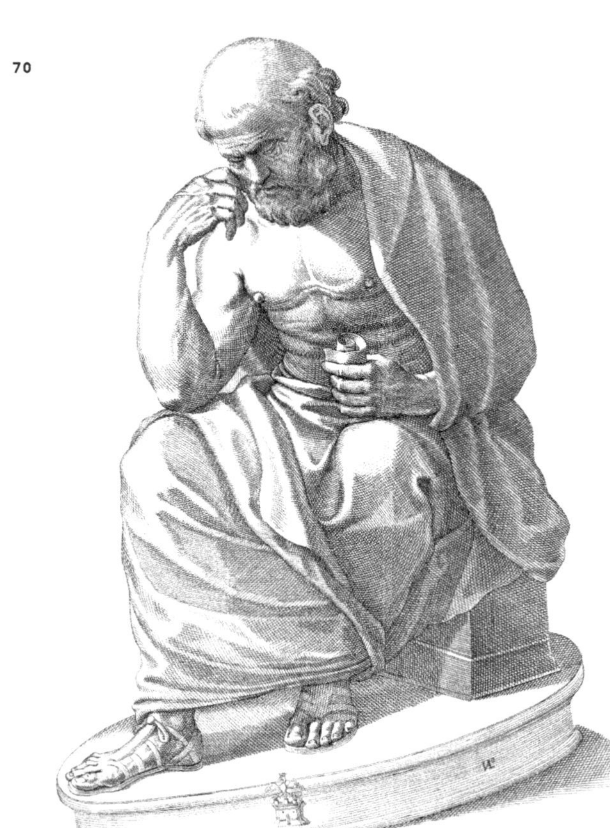

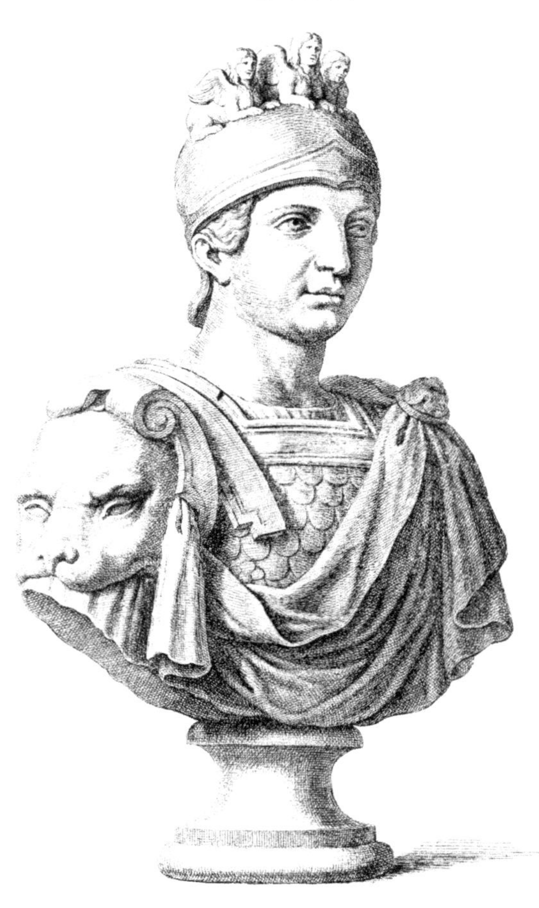

68. Marble bust of a woman, Ernest Haets, 1886.

69. Bust of Emperor Tiberius, Hubert Quellinus, 1646 – 1670.

70. Statue of a Seated Man possibly Diogenes, Giovanni Luigi Valesio, 1636 – 1647.

71. Bust of Minerva, Hubert Quellinus, 1646 – 1670.

72

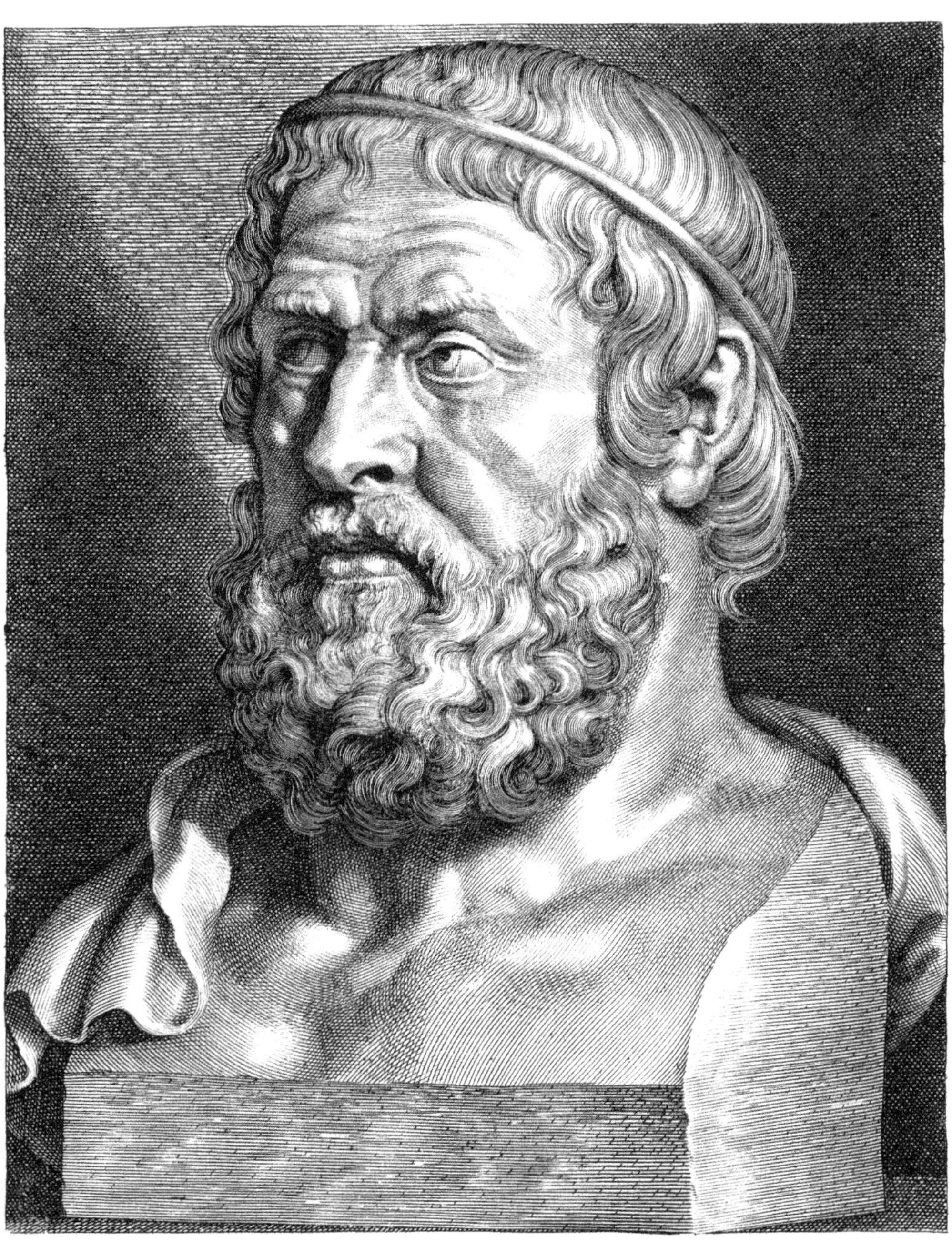

72. Antique bust of Sophocles, Paulus Pontius,
after Peter Paul Rubens, 1638.

73

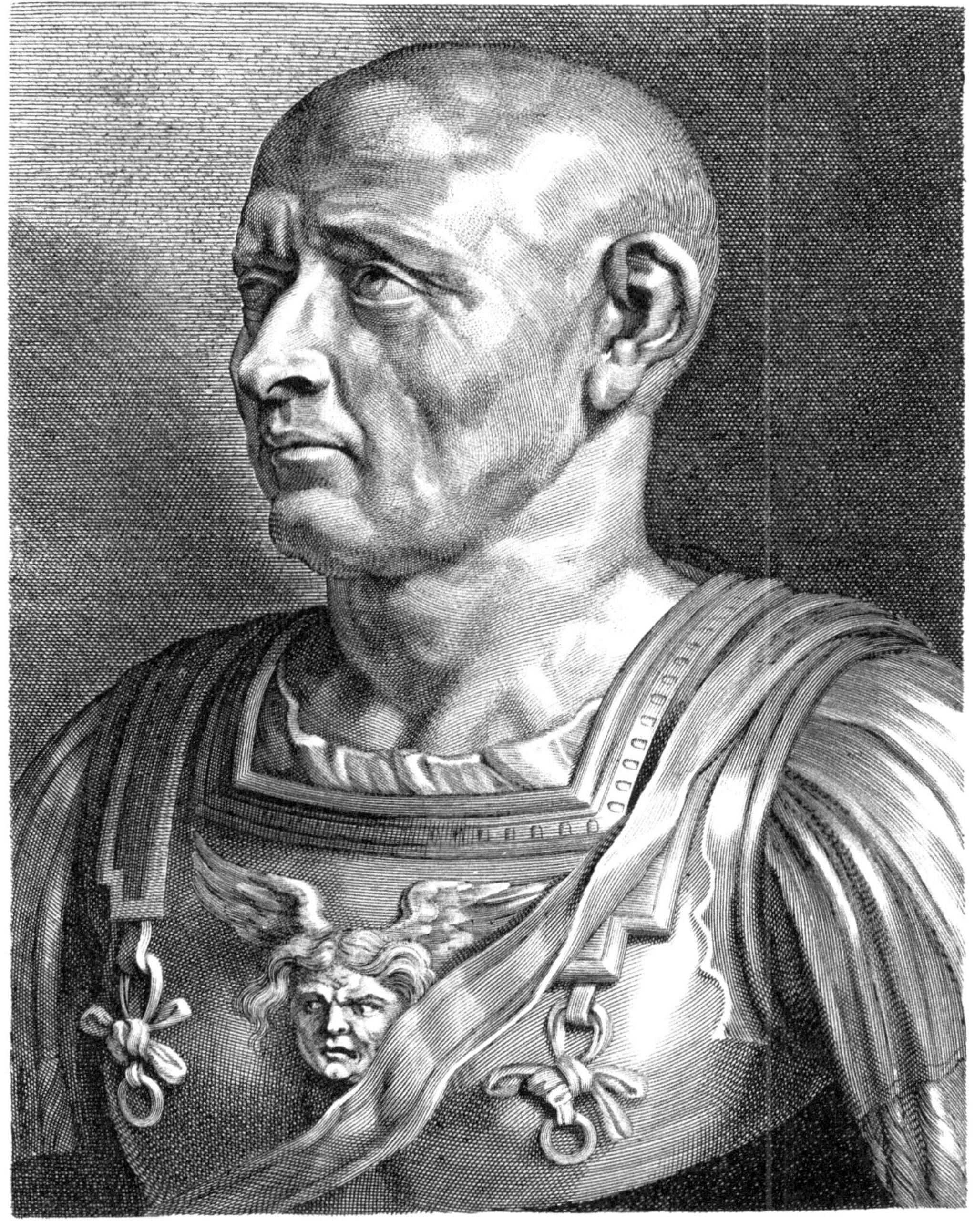

73. Antique bust of Scipio Africanus, Paulus
Pontius, after Peter Paul Rubens, 1638.

74

75

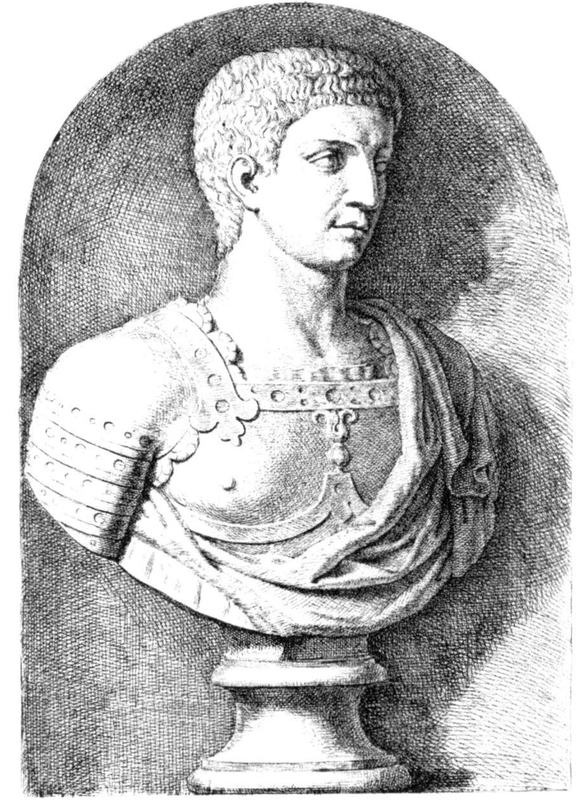

76

77

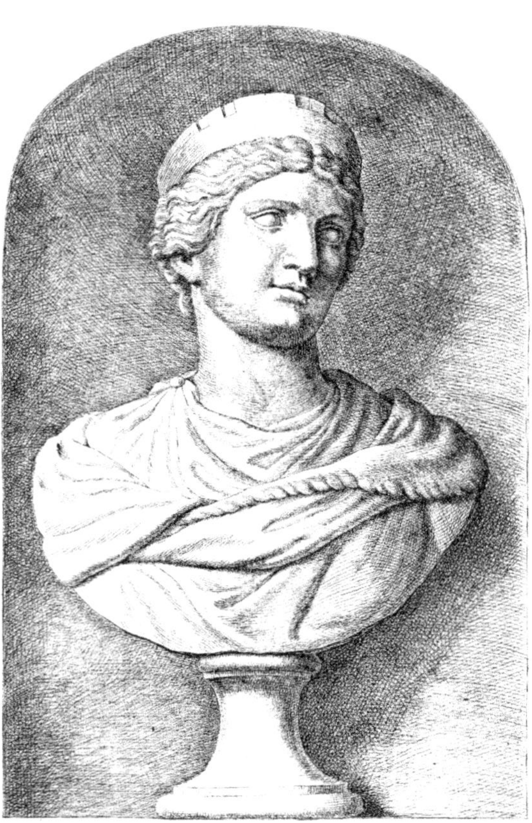

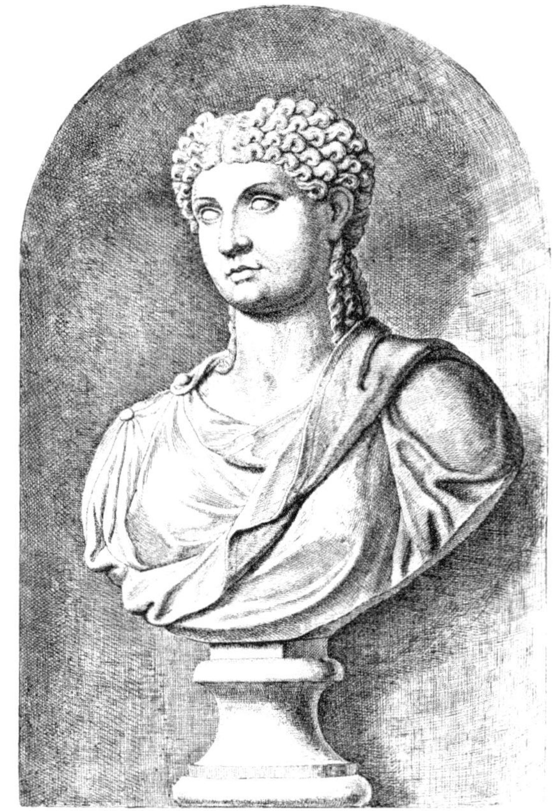

74. Bust of Agrippina the Elder, Hubert Quellinus, 1646 – 1670.

75. Bust of Emperor Augustus, Hubert Quellinus, 1646 – 1670.

76. Bust of the goddess Cybele, Hubert Quellinus, 1646 – 1670.

77. Bust of Poppaea Sabina, Hubert Quellinus, 1646 – 1670.

78

79

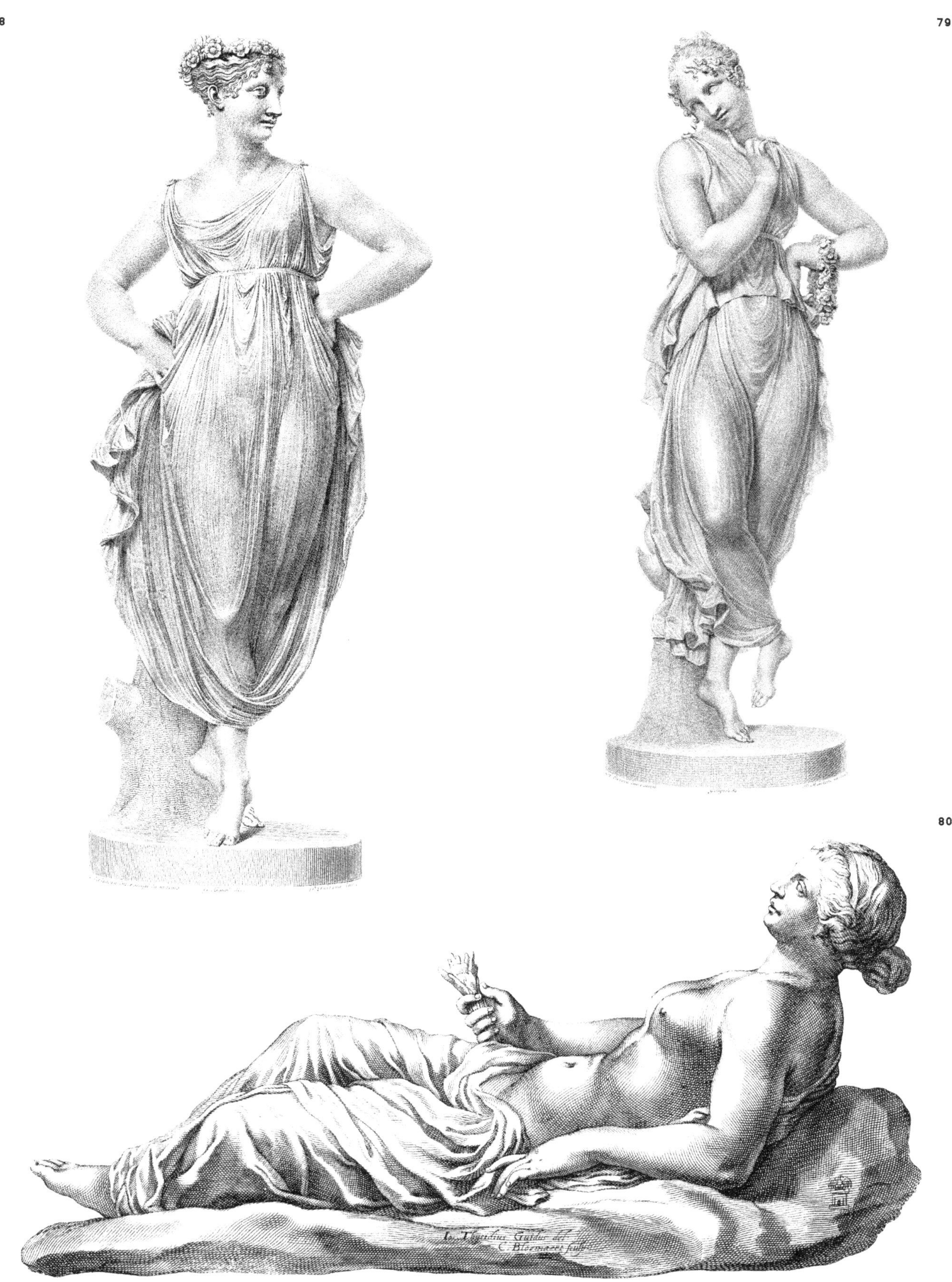

80

78. Dancer, Pietro Fontana, after Antonio Canova,
after Giovanni Tognolli, 1772 – 1837.

79. Dancer, Domenico Marchetti, after Giovanni
Tognolli, after Antonio Canova, 1790 – 1844.

80. Half–naked woman, Cornelis Bloemaert (II),
after Giovanni Citosibio Guidi, 1636 – 1647.

81

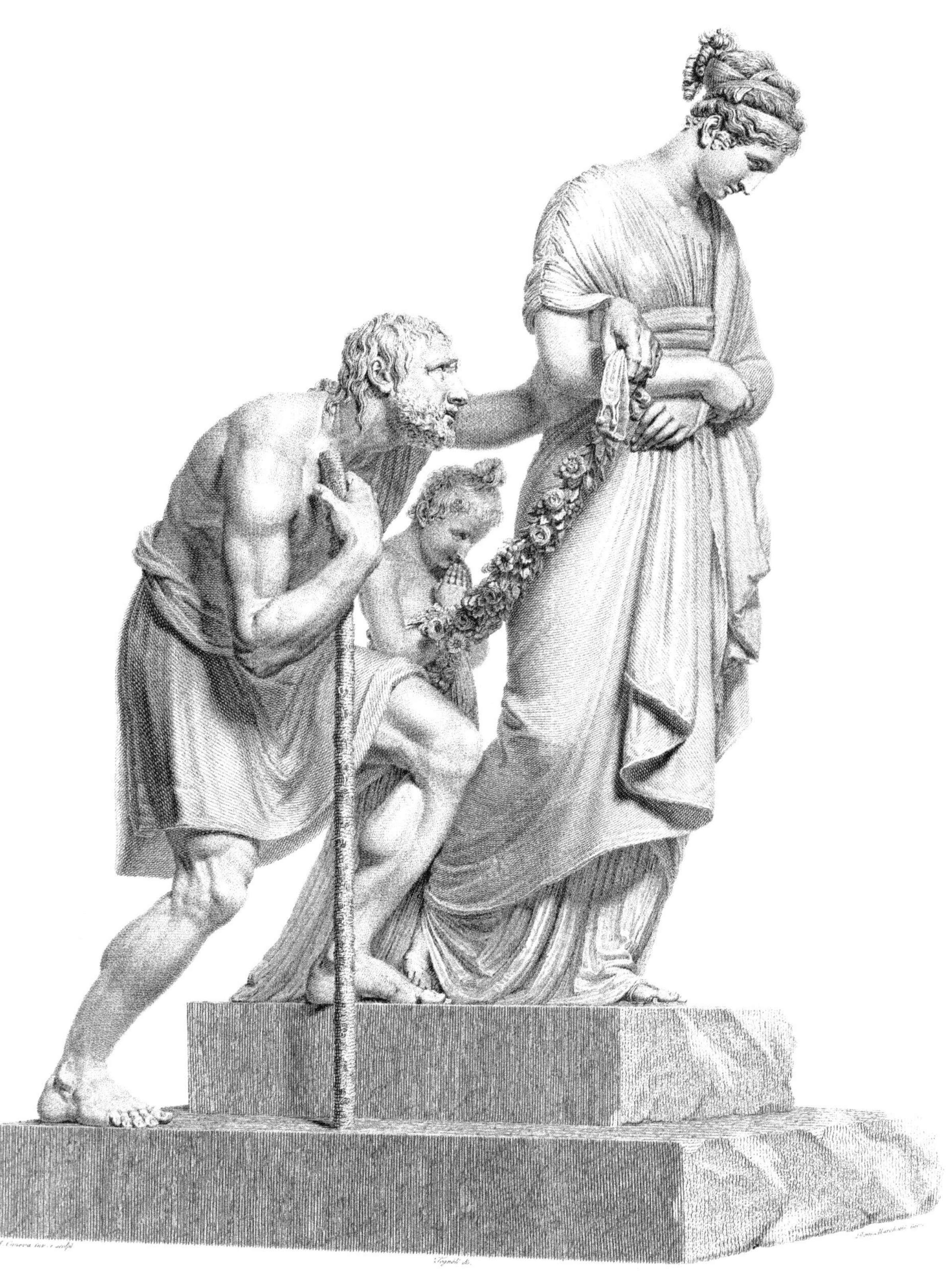

81. Charity in the Funerary Monument of Maria
Christina of Austria, Domenico Marchetti, c. 1805.

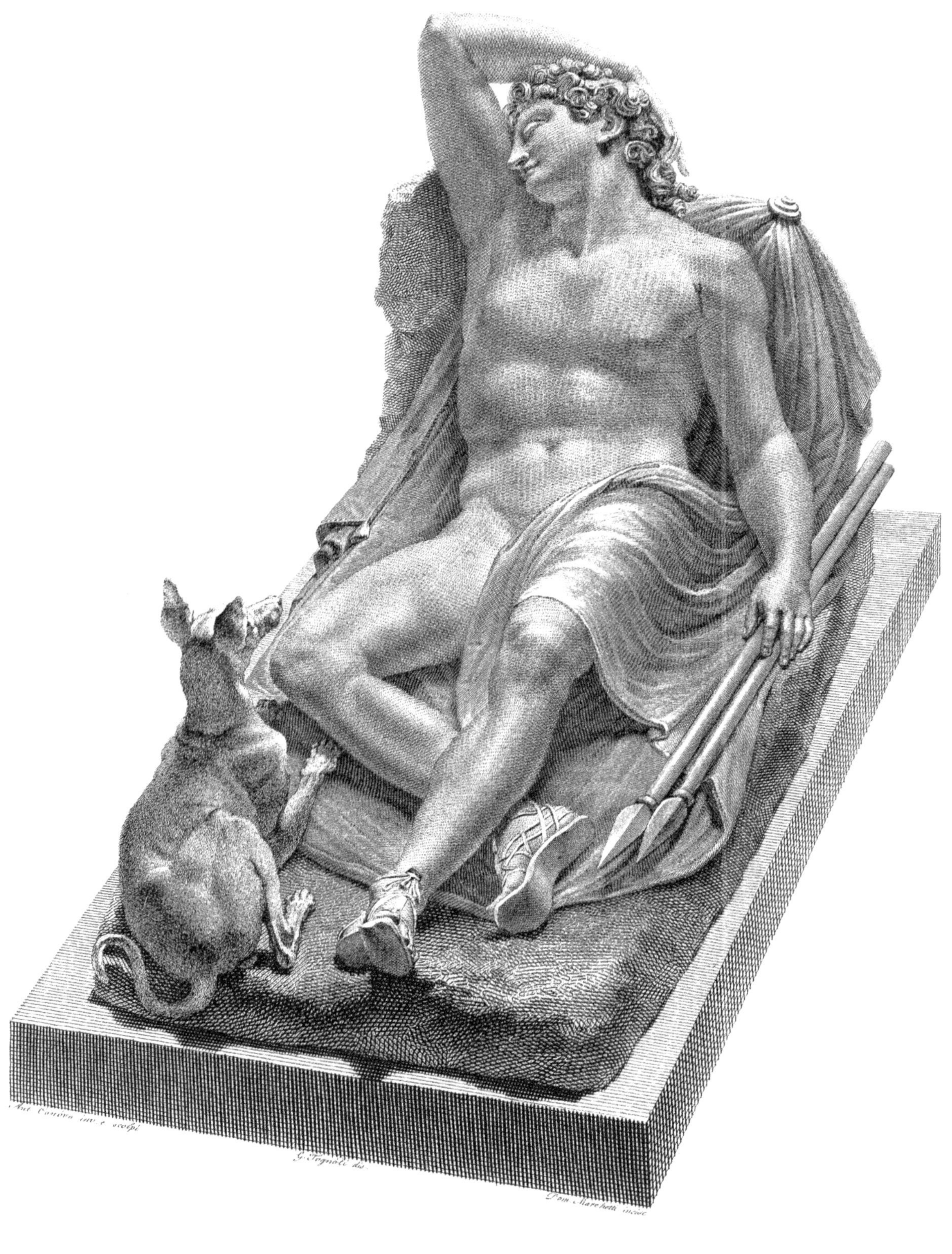

82. Endymion, Domenico Marchetti, after Giovanni
Tognolli, after Antonio Canova, 1790 – 1844.

83

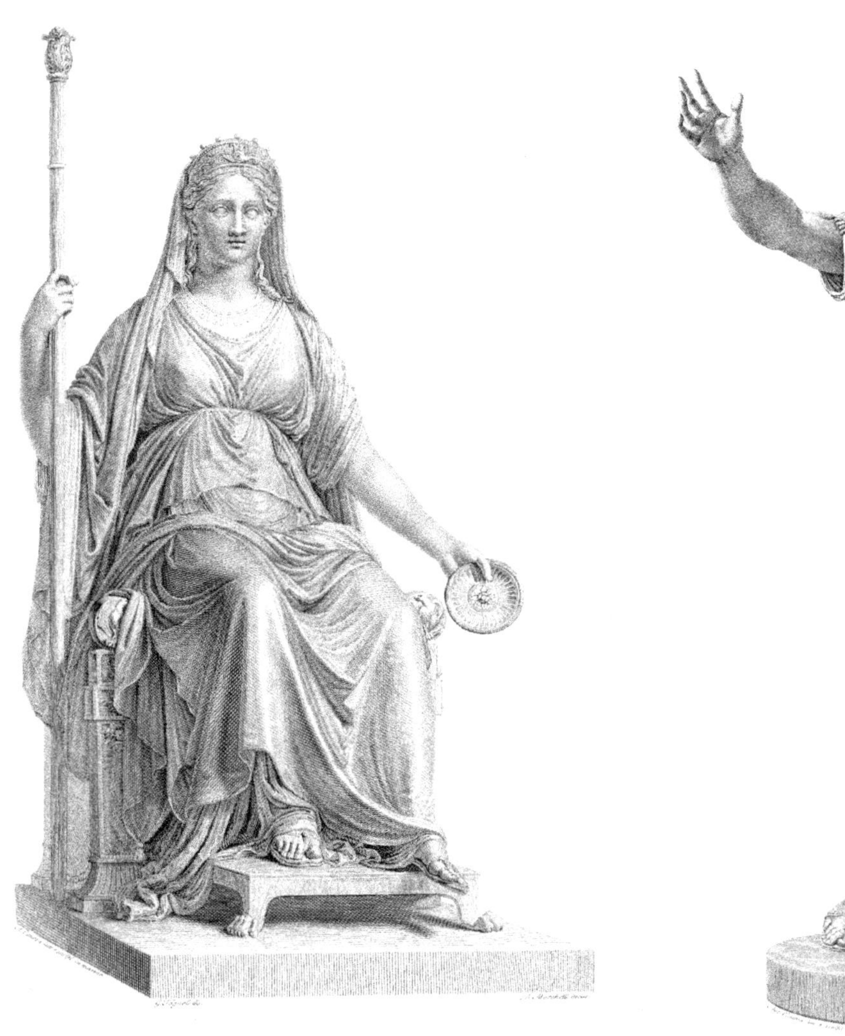

84

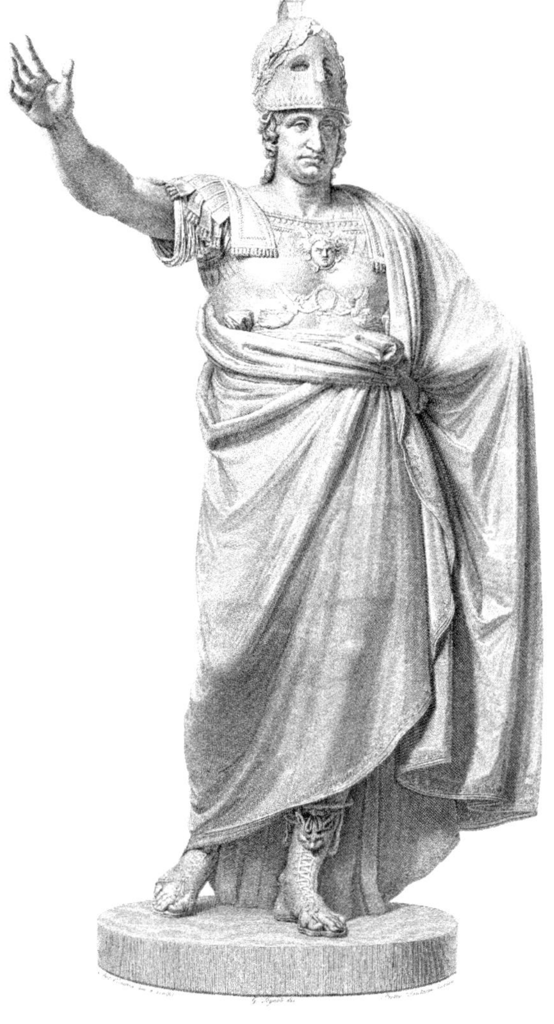

85

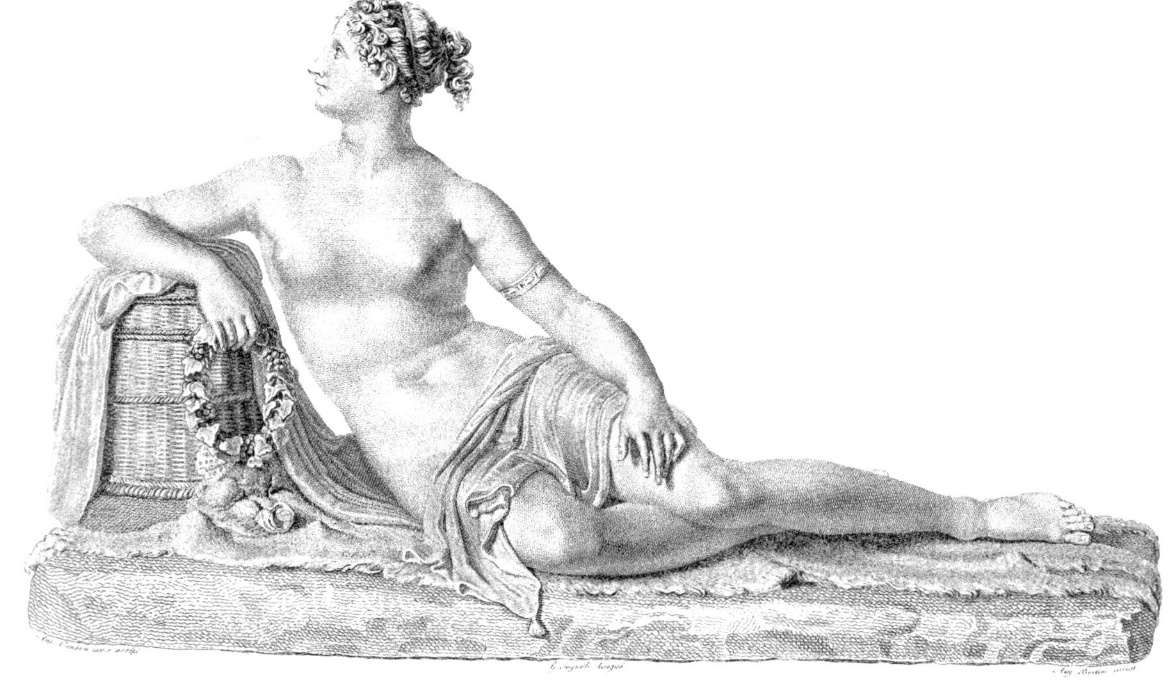

83. Concordia, Domenico Marchetti, after
Giovanni Tognolli, 1790 – 1844.

84. Ferdinand I as Minerva, Pietro Fontana, after
Giovanni Tognolli, 1772 – 1837.

85. Dirce, Angelo Bertini, after Giovanni Tognolli,
after Antonio Canova, 1793 – 1838.

86

87

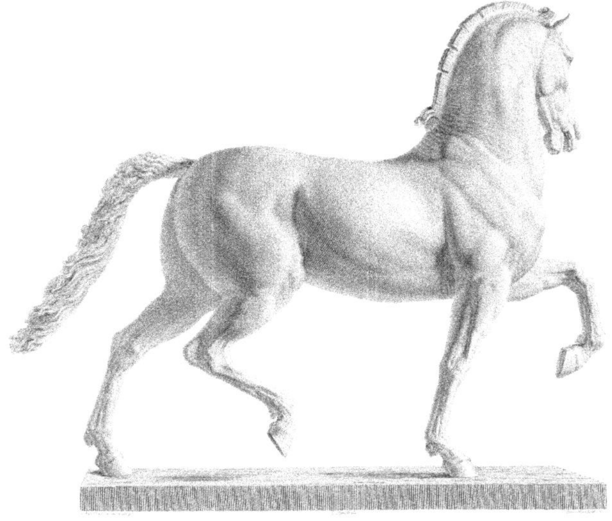

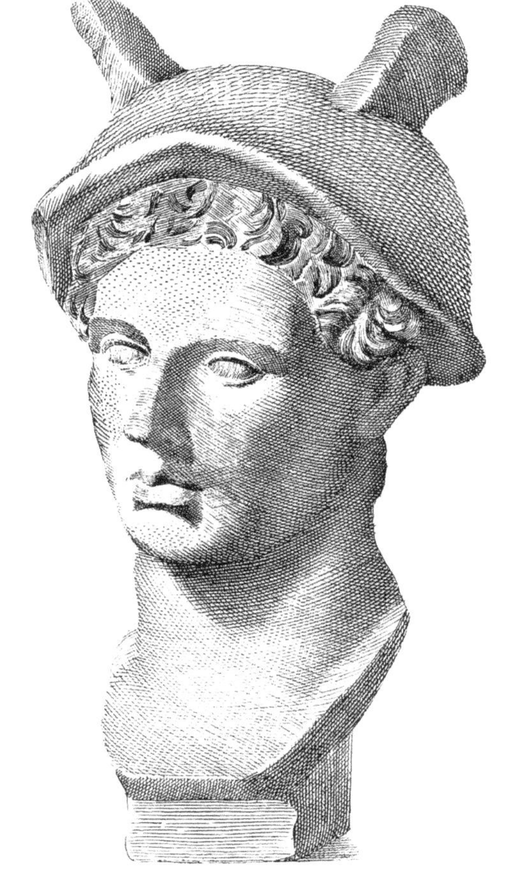

88

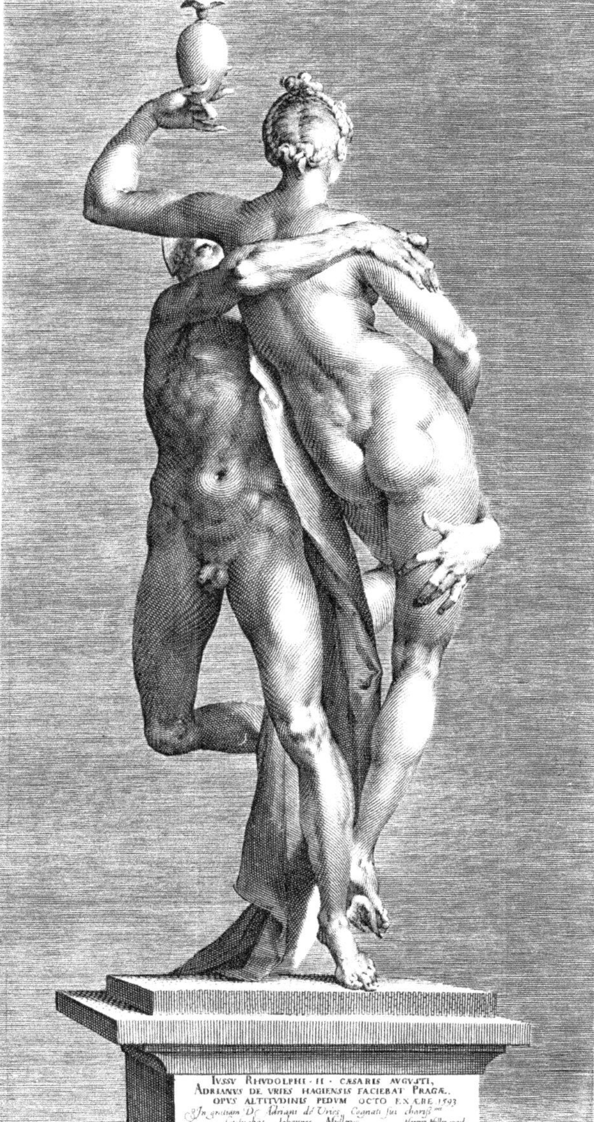

89

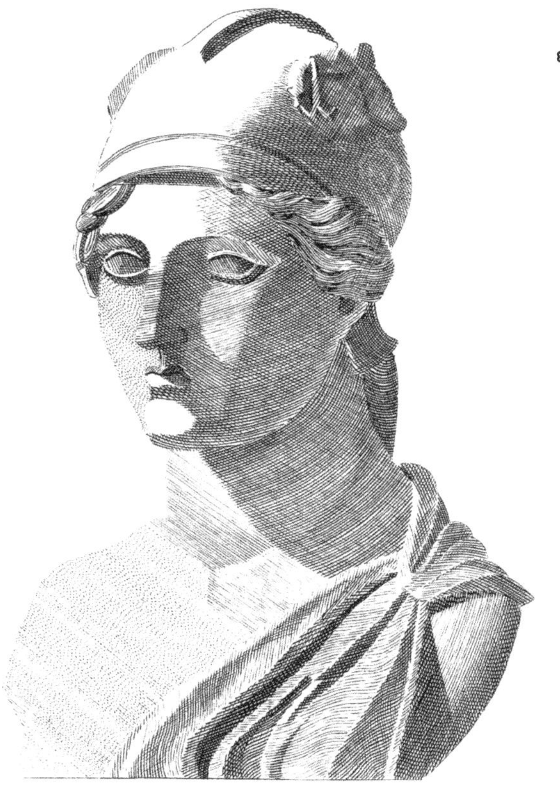

86. Horse, Domenico Marchetti, after Giovanni Tognolli, after Antonio Canova, 1790 – 1844.

87. Bust of Mercury, J. Weyn, 1888.

88. Mercury and Psyche, view with the back of Psyche, Jan Harmensz. Muller, 1595 – 1599.

89. Bust of Minerva, Eduard Augustyns, c. 1850 – in or before 1909.

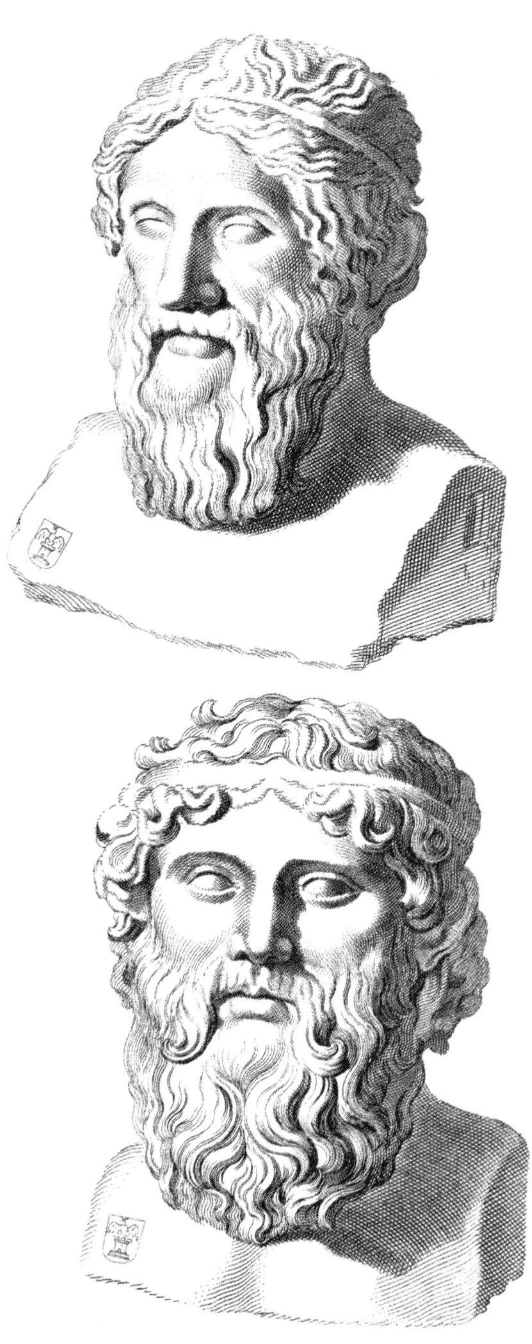

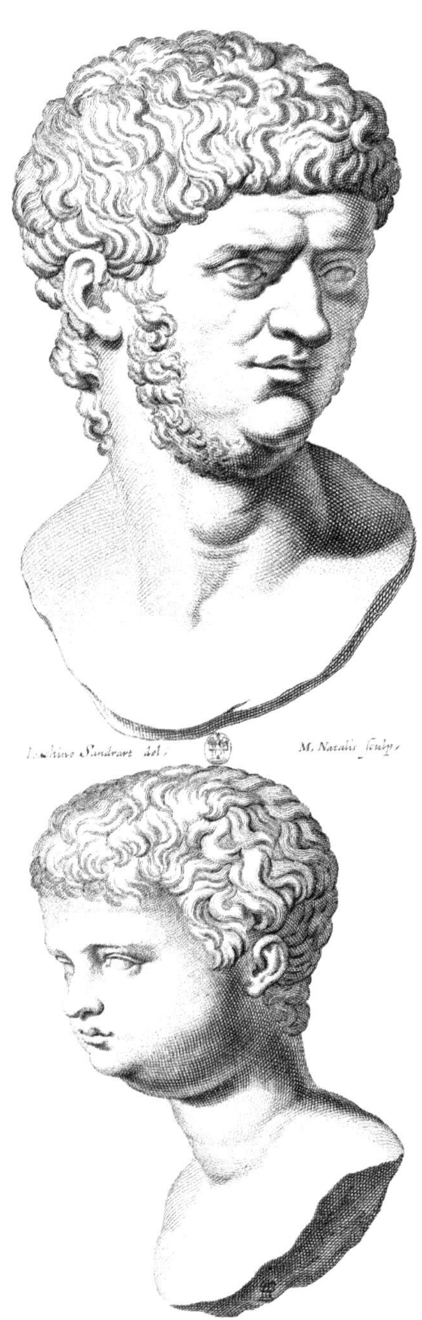

90. Two busts of Apollo, Michel Natalis, after
Joachim von Sandrart (I), 1636 – 1647.

91. Two portrait busts of Nero, Michel Natalis,
after Joachim von Sandrart (I), 1640.

92

93

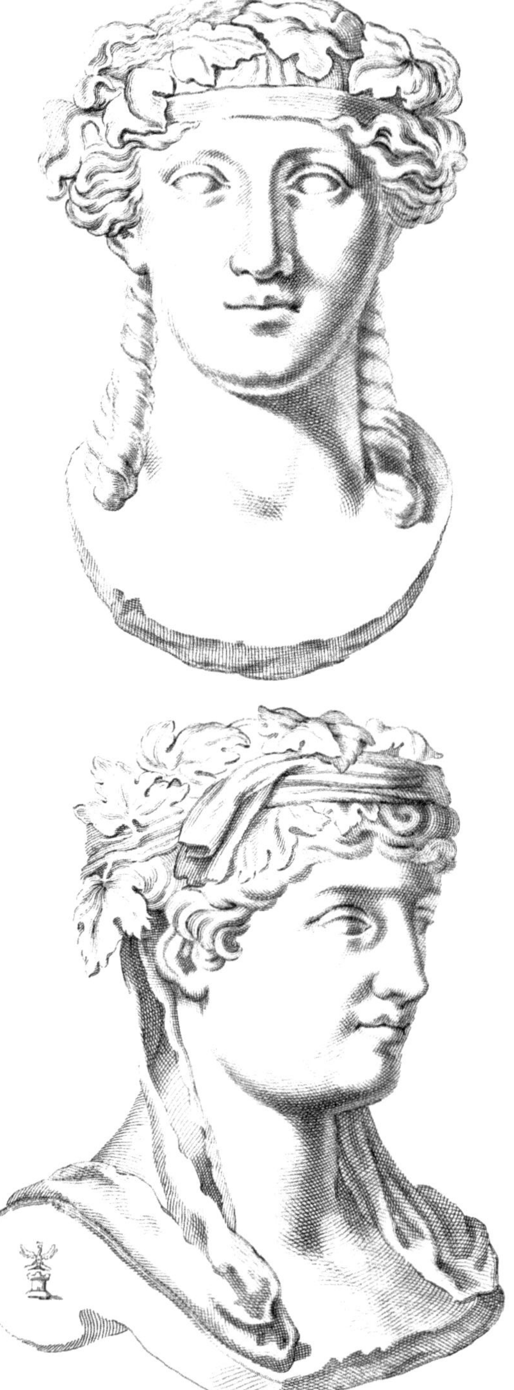

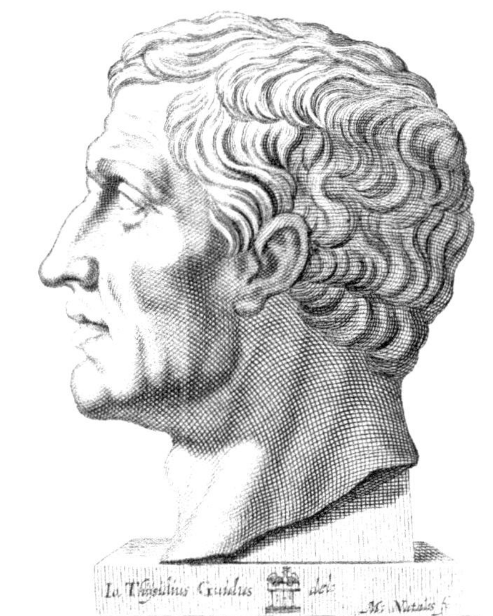

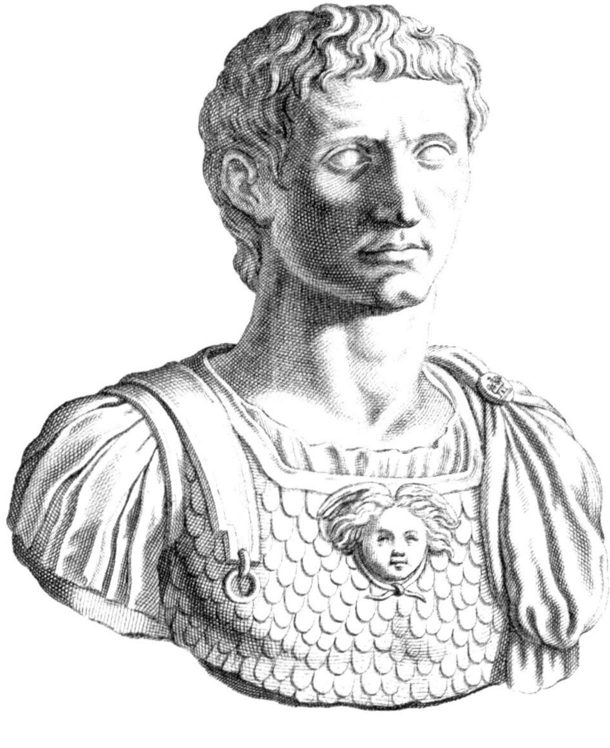

92. Two busts of Bacchantes, Reinier van Persijn, after Joachim von Sandrart (I), 1640.

93. Two busts of Emperor Augustus, Michel Natalis, after Giovanni Citosiblo Guidi, 1640.

94

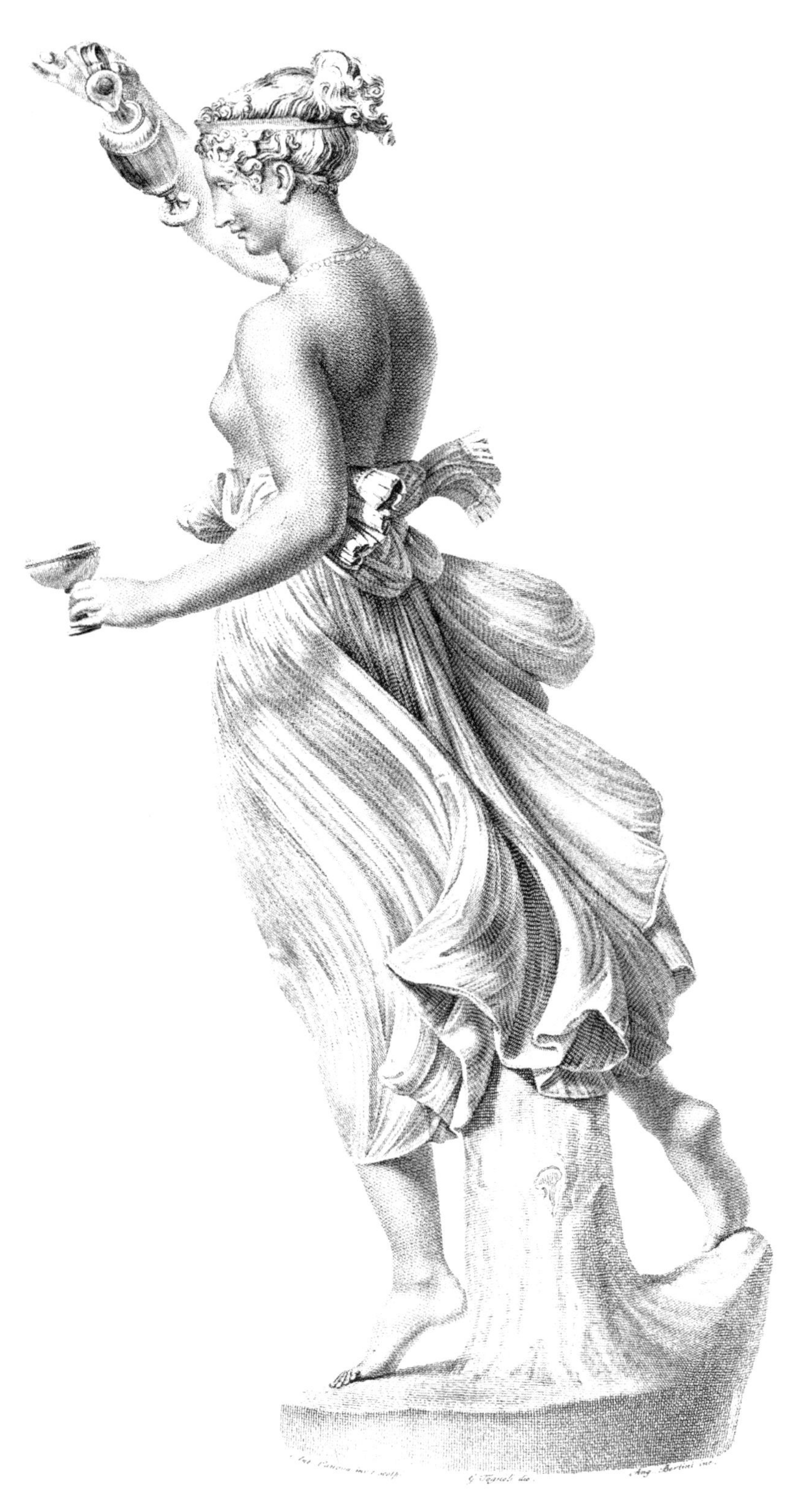

94. Sculpture of the Greek goddess Hebe, Angelo
Bertini, after Giovanni Tognolli, 1793 – 1838.

95

96

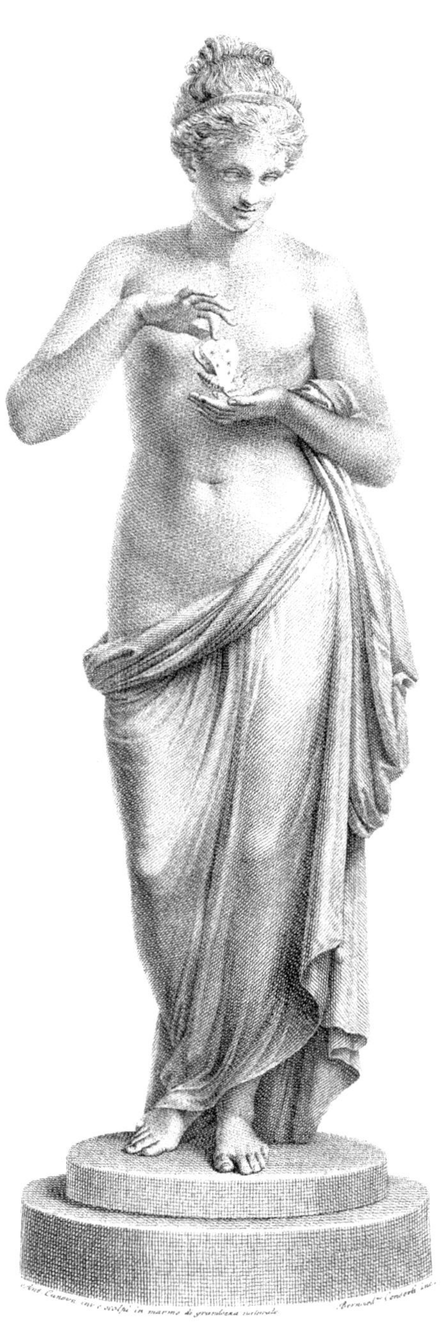

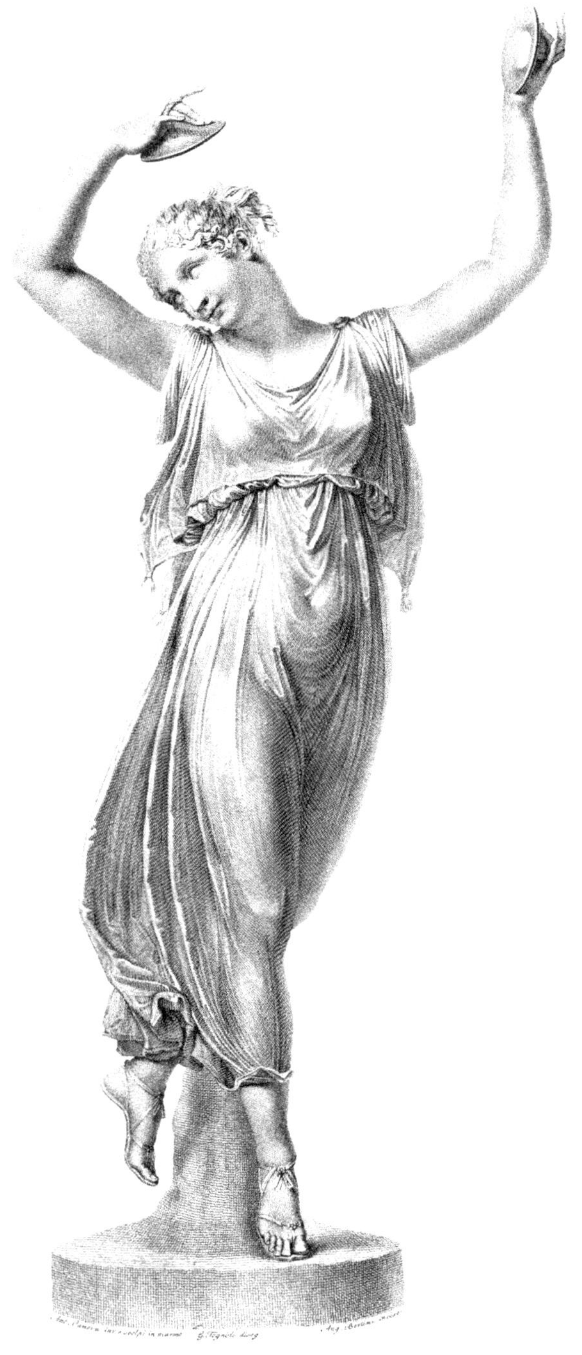

95. Sculpture of Psyche, Bernardino Consorti,
after Antonio Canova, 1790 – 1859.

96. Sculpture of a Dancer, Angelo Bertini, after
Giovanni Tognolli, 1793 – 1838.

97

98

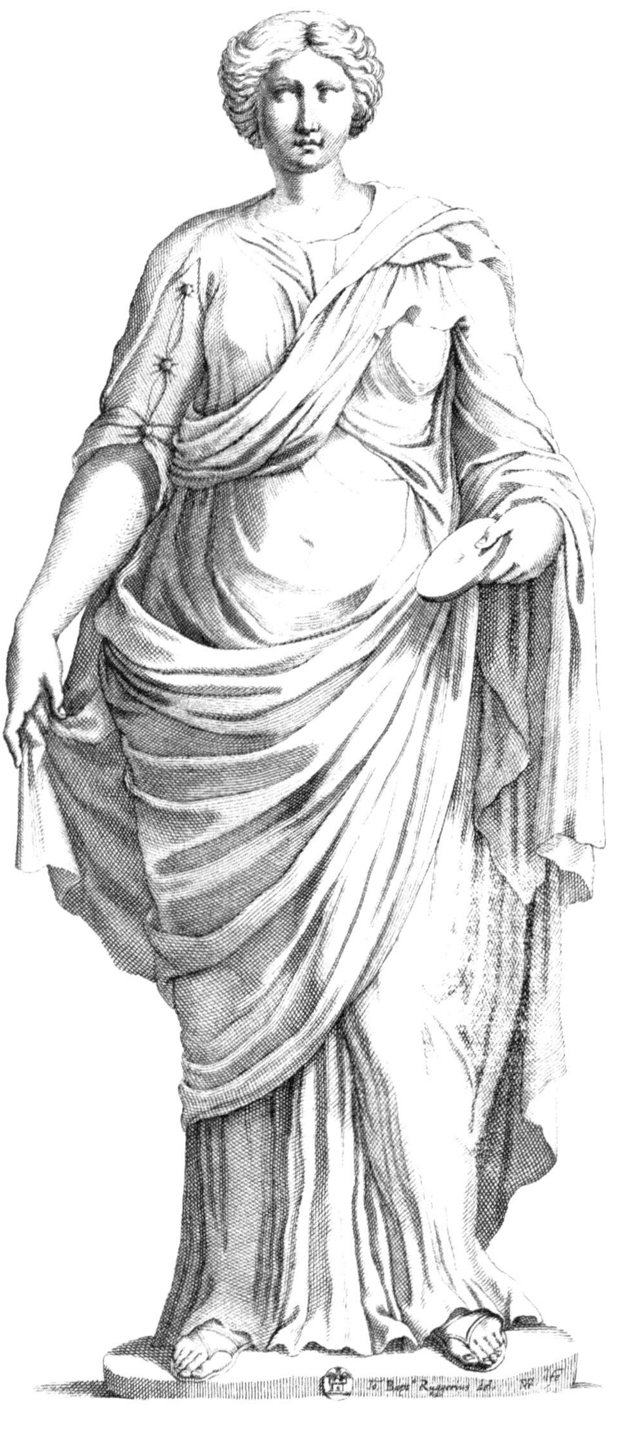

97. Statue of a Woman in a Cloak, Cornelis
Bloemaert (II), 1636 – 1647.

98. Statue of a Woman in Roman Clothing,
Cornelis Bloemaert (II), 1636 – 1647.

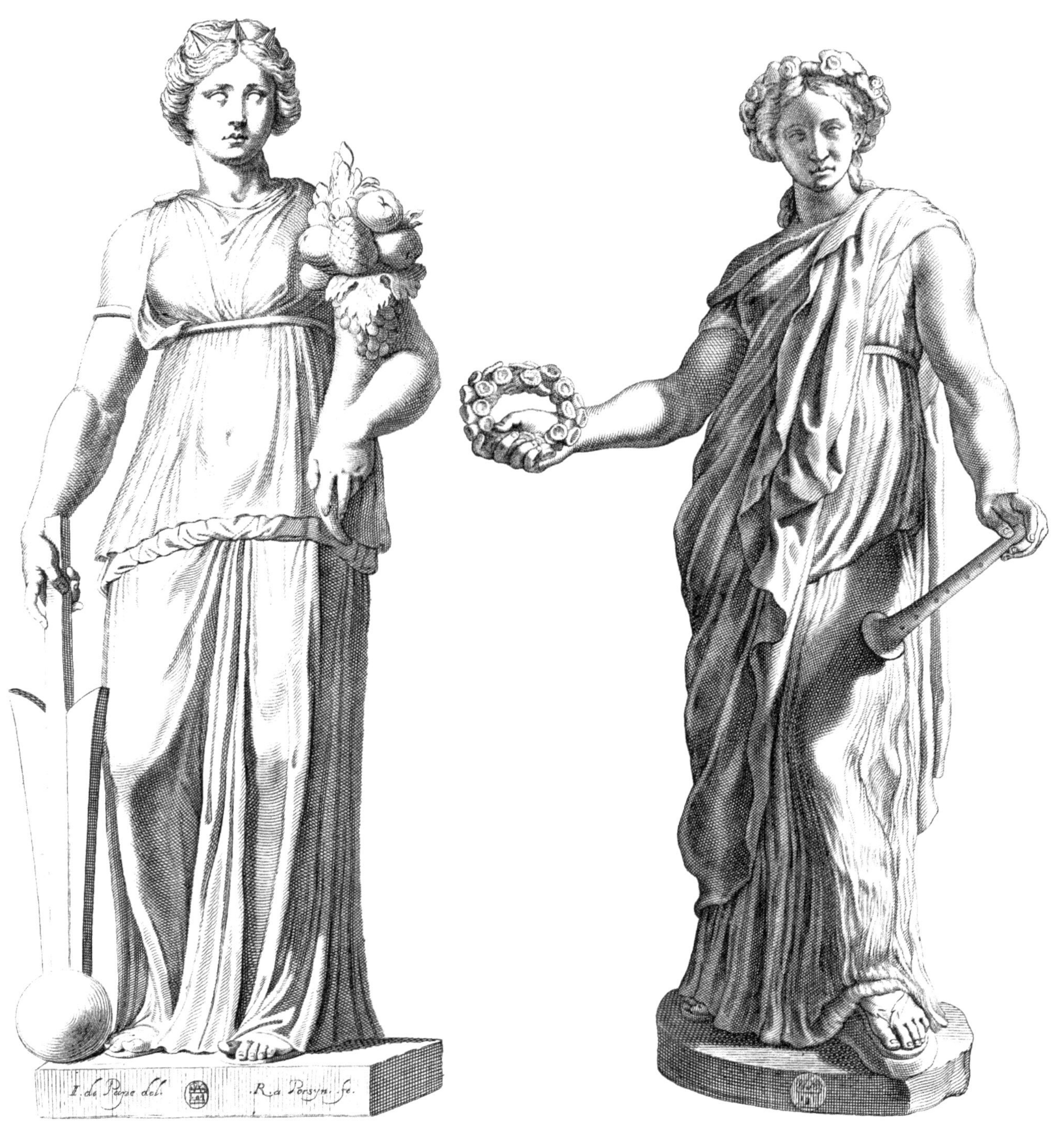

99. Statue of a Woman with a Cornucopia, Reinier van Persijn, after Joos de Pape, 1640.

100. Statue of a woman with a flower in her hand, Cornelis Bloemaert (II), 1636 – 1647.

101

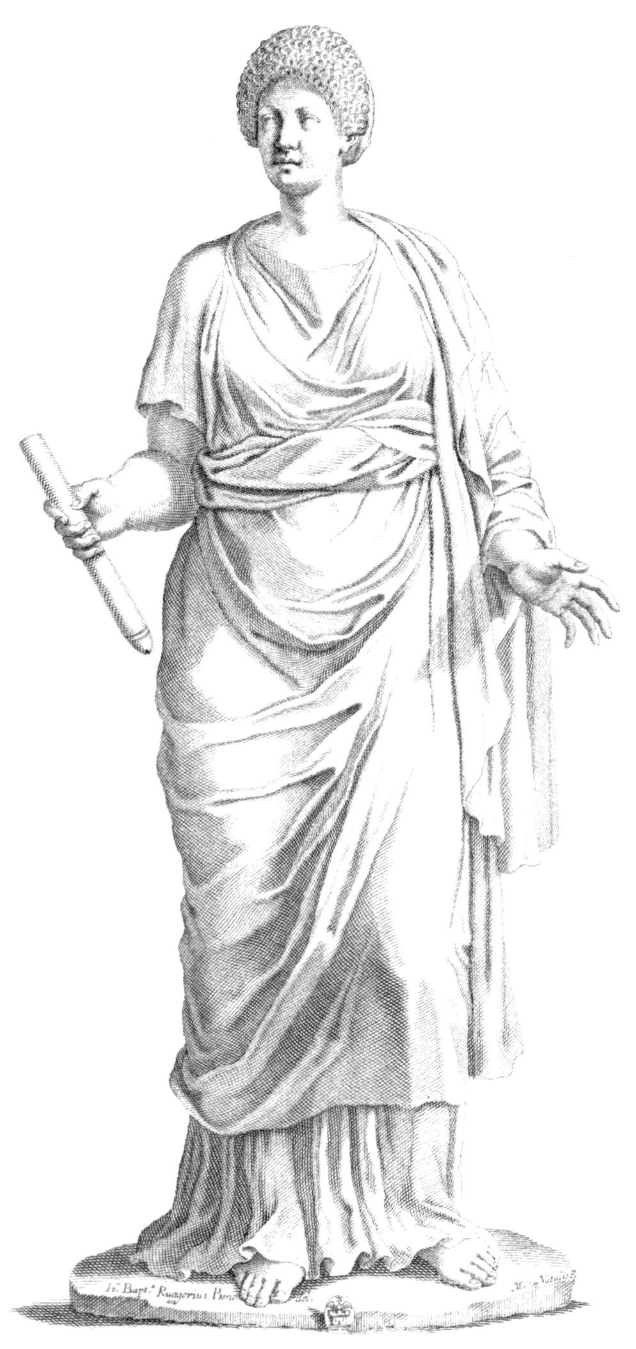

102

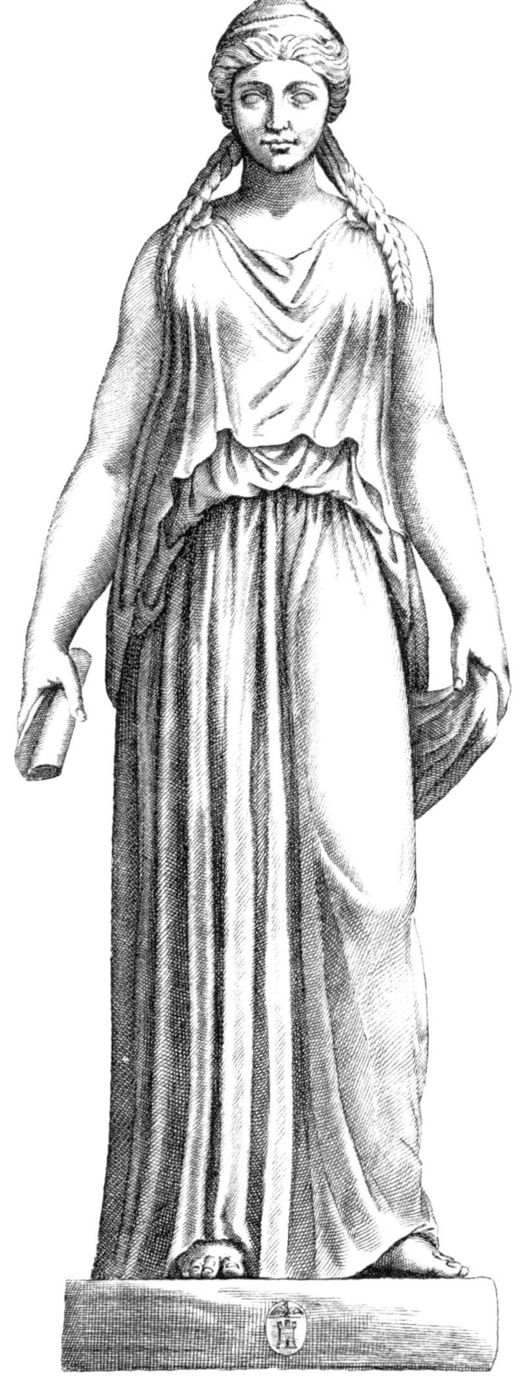

101. Statue of a Woman with a Staff, Michel
Natalis, after Giovanni Battista Ruggieri, 1640.

102. Statue of a Woman with Braids in Her Hair,
Luca Ciamberlano, 1636 – 1647.

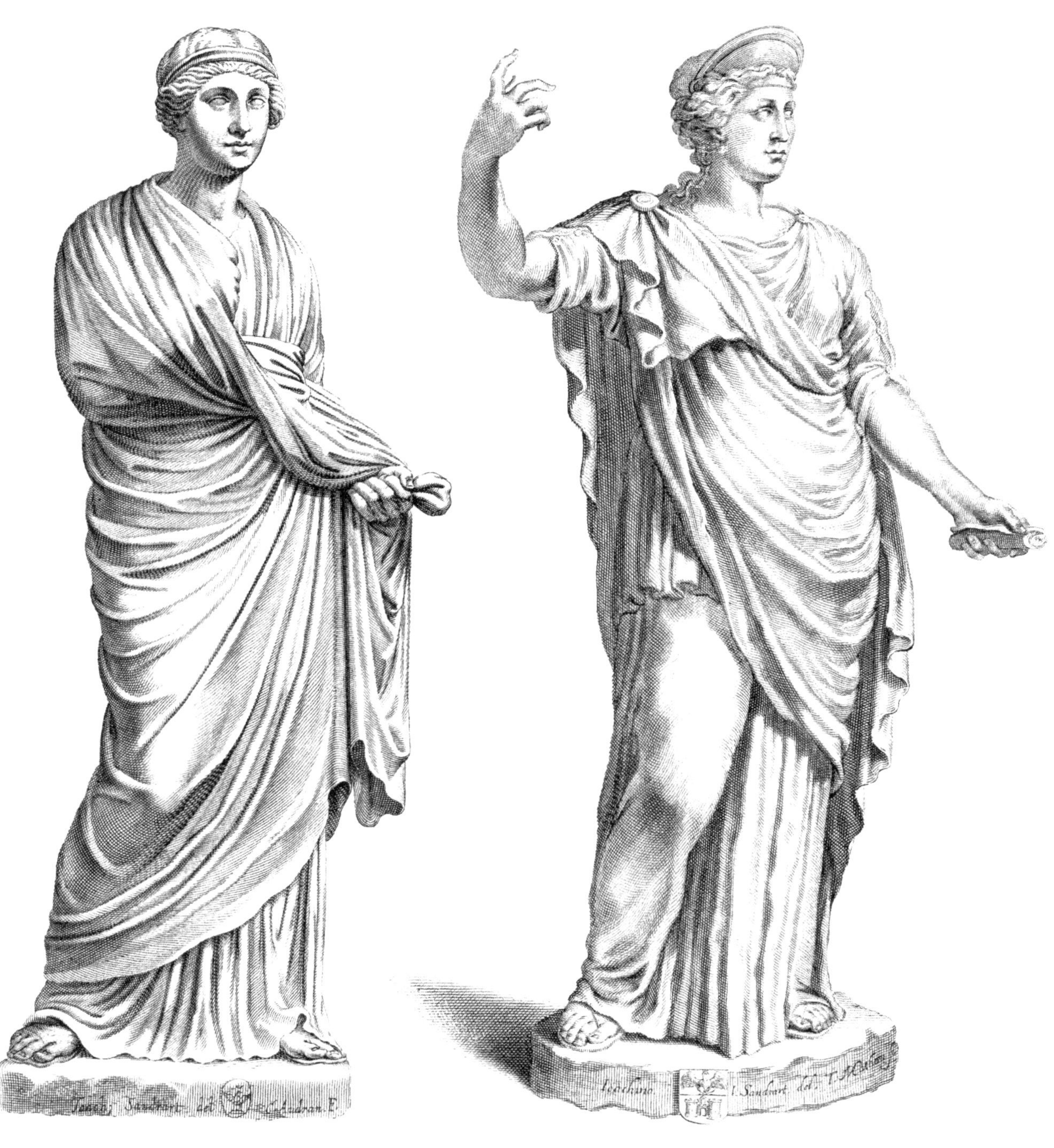

103. Statue of a Woman, Charles Audran, after
Joachim von Sandrart (I), 1636 – 1647.

104. Statue of a Woman with Raised Right Arm,
Theodor Matham, 1640.

105

106

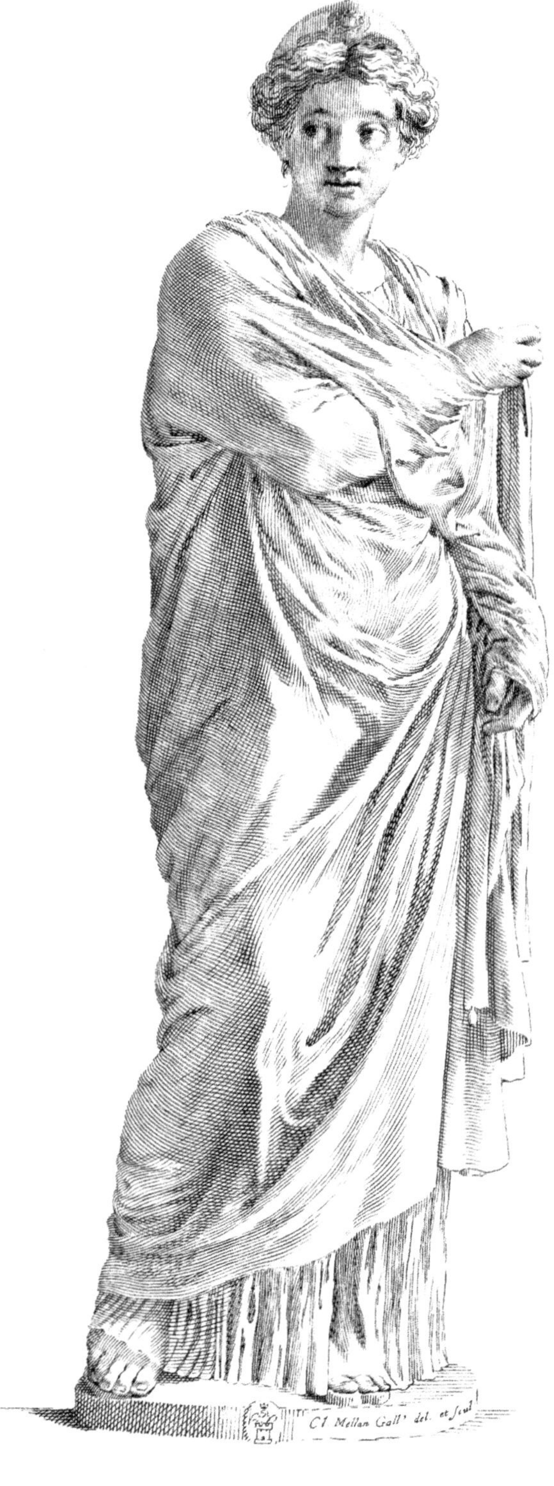

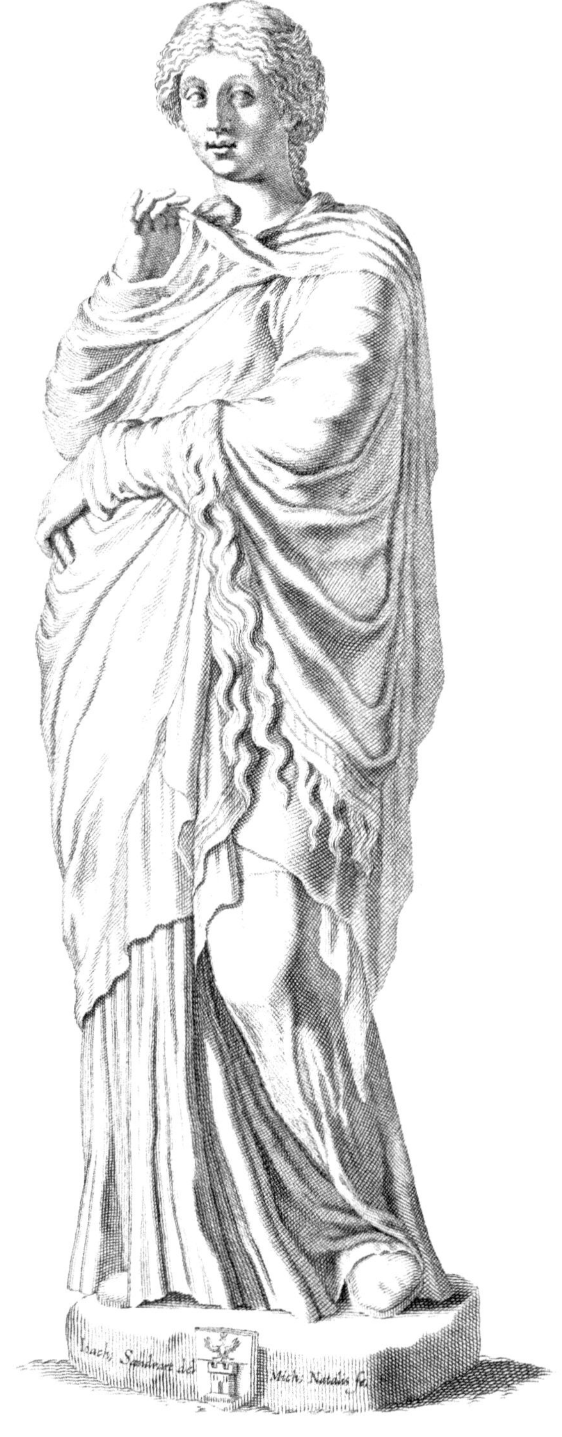

105. Statue of a Woman, Claude Mellan, 1636
– 1647.

106. Statue of a Woman, Michel Natalis, after
Joachim von Sandrart (I), 1640.

107   108

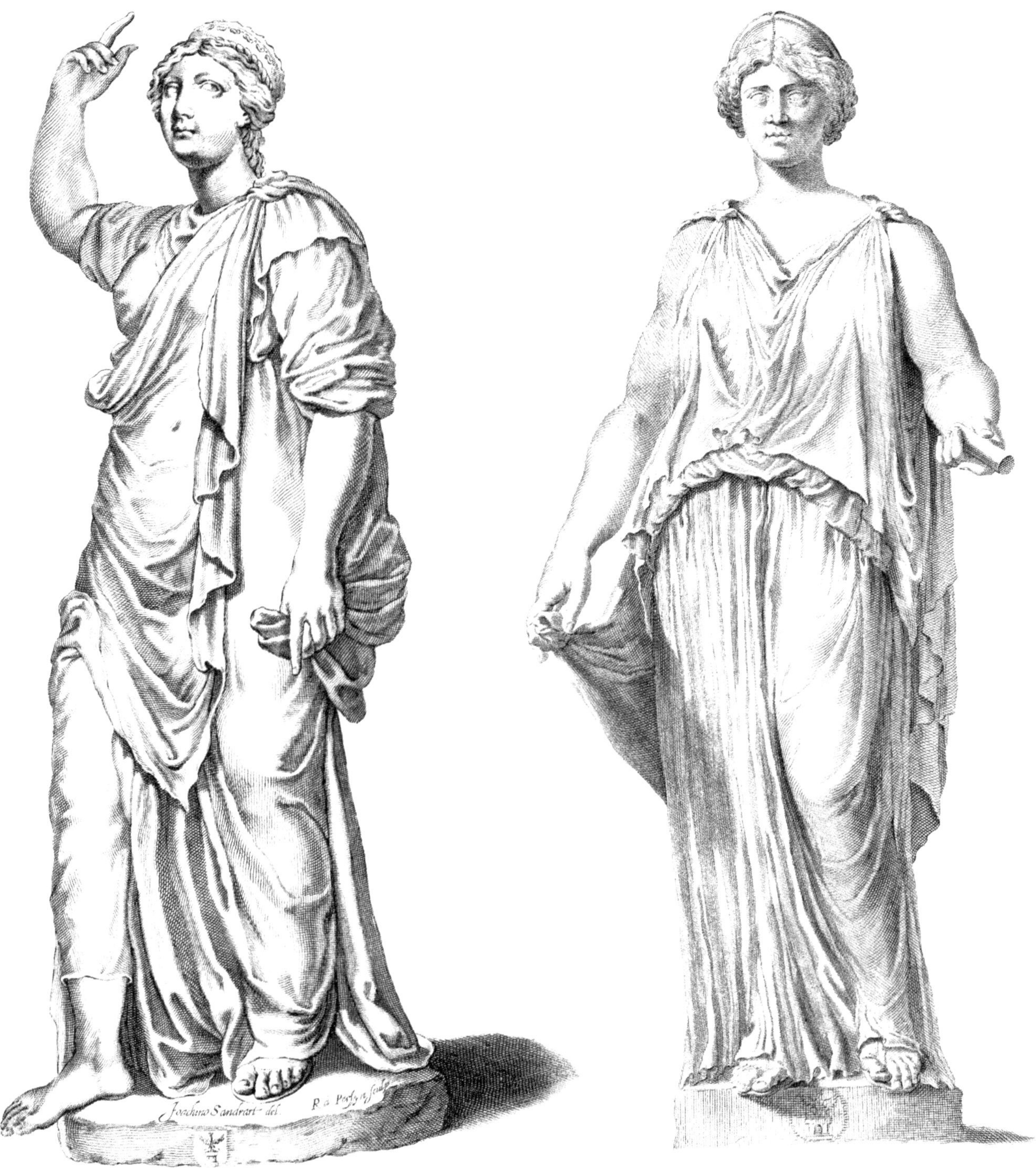

GREEK AND ROMAN SCULPTURE

107. Statue of a woman, Reinier van Persijn, after
Joachim von Sandrart (I), 1636 – 1647.

108. Statue of a woman, Theodor Matham, after
Pietro Testa, 1640.

109

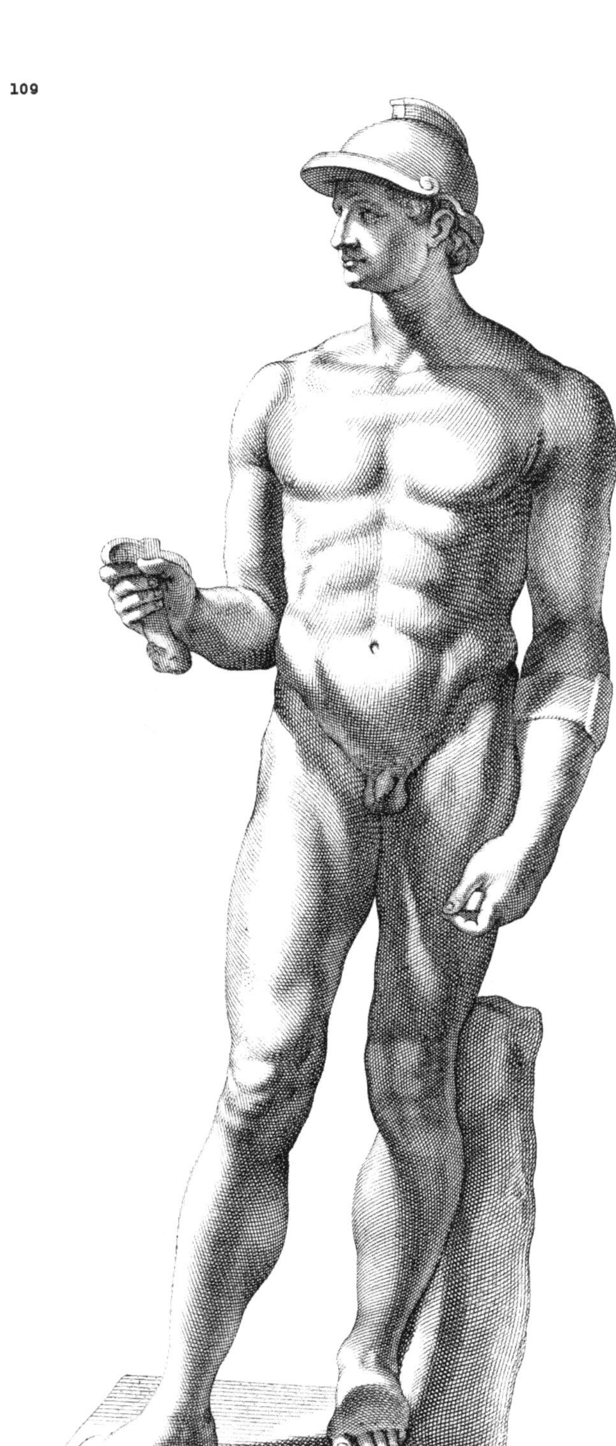

110

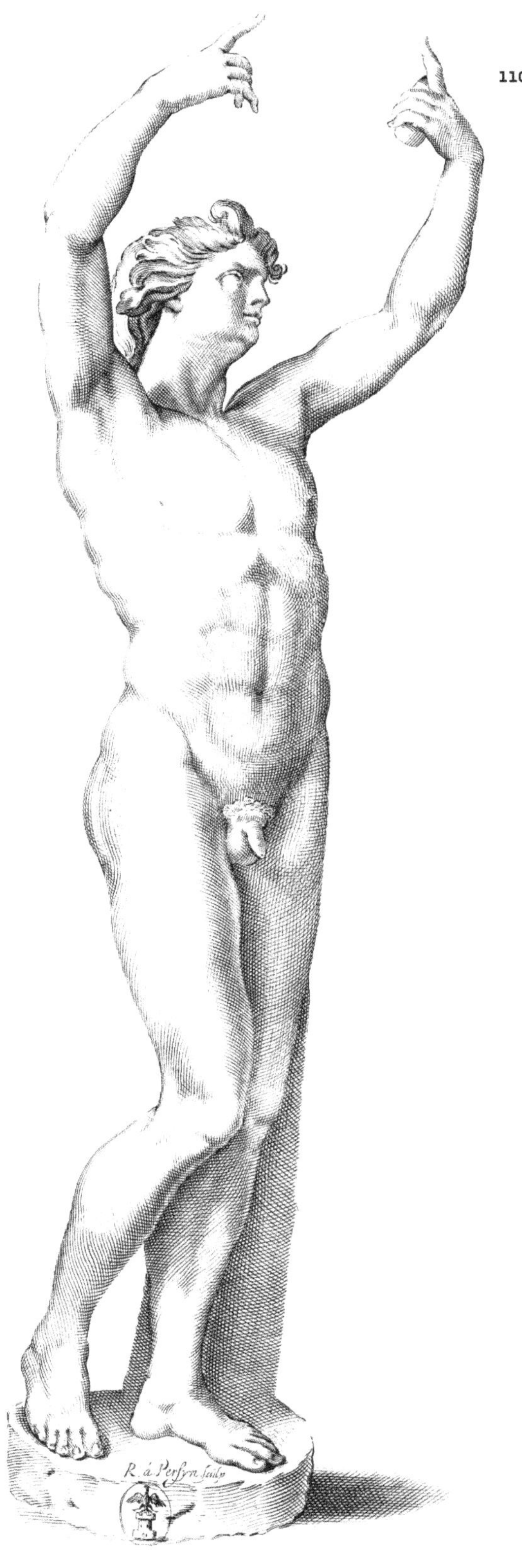

109. Statue of a young gladiator, Cornelis
Bloemaert (II), 1636 – 1647.

110. Statue of a Young Man, Reinier van Persijn,
1640.

111

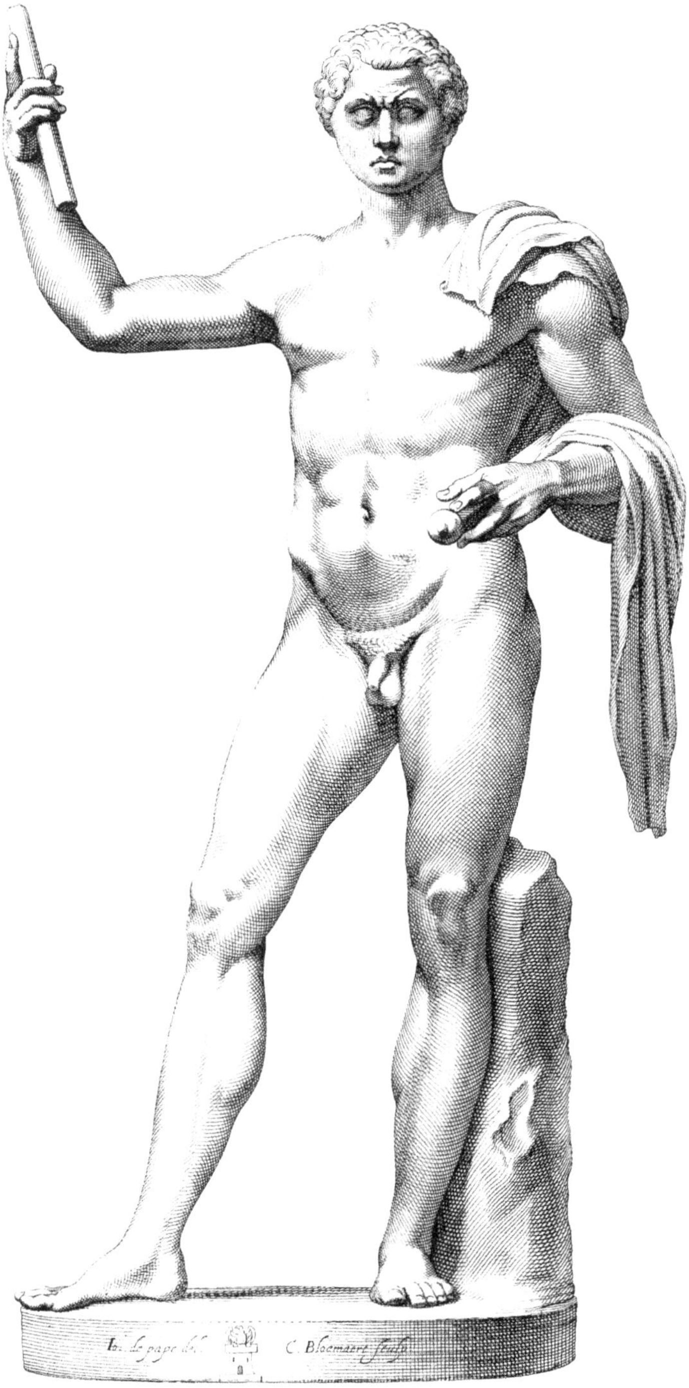

112

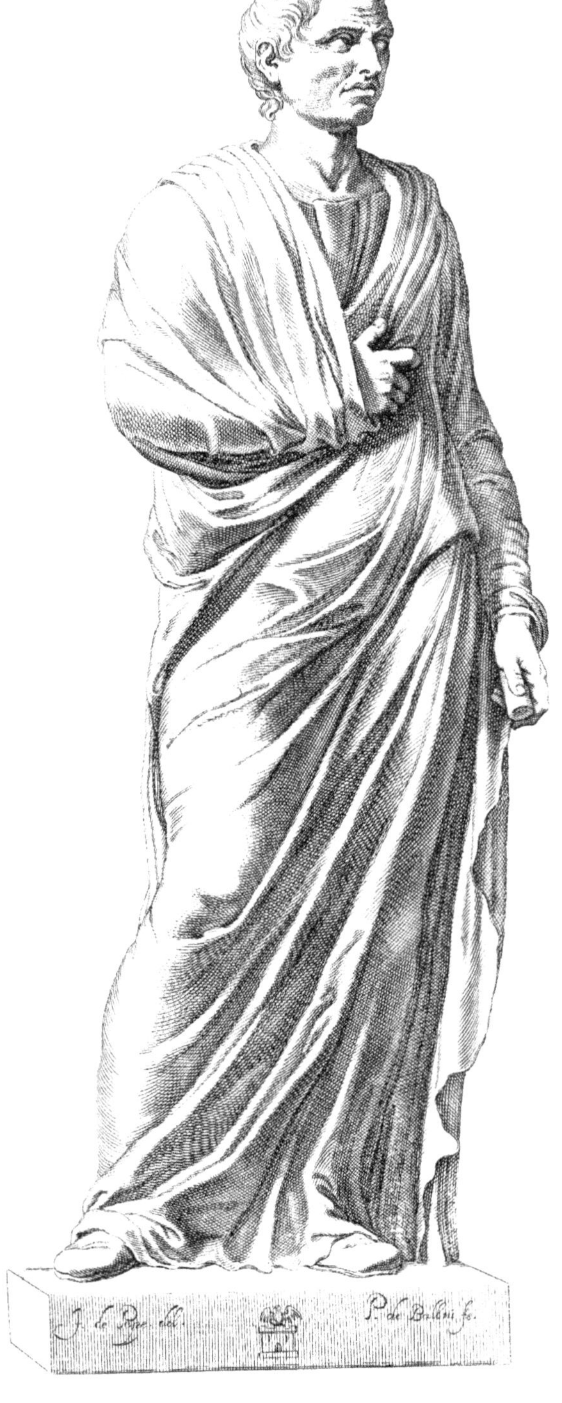

111. Statue of a young soldier with command staff, Cornelis Bloemaert (II), 1636 – 1647.

112. Statue of a Consul in Toga with Scroll, Pieter de Bailliu (I), after Joos de Pape, 1636 – 1647.

113

114

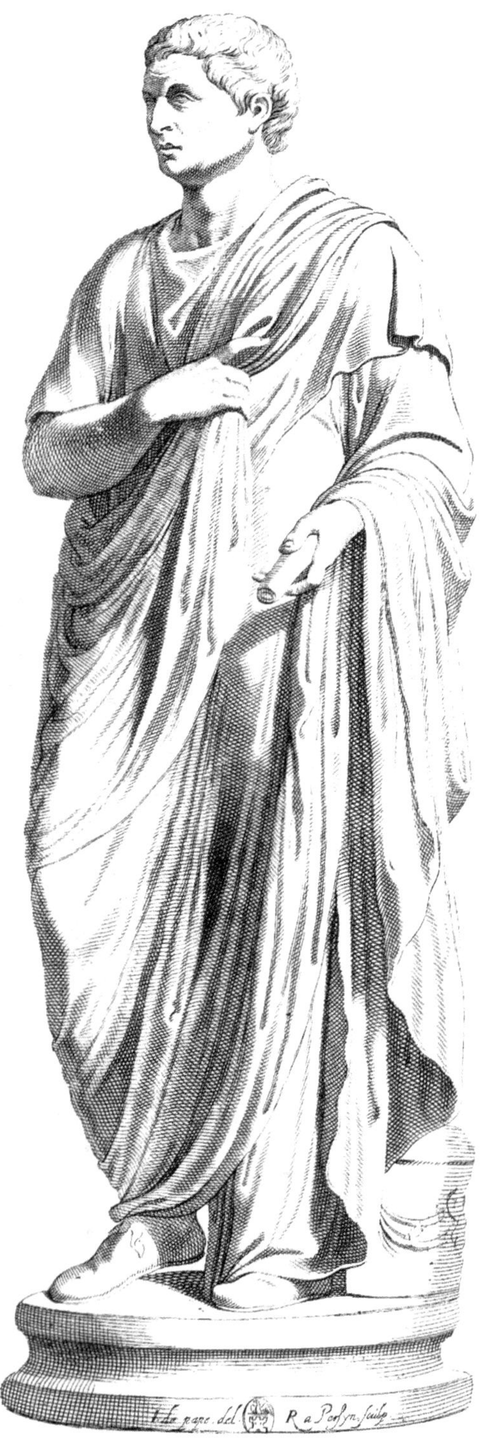

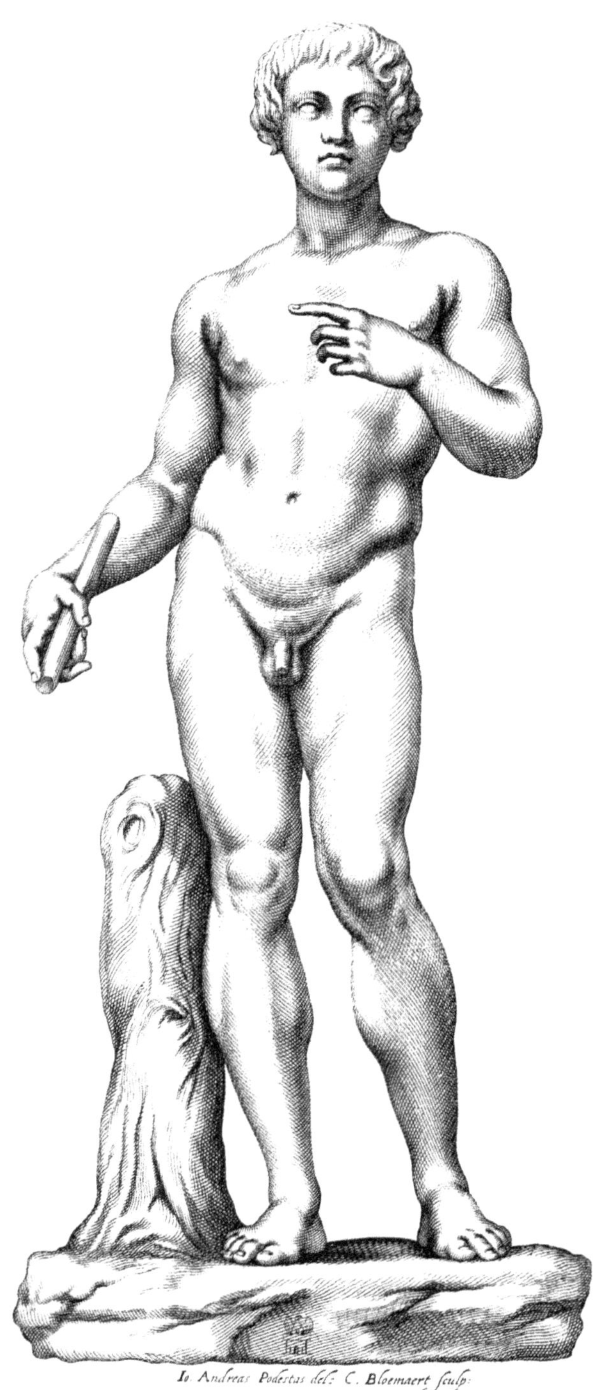

113. Statue of a Consul, Reinier van Persijn, after
Joos de Pape, 1640.

114. Statue of a boy with an officer's baton,
Cornelis Bloemaert (II), 1636 – 1647.

115

116

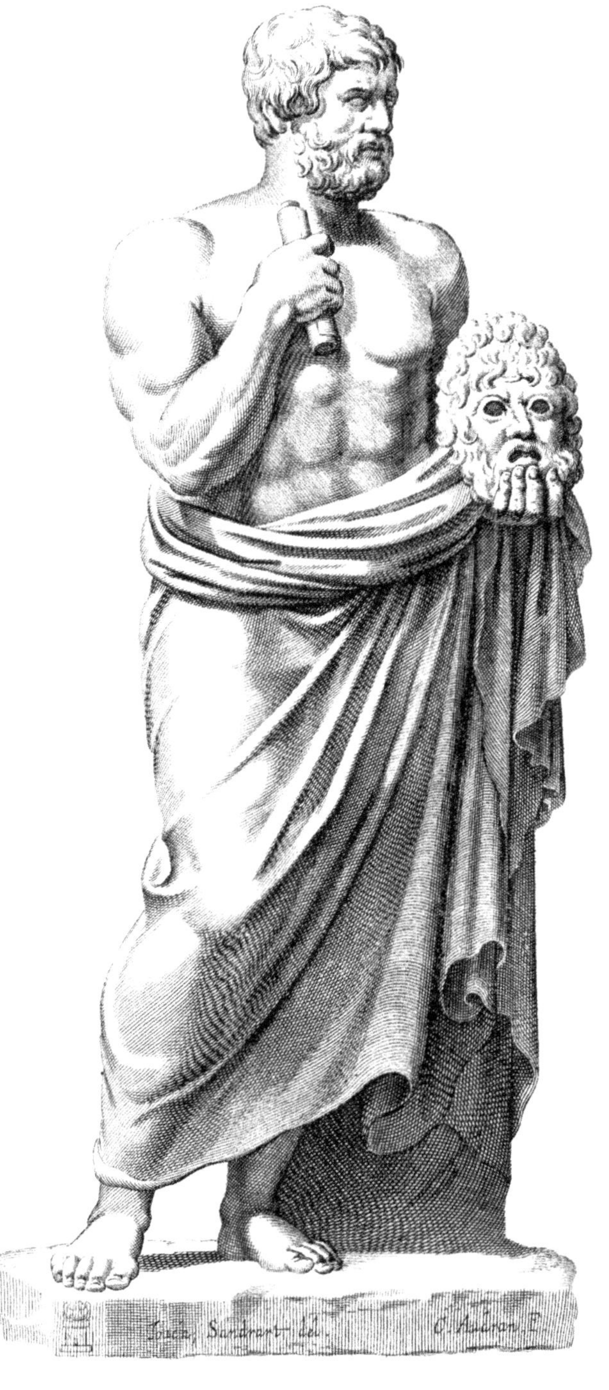

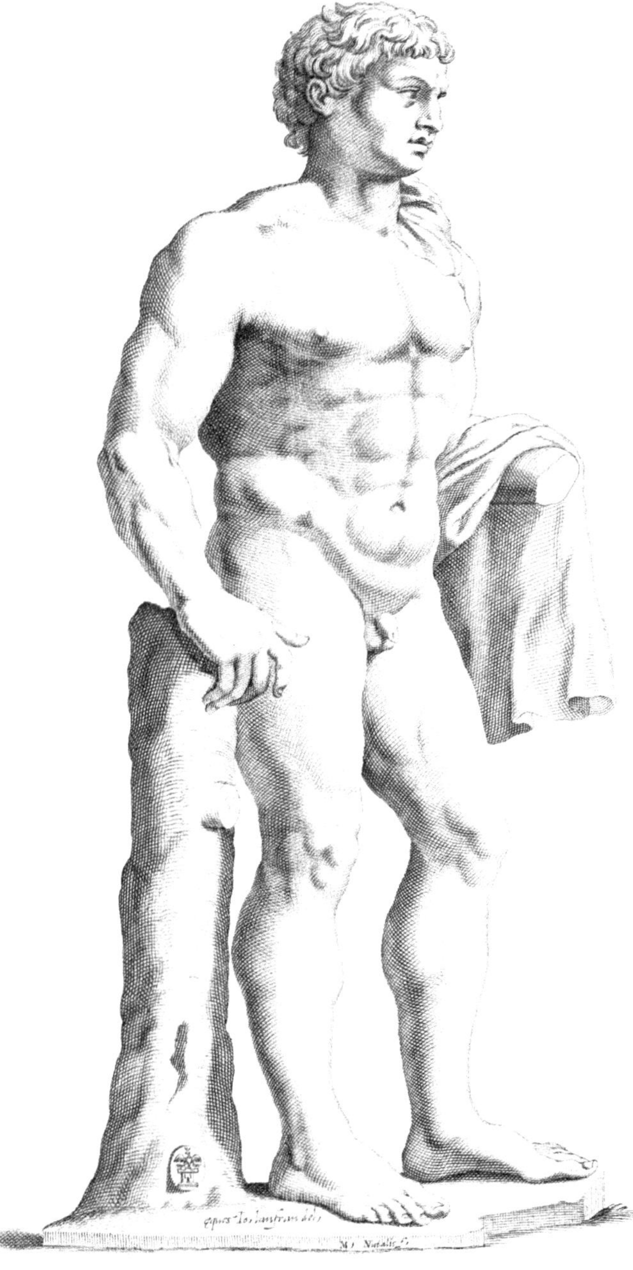

115. Statue of a Man with Mask Possibly Terentius, Charles Audran, 1636 – 1647.

116. Statue of a Young Man, Michel Natalis, after Giovanni Lanfranco, 1640.

117   118

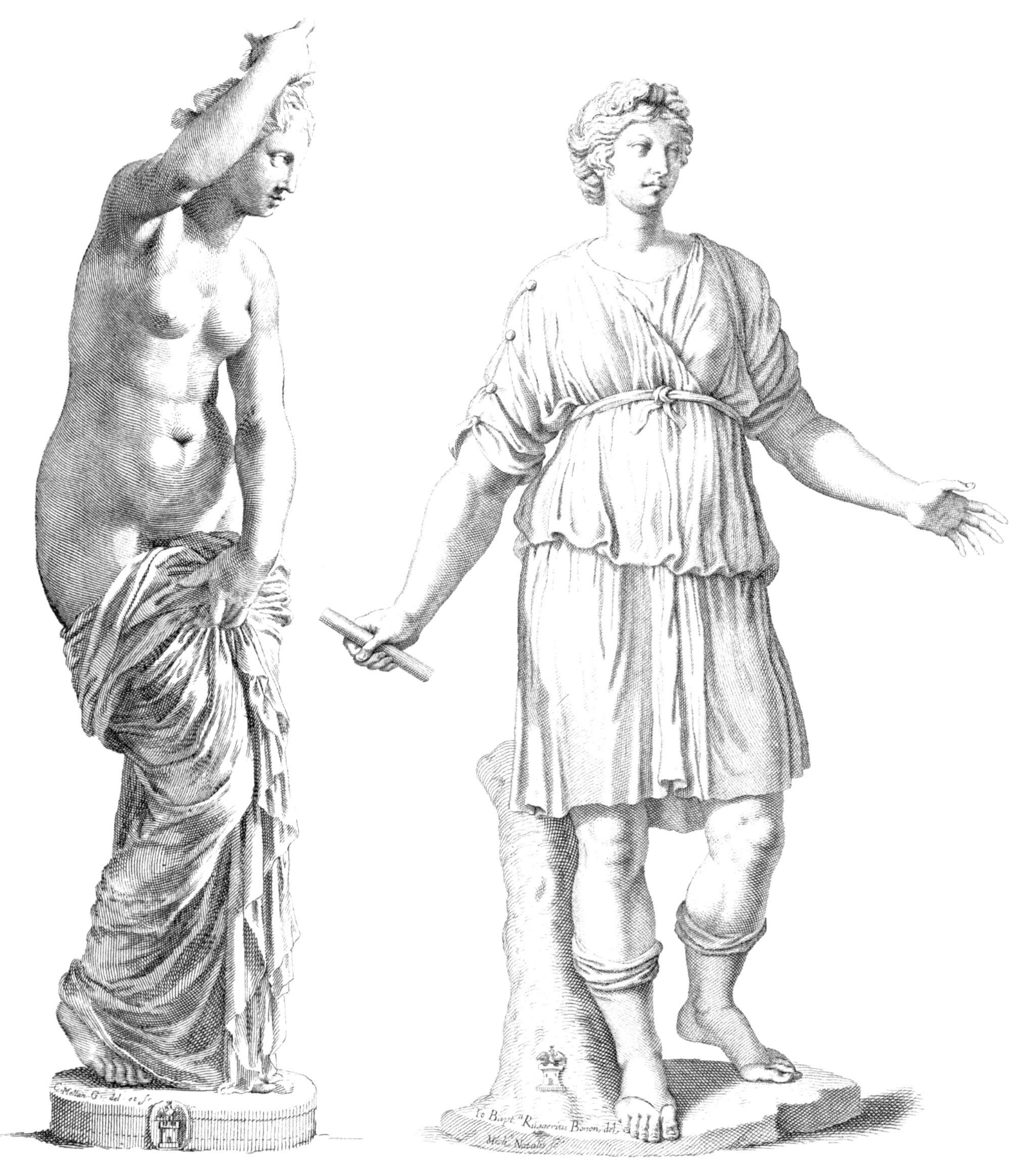

117. Statue of Venus with a Hand Above Her
Head, Claude Mellan, 1636 – 1647.

118. Statue of Standing Woman, Michel Natalis,
after Giovanni Battista Ruggieri, 1640.

119

120

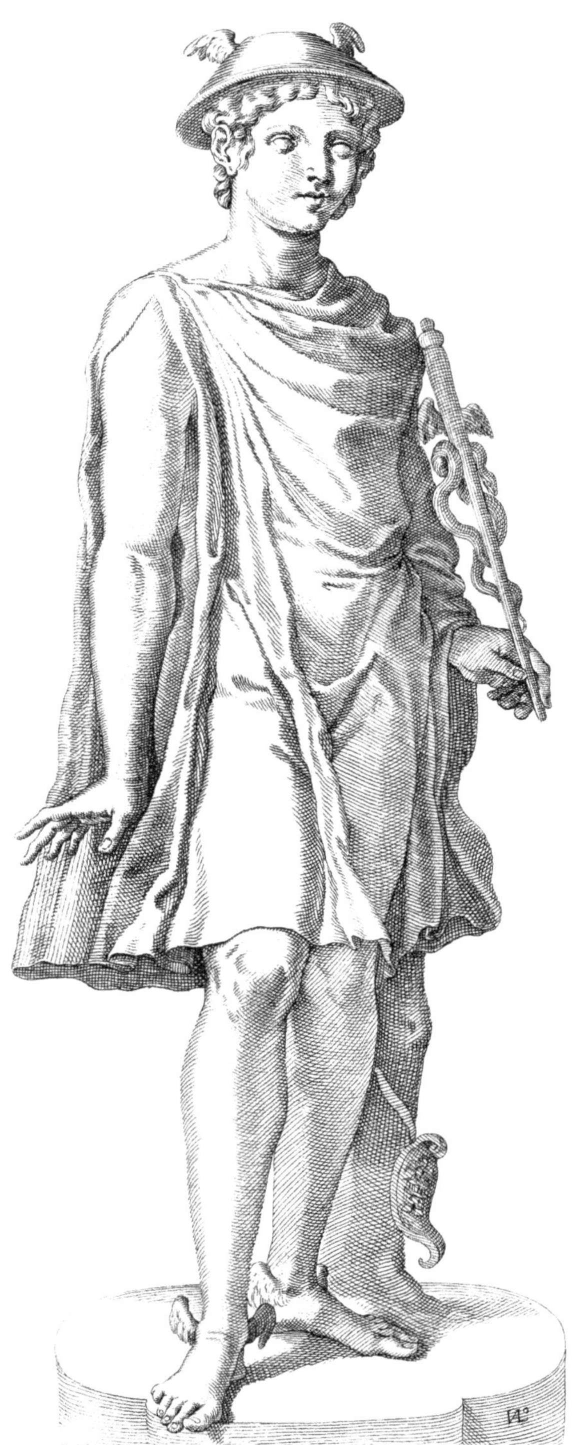

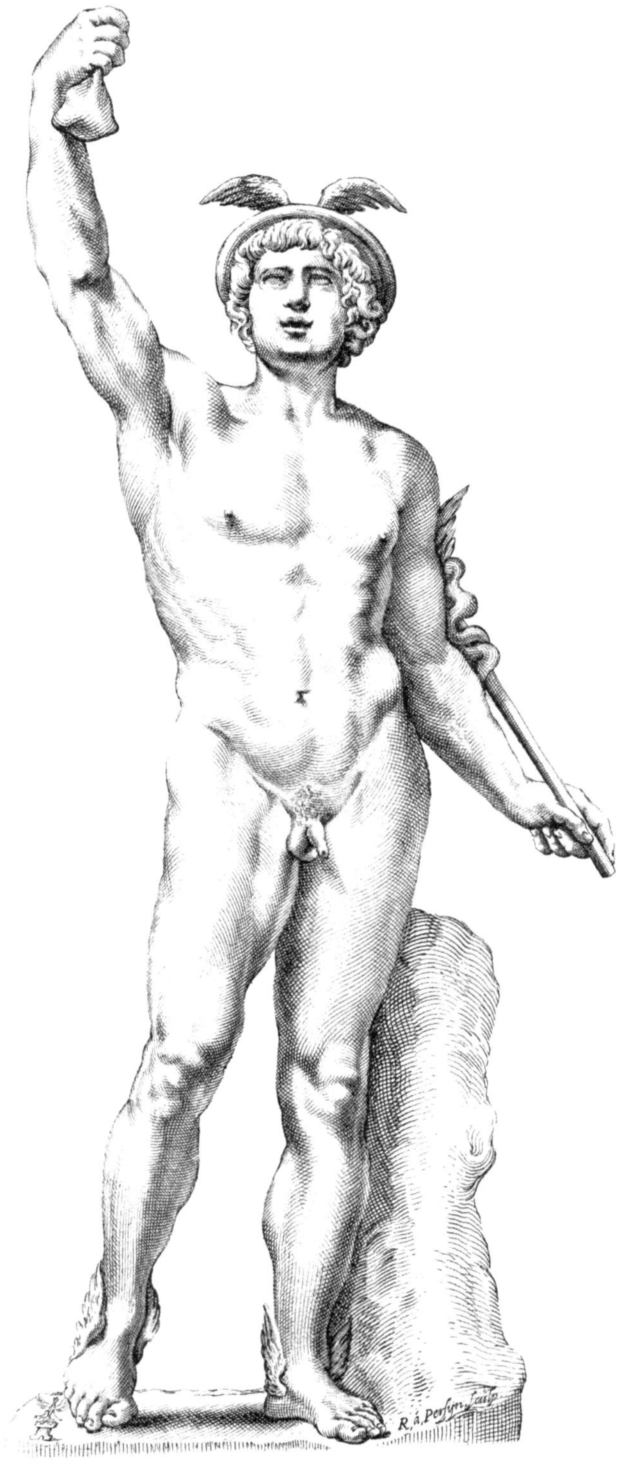

119. Statue of Mercury with Caduceus and Bag of Money, Valérien Regnard, 1636 – 1647.

120. Statue of Mercury with a Putto at His Feet, Claude Mellan, 1636 – 1647.

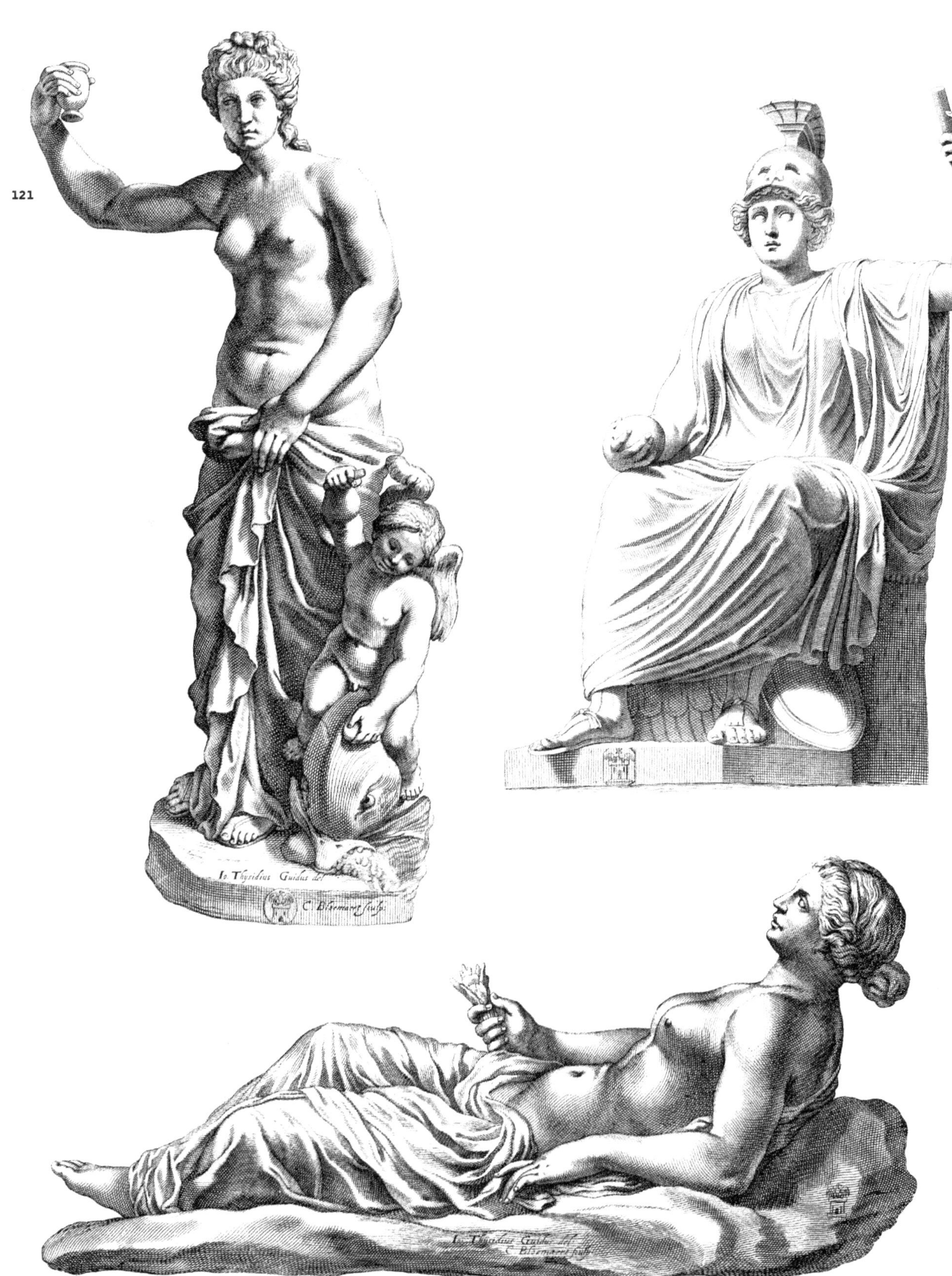

121. Statue of Venus with Amor Sitting on a Dolphin, Cornelis Bloemaert (II), 1636 – 1647.

122. Statue of the goddess Roma, Michel Natalis (attributed to), after Joos de Pape, 1636 – 1647.

123. Sleeping Woman with Putto, Cornelis Bloemaert (II), 1636 – 1647.

124

125

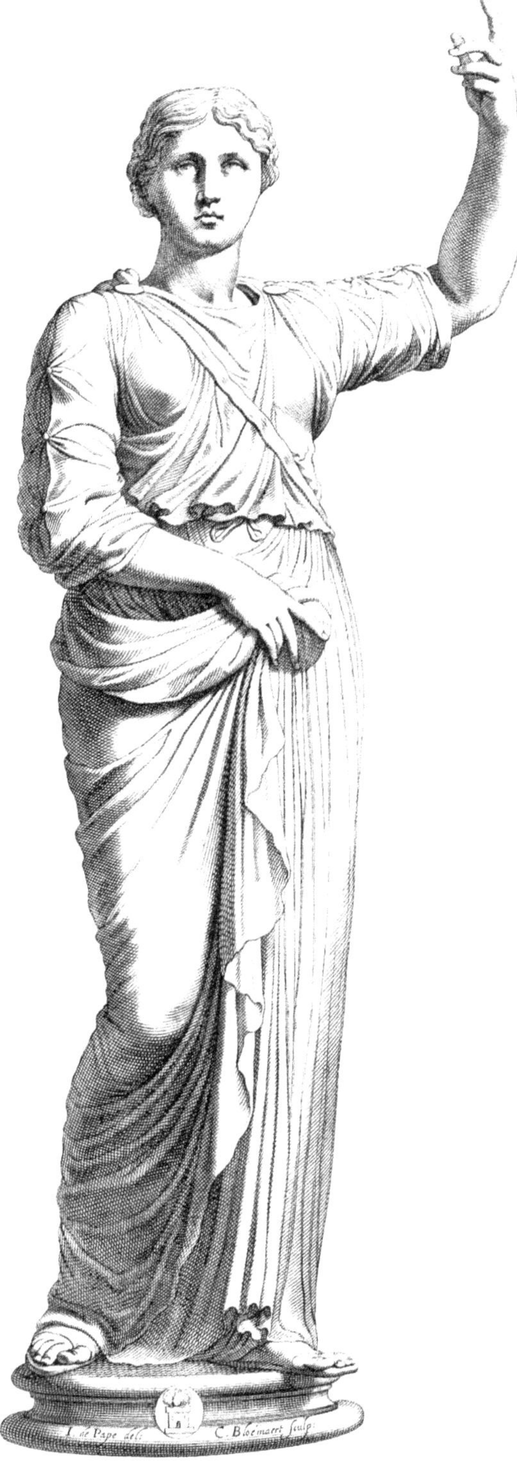

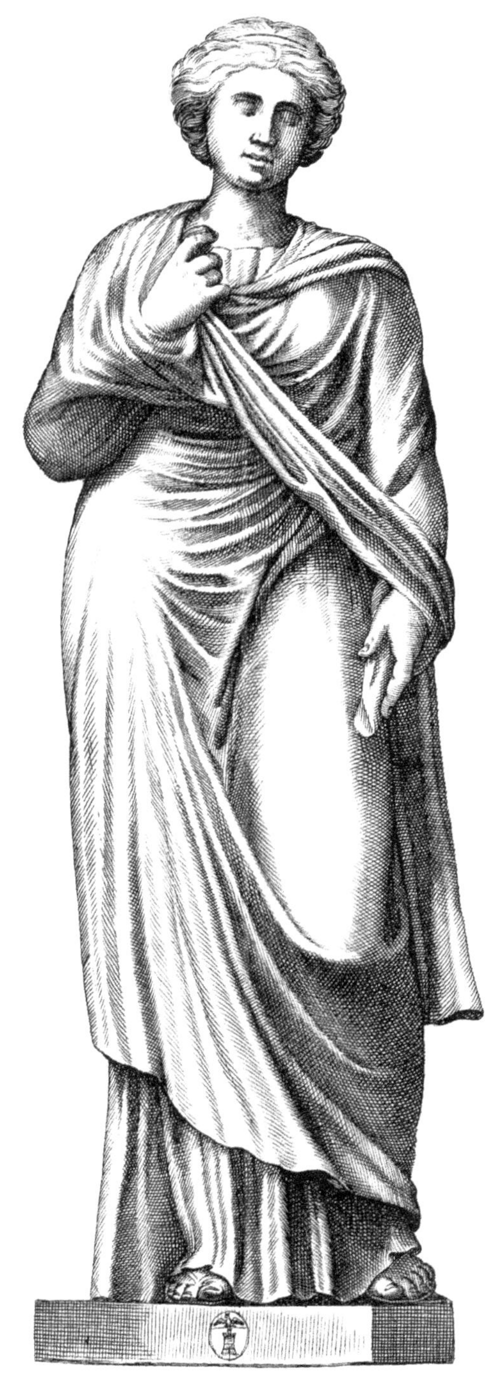

124. Statue of a Standing Woman, Cornelis
Bloemaert (II), after Joos de Pape, 1636 – 1647.

125. Statue of a Standing Woman Pointing with
the Left Hand, Joan Comin, 1636 – 1647.

126

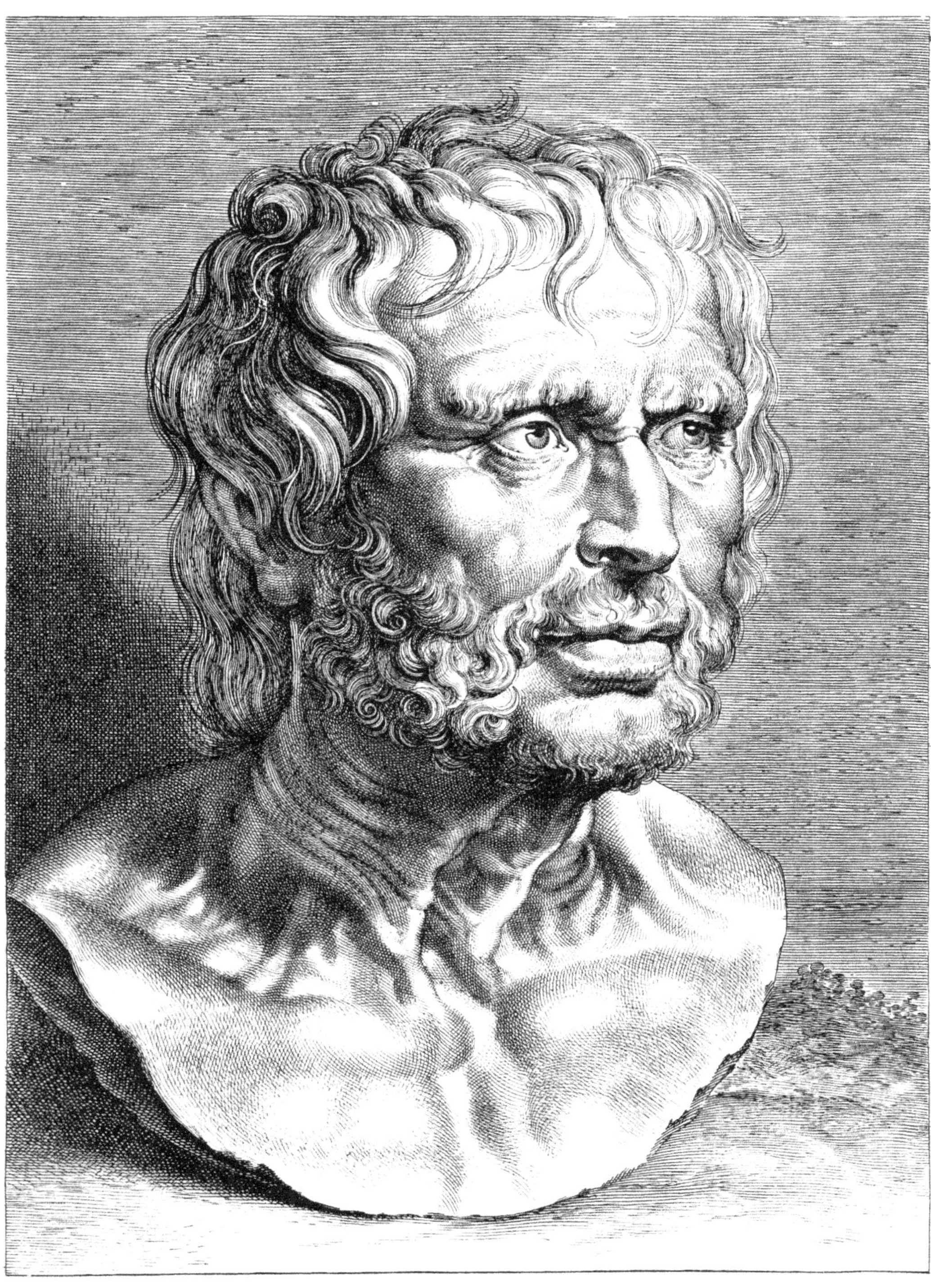

126. Bust of Seneca, Lucas Vorsterman (I), after
Peter Paul Rubens, after anonymous, 1638.

127

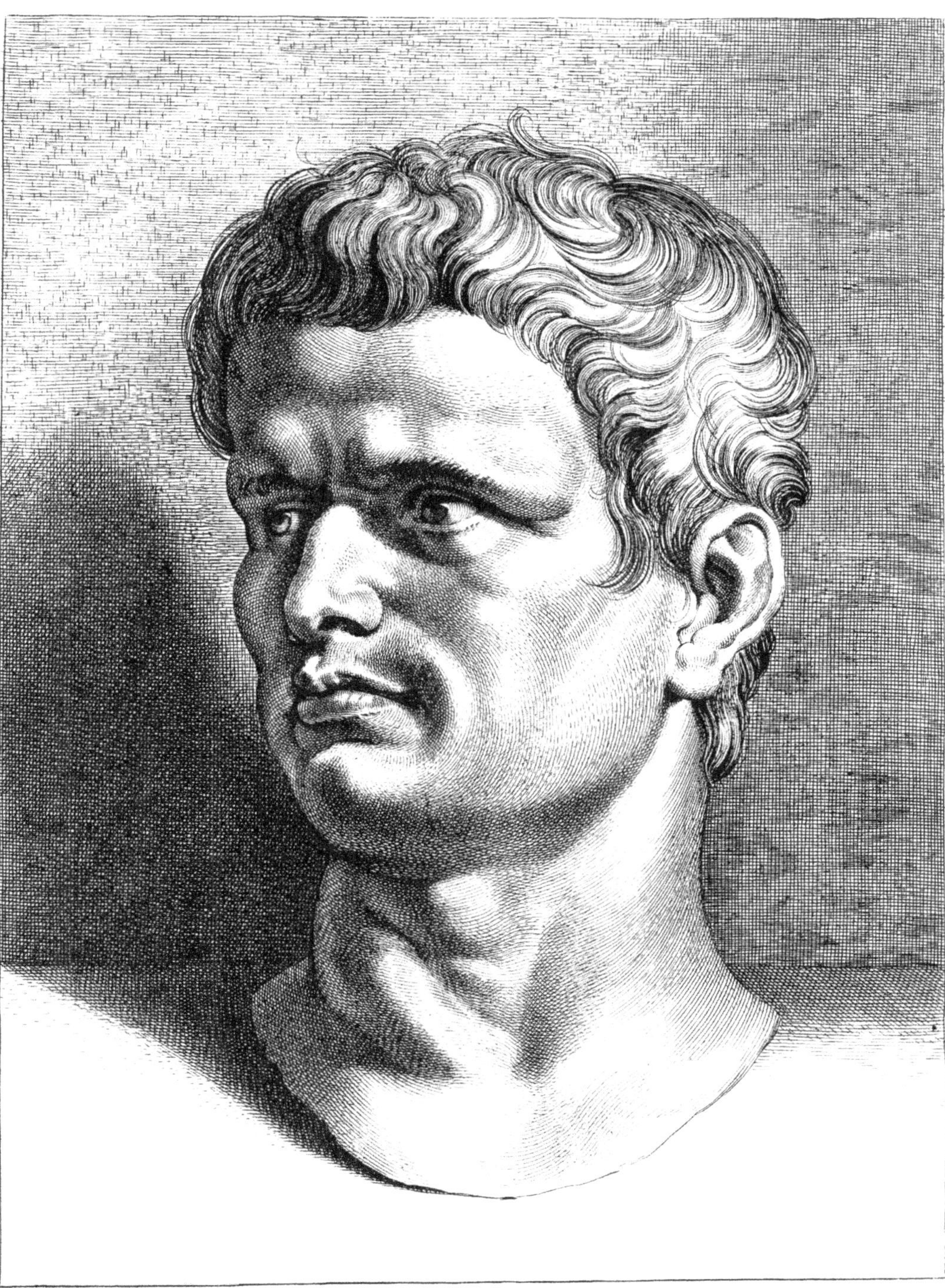

127. Bust of Marcus Junius Brutus, Lucas
Vorsterman (I), after Peter Paul Rubens, 1638.

128

129

130

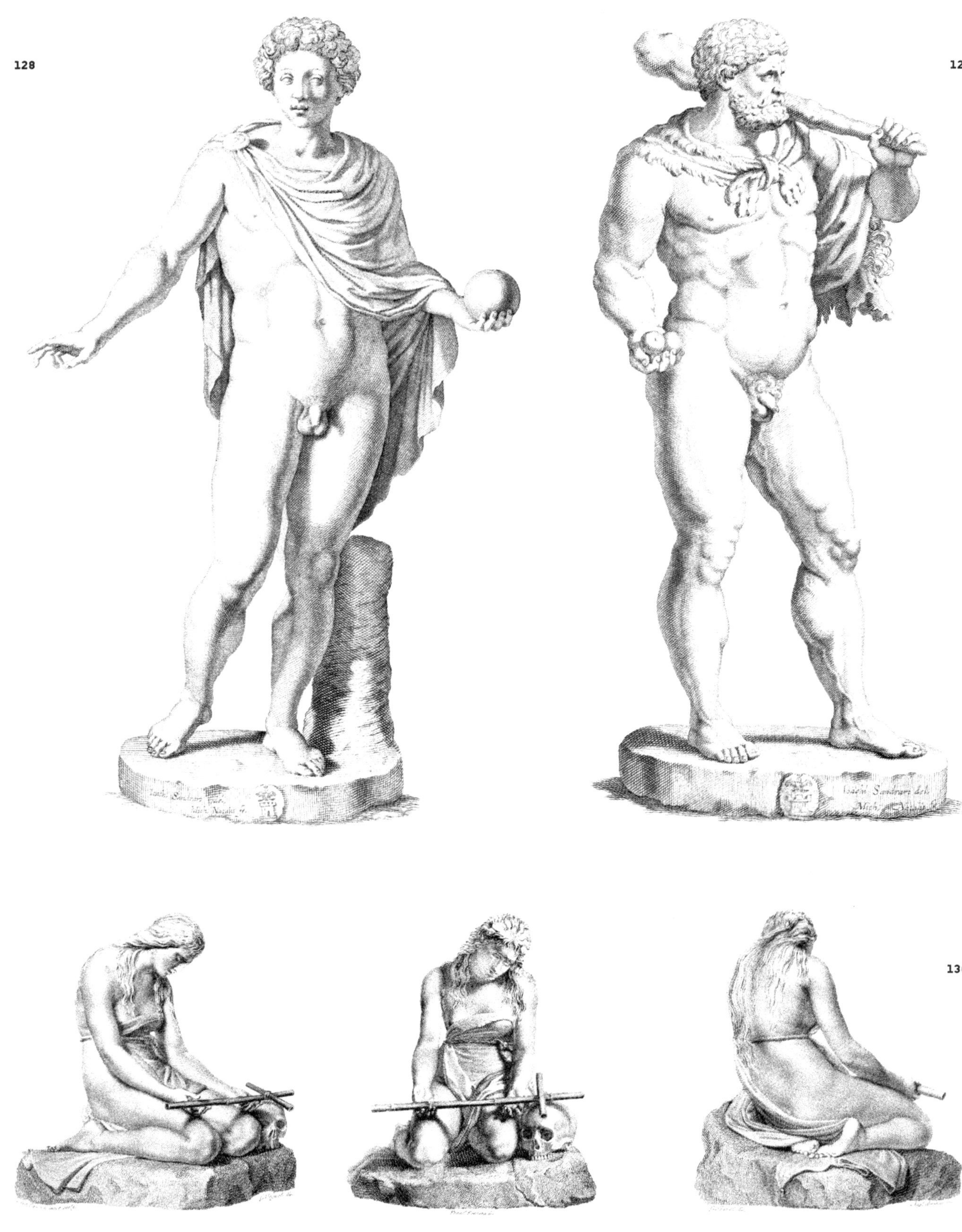

128. Statue of the Young Marcus Aurelius, Michel Natalis, after Joachim von Sandrart (I), 1640.

129. Statue of the Old Hercules, Michel Natalis, after Joachim von Sandrart (I), 1640.

130. The Penitent Mary Magdalene, Angelo Bertini, 1793 – 1838.

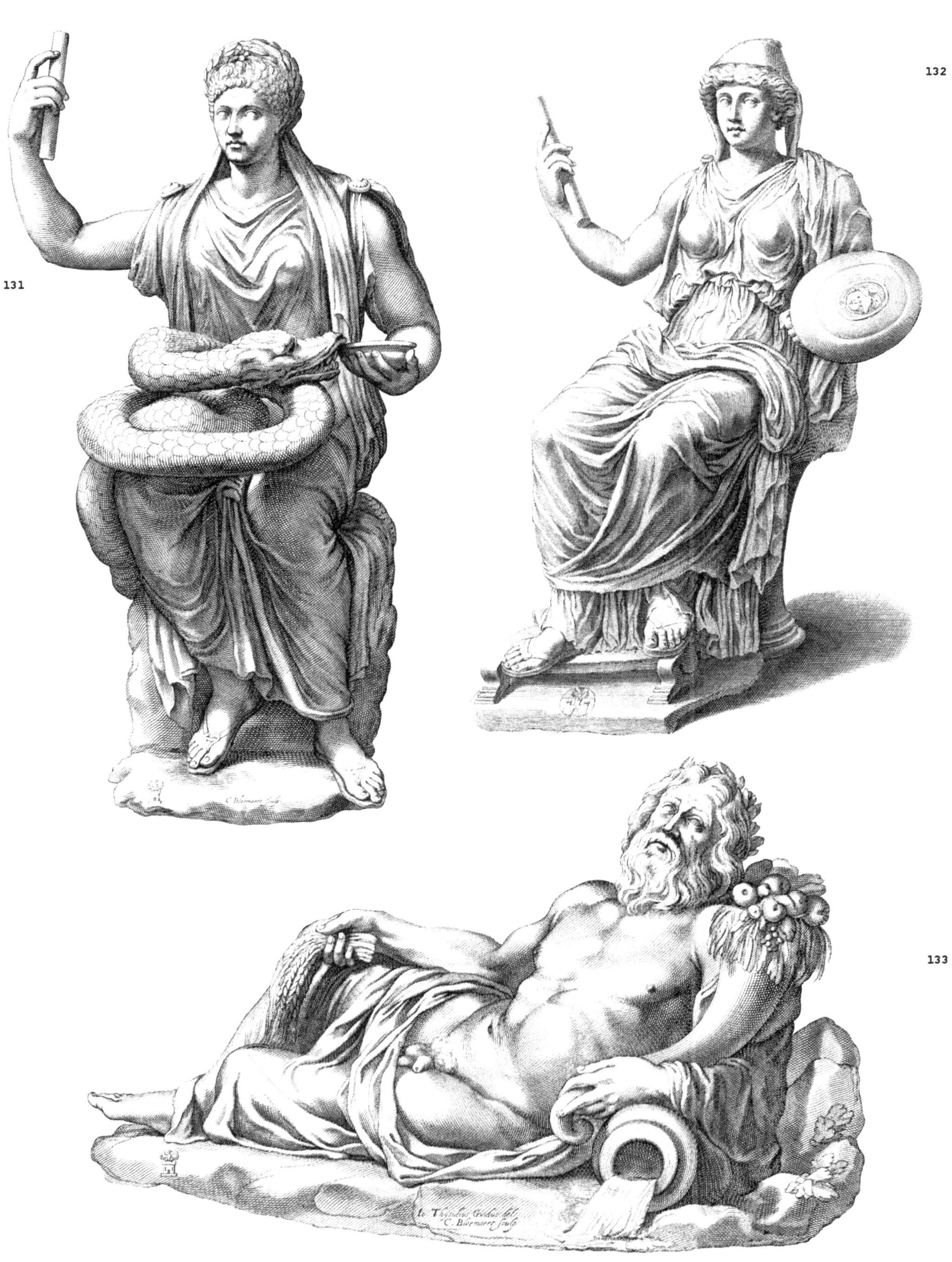

131. Statue of Seated Goddess with Serpent, Cornelis Bloemaert (II), 1636 – 1647.

132. Statue of Seated Minerva, Theodor Matham (attributed to), 1636 – 1647.

133. Reclining River God, Cornelis Bloemaert (II), after Giovanni Citosibio Guidi, 1636 – 1647.

134

135

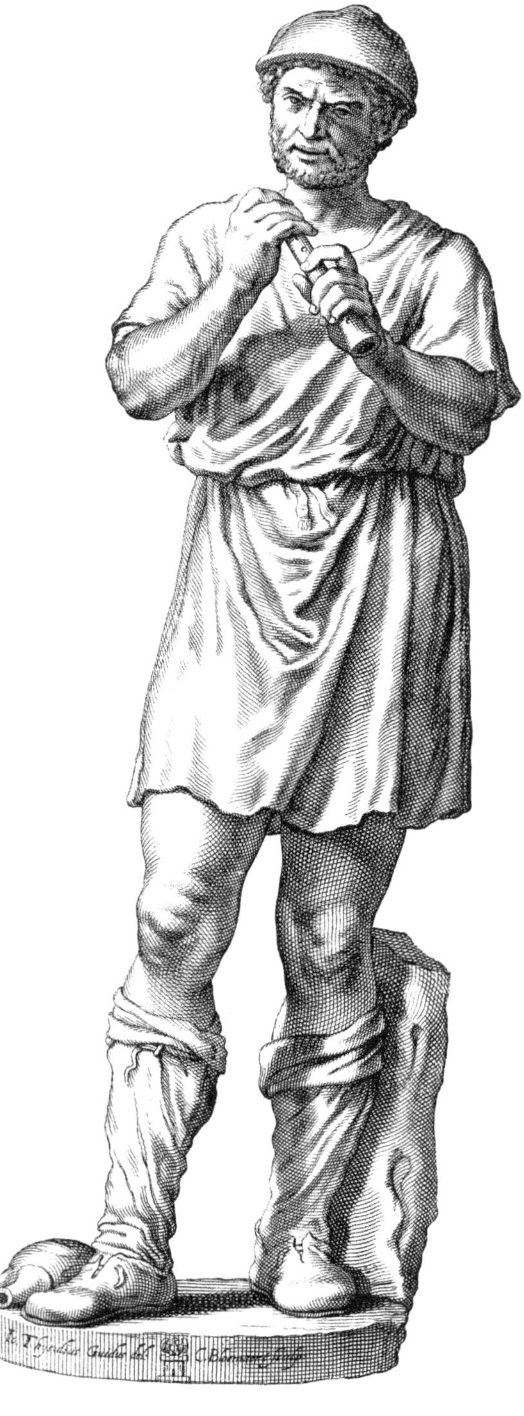

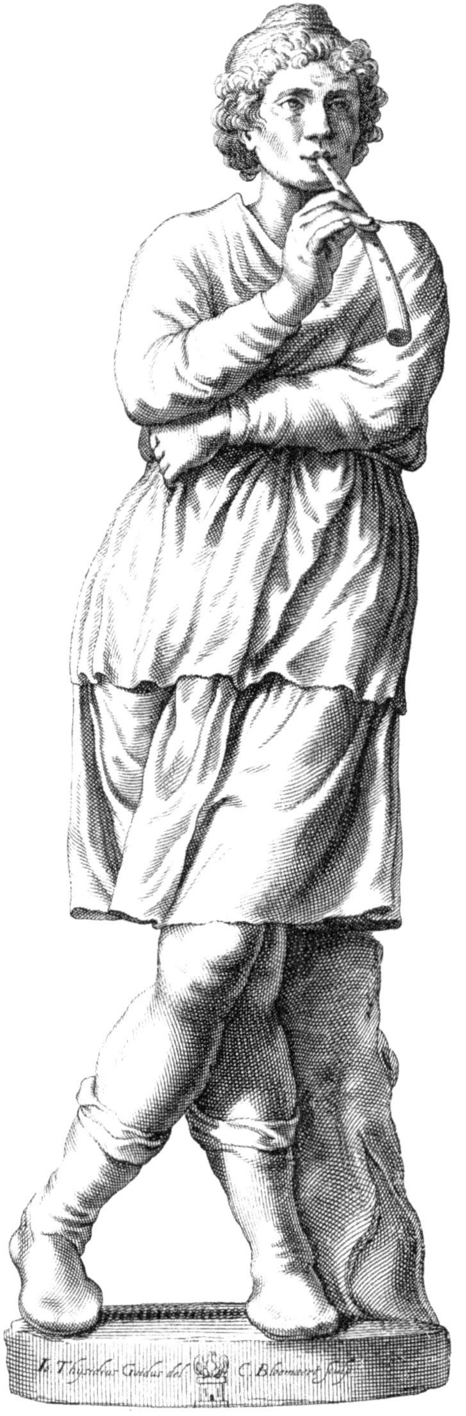

134. Statue of a Standing Man with Flute,
Cornelis Bloemaert (II), 1636 – 1647.

135. Statue of a flute player, Cornelis Bloemaert
(II), after Giovanni Citosibio Guidi, 1636 – 1647.

136

137

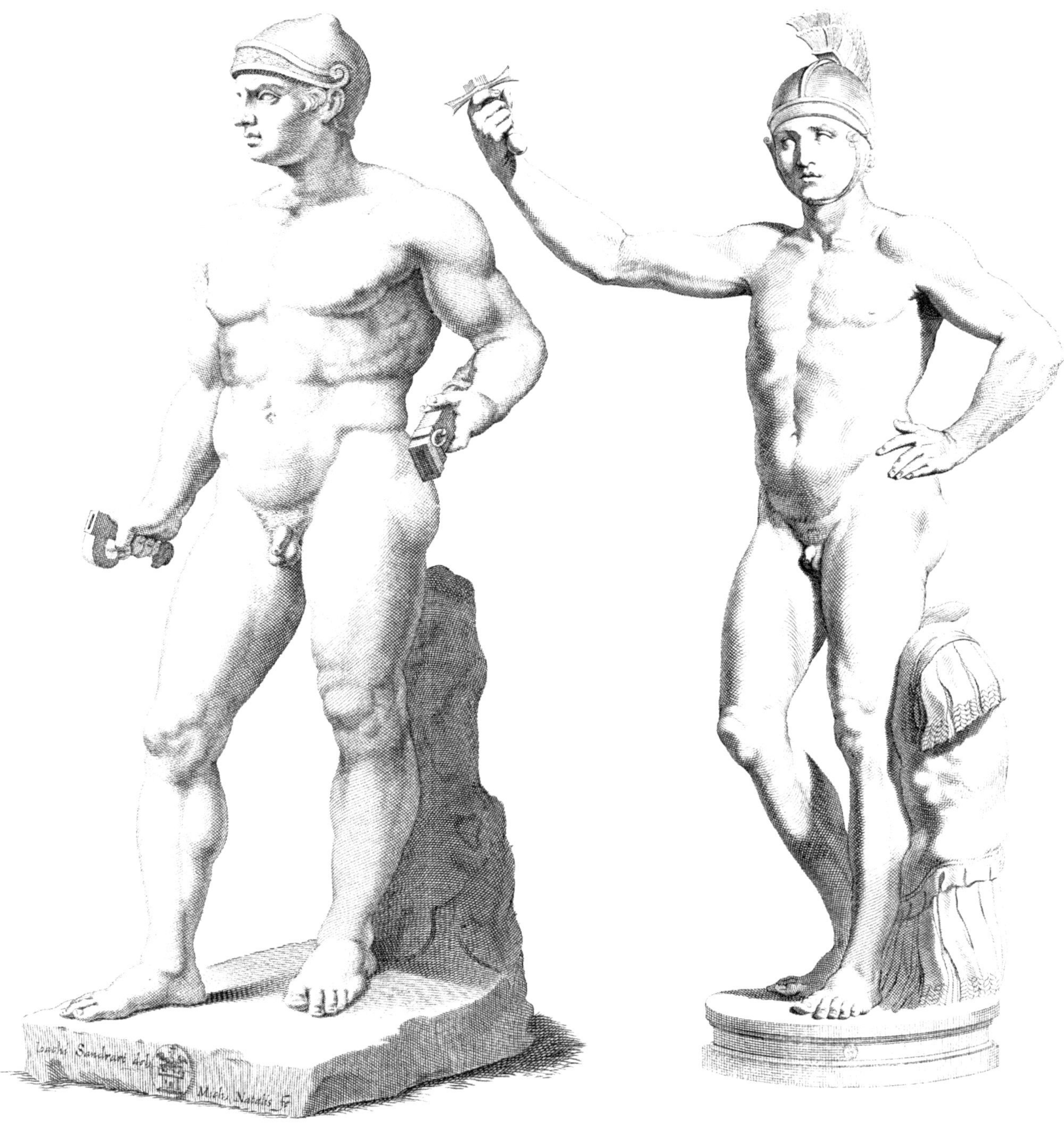

136. Statue of a gladiator, Michel Natalis, after
Joachim von Sandrart (I), 1640.

137. Statue of a gladiator, Theodor Matham, after
Joos de Pape 1636–1647.

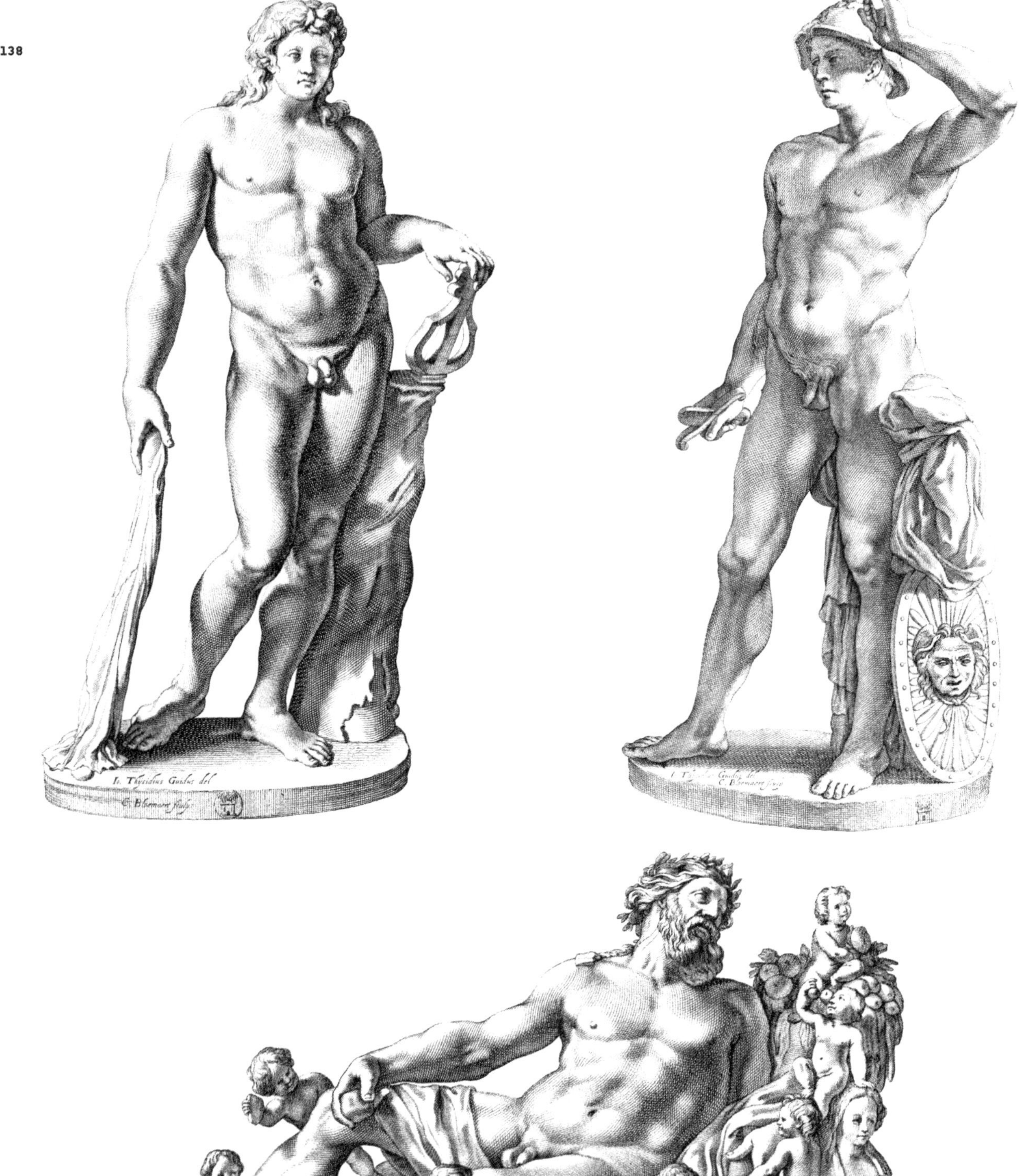

138. Statue of a Naked Boy with Torch, Cornelis Bloemaert (II), 1636 – 1647.

139. Statue of a Nude Gladiator with Helmet and Shield, Cornelis Bloemaert (II), 1636 – 1647.

140. River God of the Nile, Cornelis Bloemaert (II), after Giovanni Citosiblo Guidi, 1636 – 1647.

141

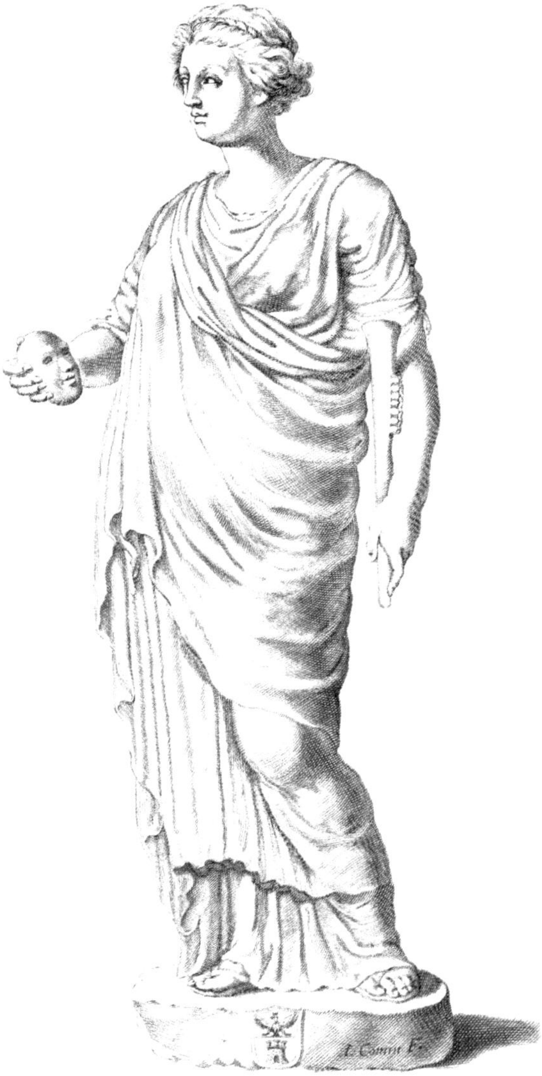

142

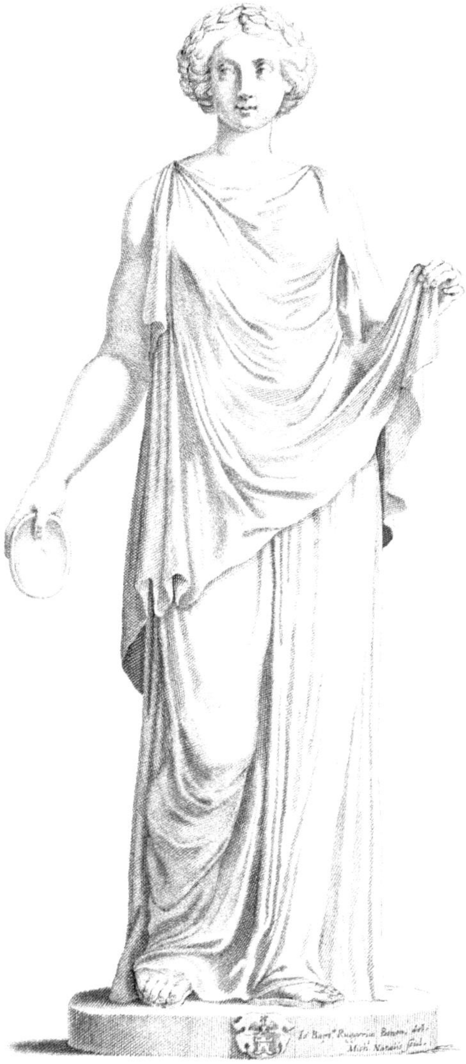

143

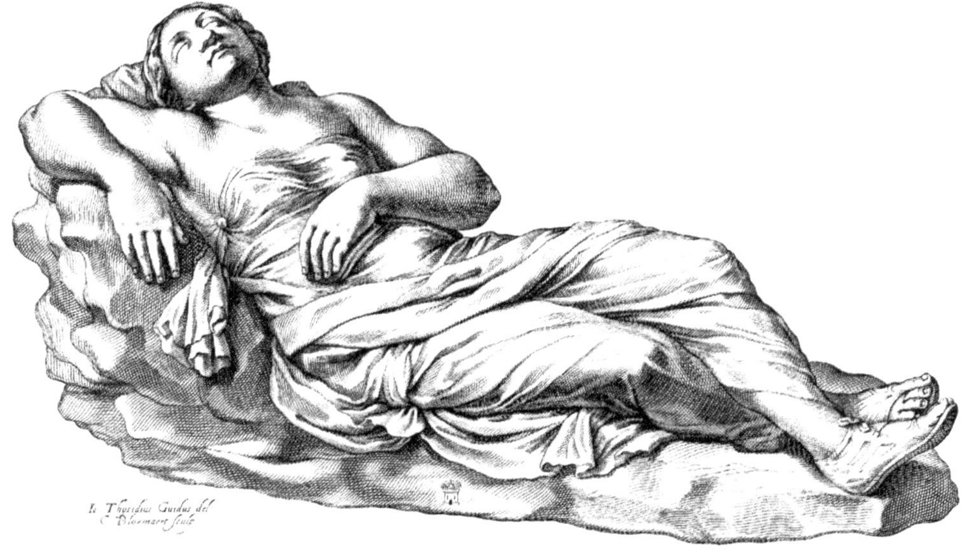

141. Statue of a Muse, Joan Comin, 1636.

142. Statue of a Young Woman, Michel Natalis, after Giovanni Battista Ruggieri, 1640.

143. Sleeping woman, Cornelis Bloemaert (II), after Giovanni Citosibio Guidi, 1636 – 1647.

144

145

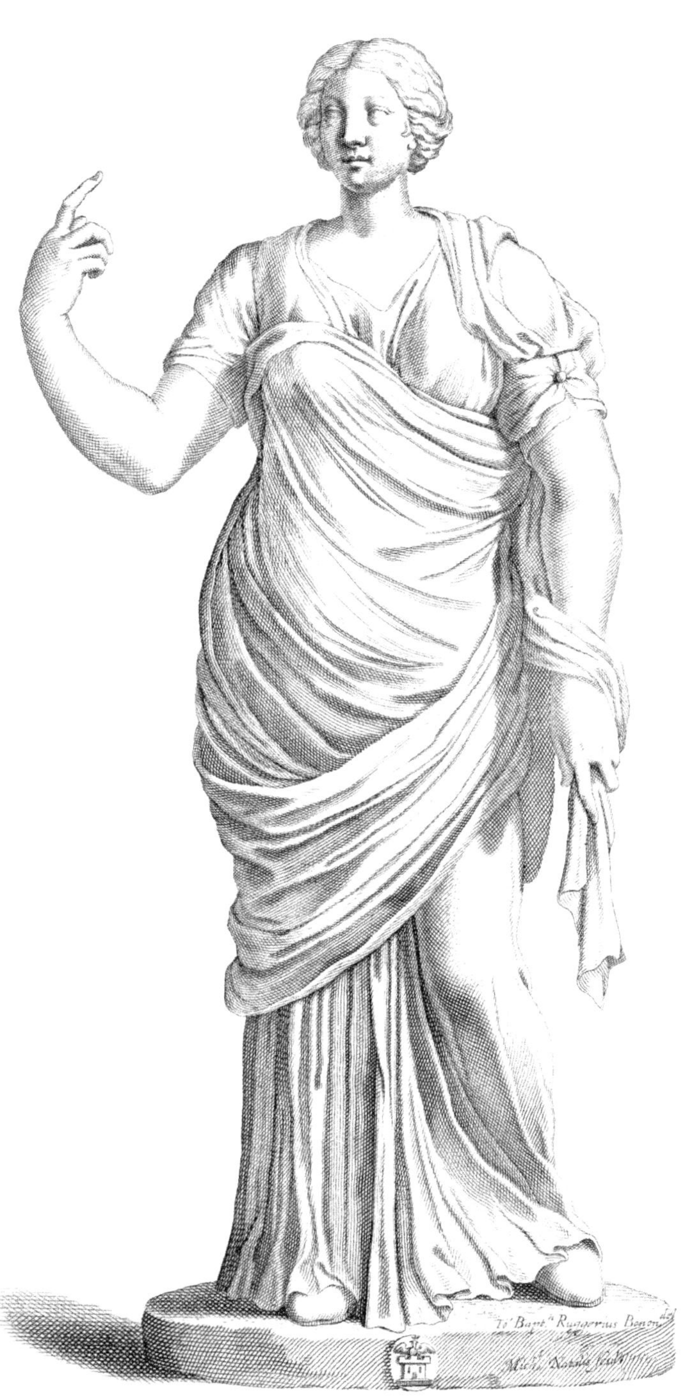

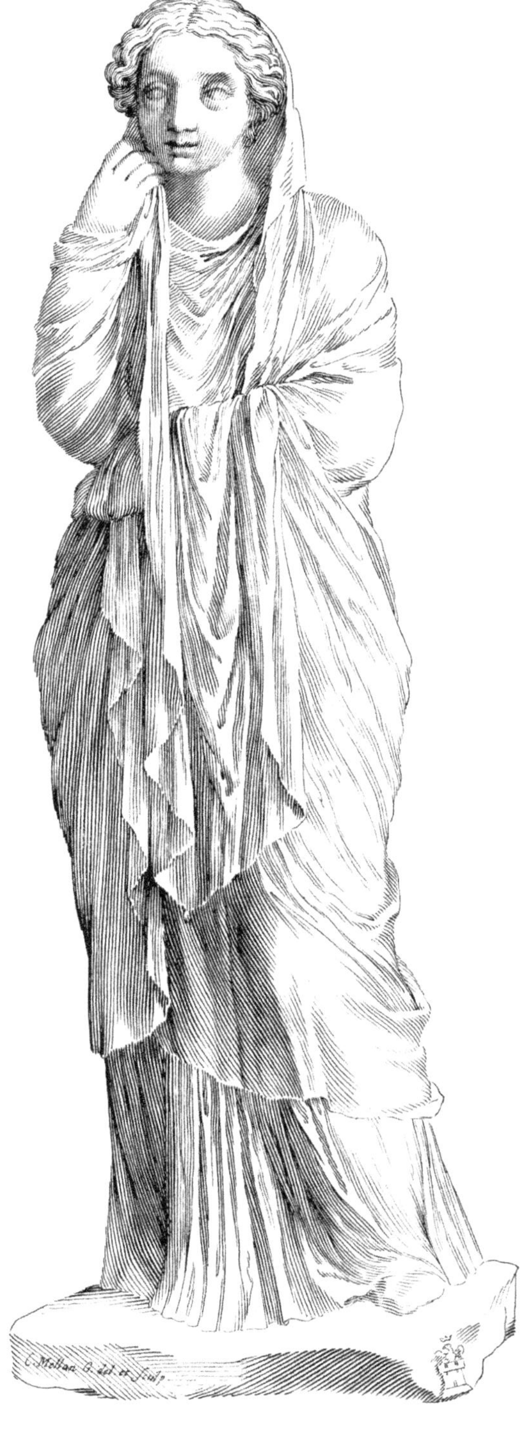

144. Statue of a Standing Woman, Michel Natalis, after Giovanni Battista Ruggieri, 1640.

145. Statue of a Standing Woman Draped, Claude Mellan, 1636 – 1647.

146

147

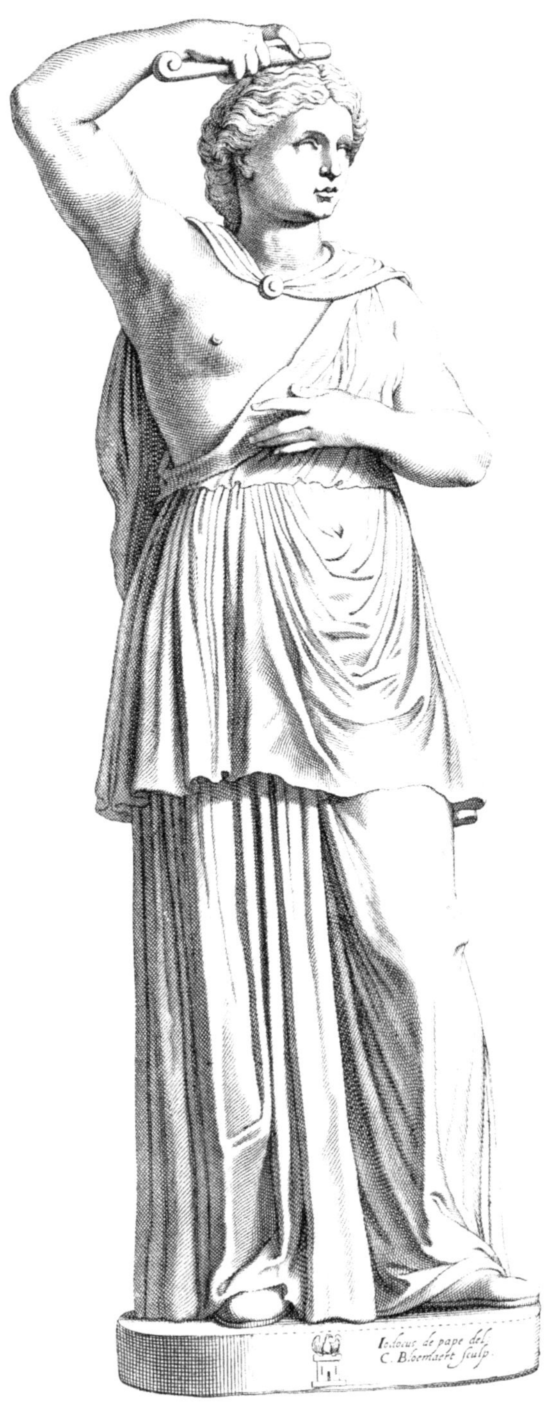

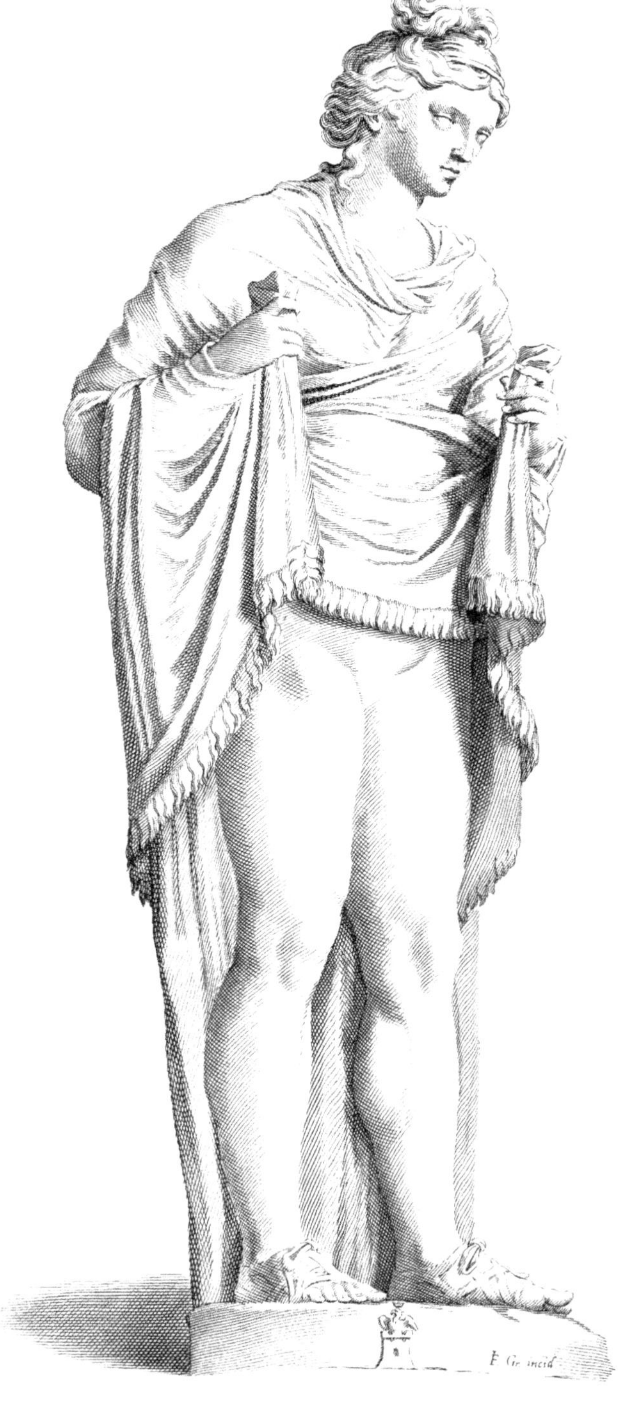

146. Statue of a woman combing her hair,
Cornelis Bloemaert (II), 1636 – 1647.

147. Unchained woman, Johann Friedrich Greuter,
1636.

148

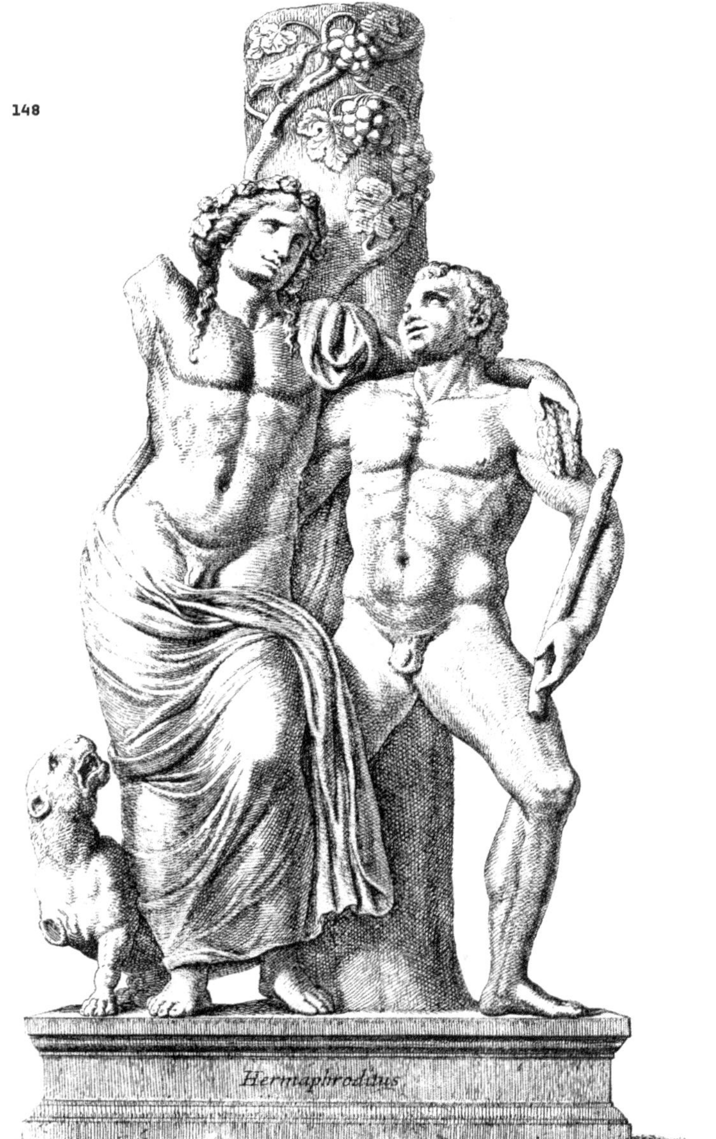

149

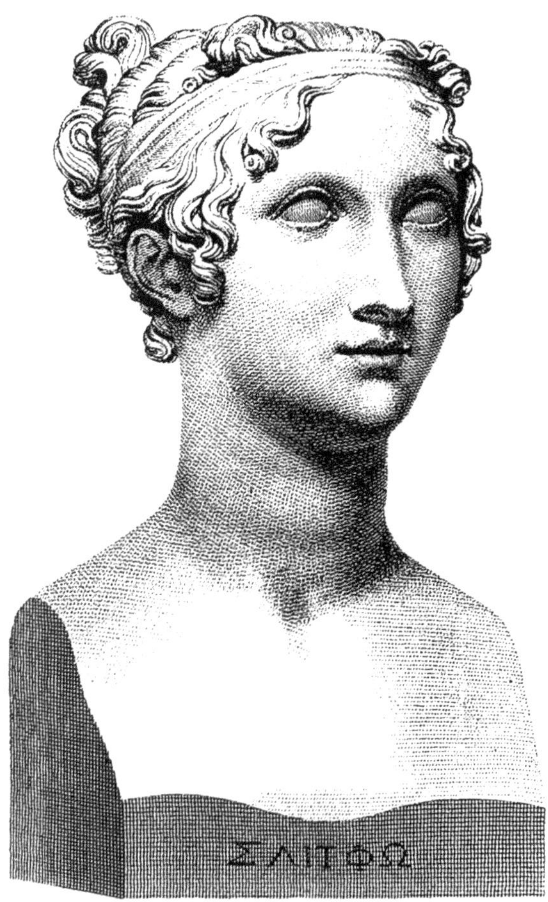

150

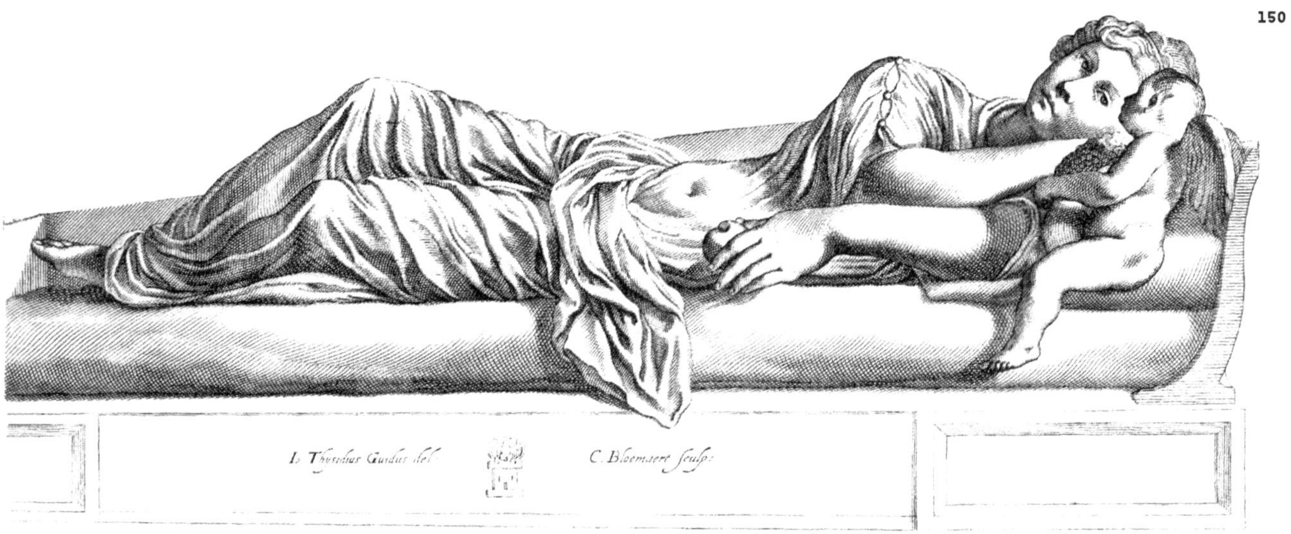

148. Sculpture of Bacchus, with Satyr and
Panther, Hubert Quellinus, 1646 – 1670.

149. Sappho, Domenico Marchetti, after
Ferdinando, 1790 – 1844.

150. Reclining Woman with Putto, Cornelis
Bloemaert (II), 1636 – 1647.

151

152

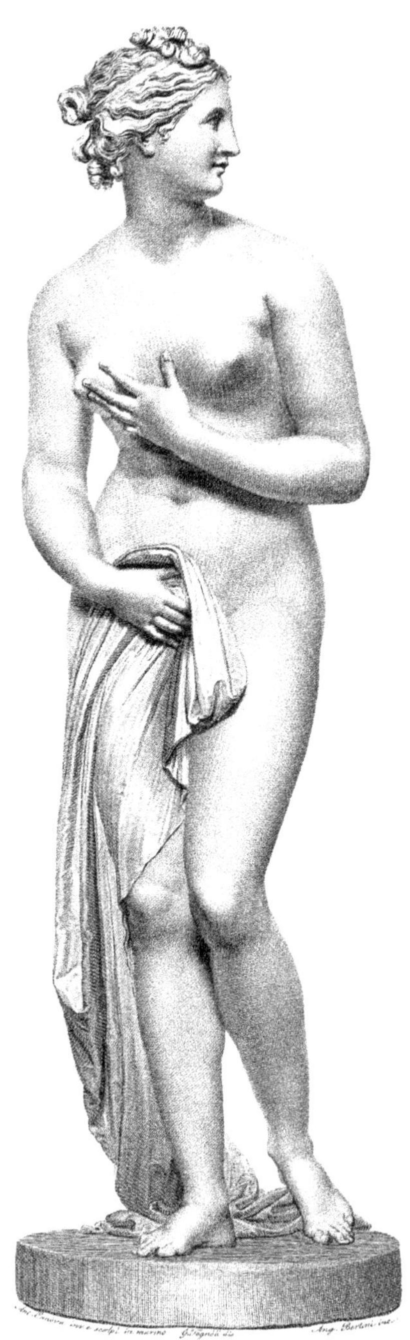

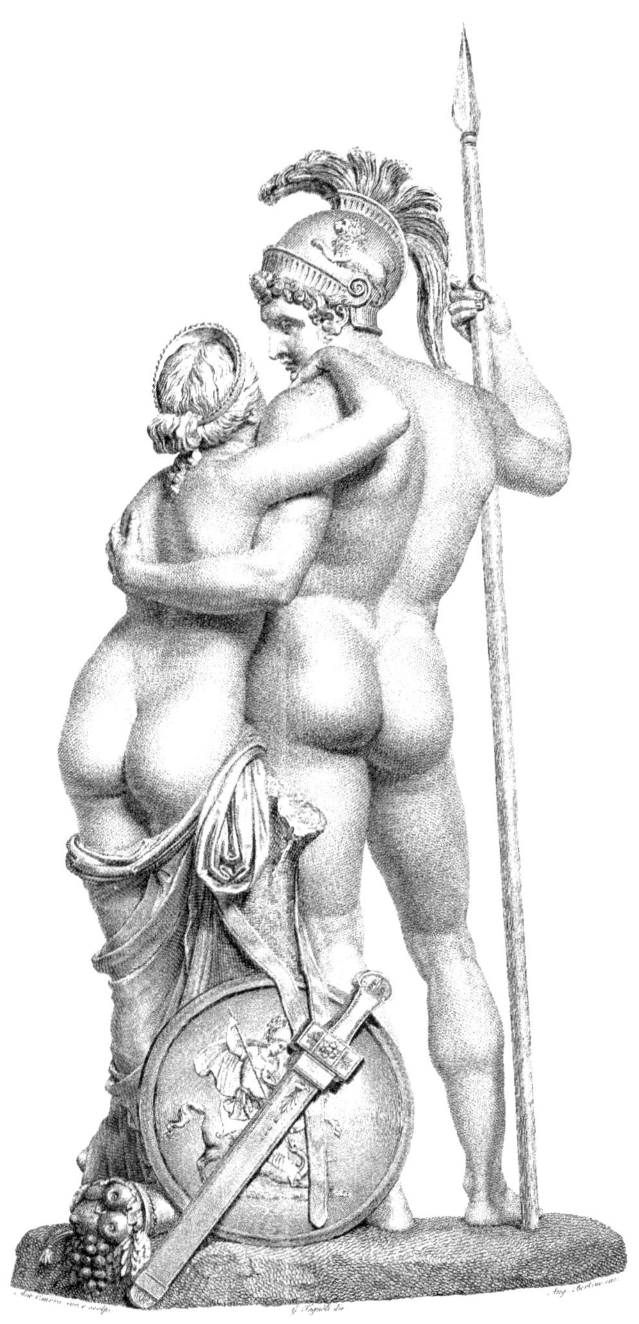

151. Venus, Angelo Bertini, after Giovanni
Tognolli, after Antonio Canova, 1793 – 1838.

152. Venus and Mars, Angelo Bertini, after
Giovanni Tognolli, 1793 – 1838.

153

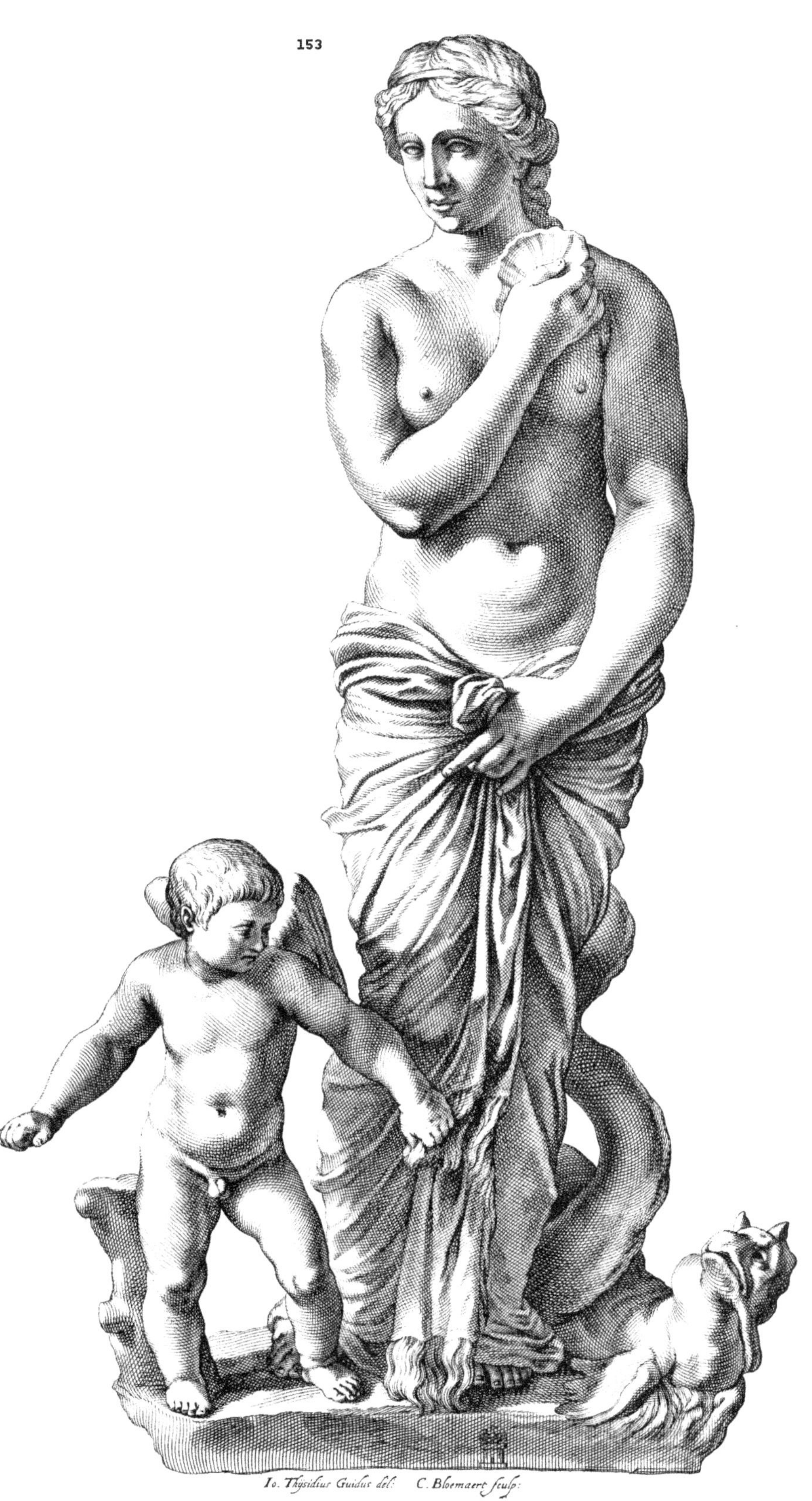

153. Statue of Venus with Amor, Cornelis
Bloemaert (II), 1636 – 1647.

154

155

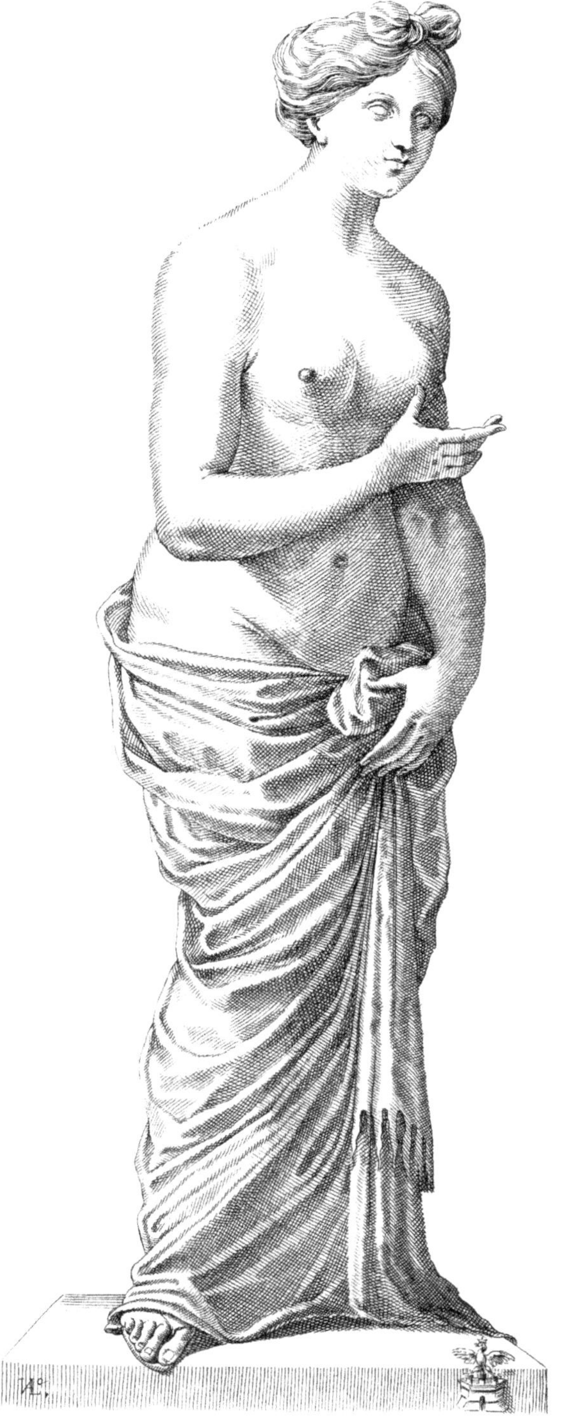

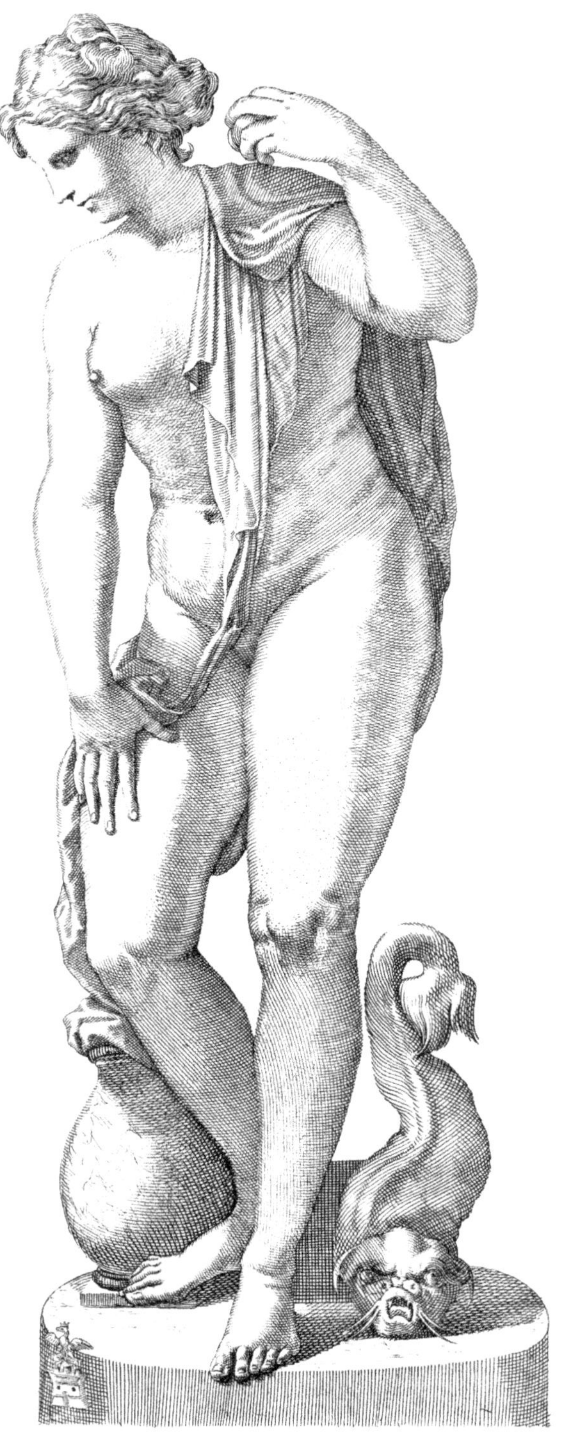

154. Statue of Venus, Giovanni Luigi Valesio,
1636 – 1647.

155. Statue of Venus, Giovanni Luigi Valesio,
1636 – 1647.

156

157

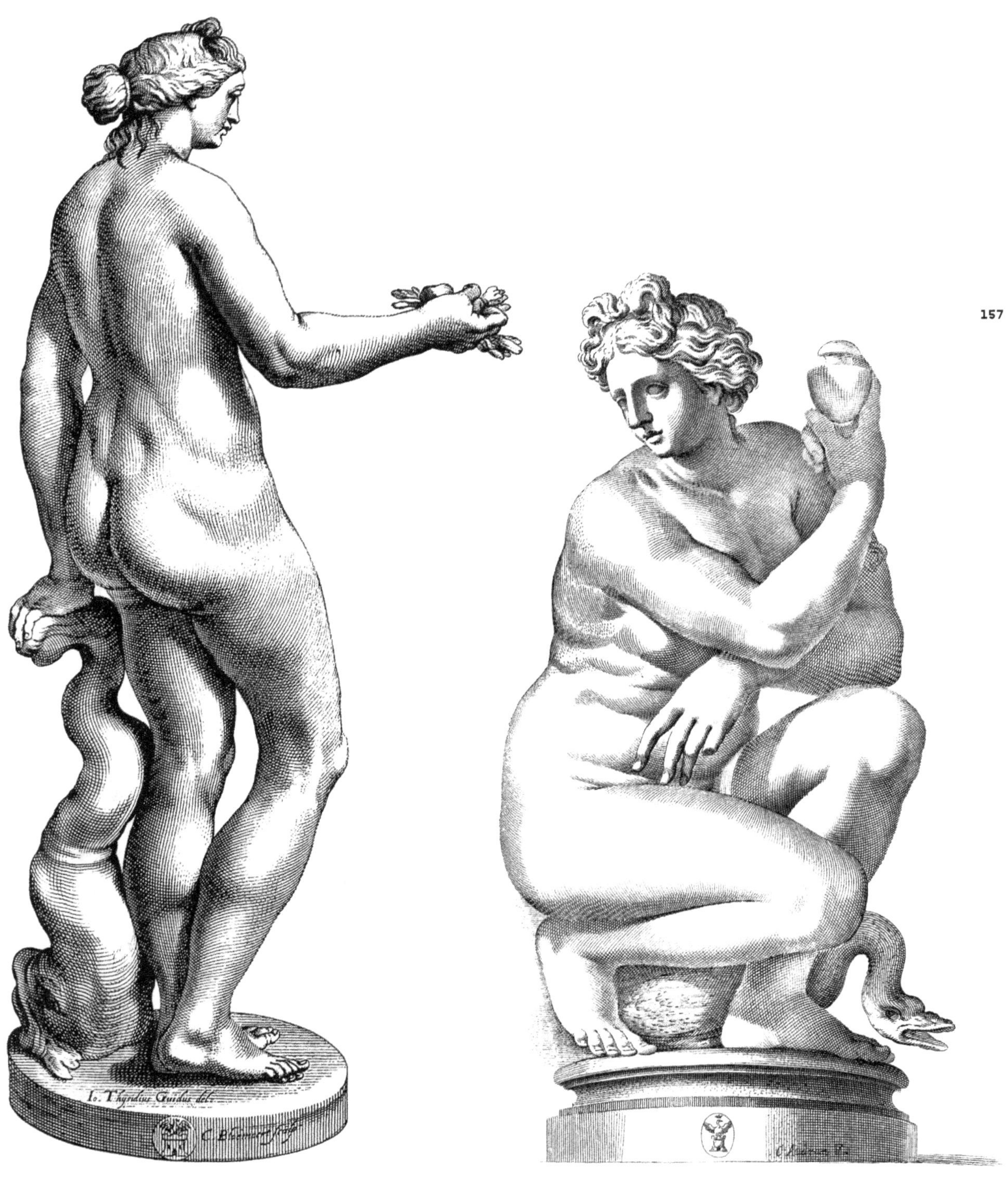

158

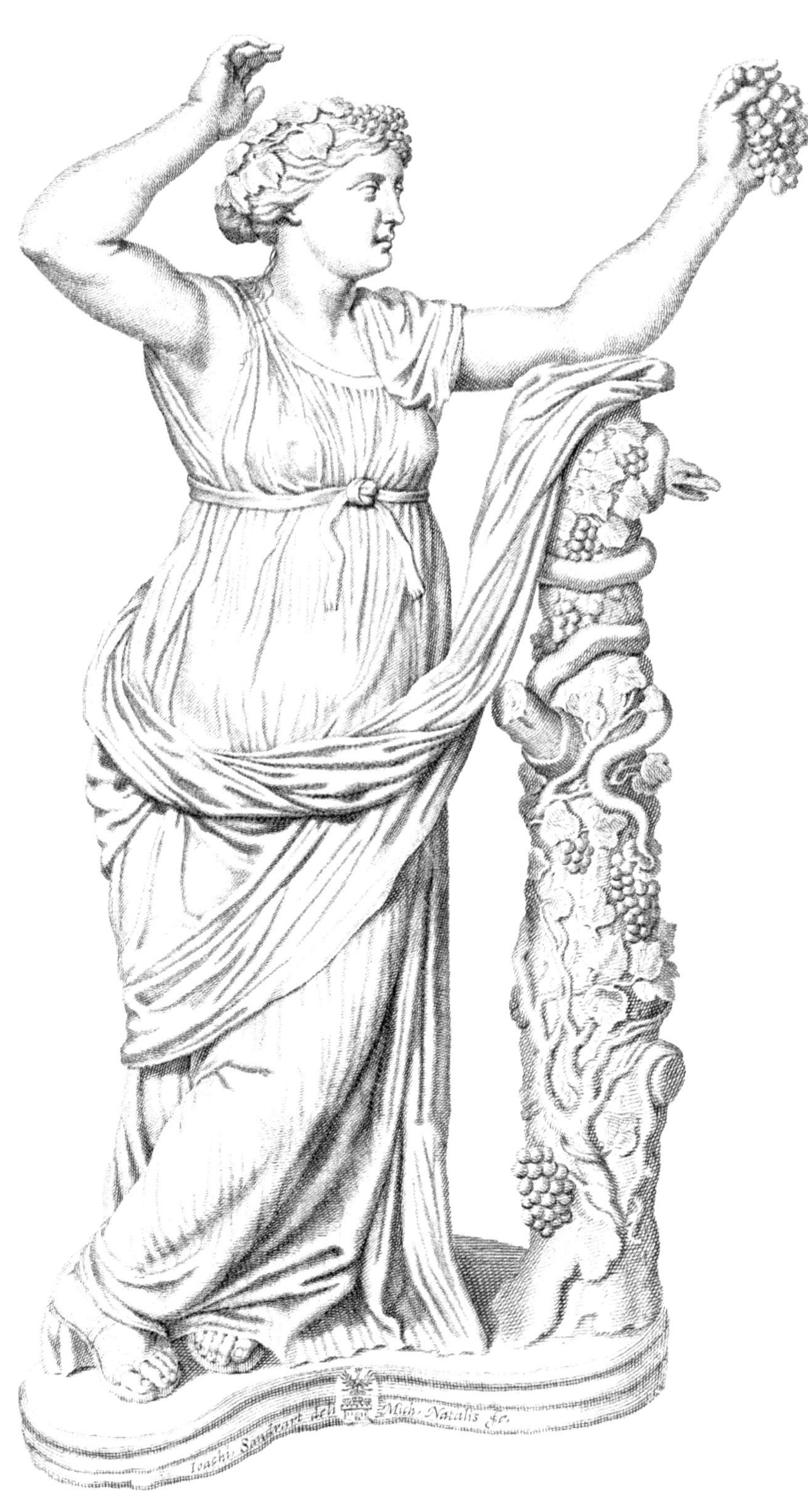

158. Statue of a Bacchante, Michel Natalis, after
Joachim von Sandrart (I), 1640.

159

160

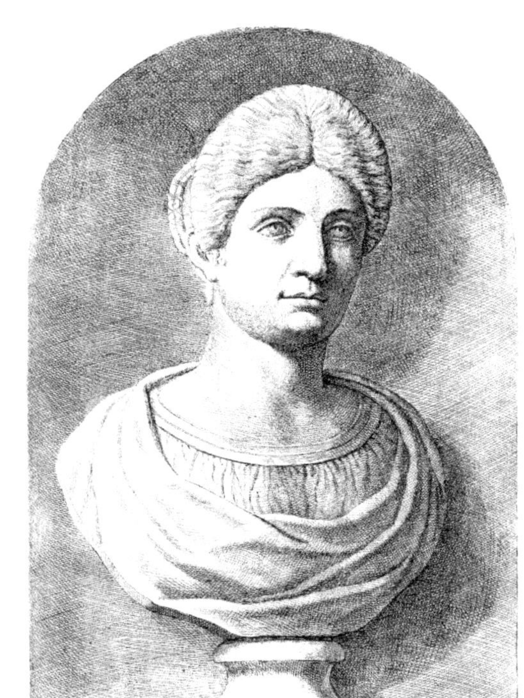

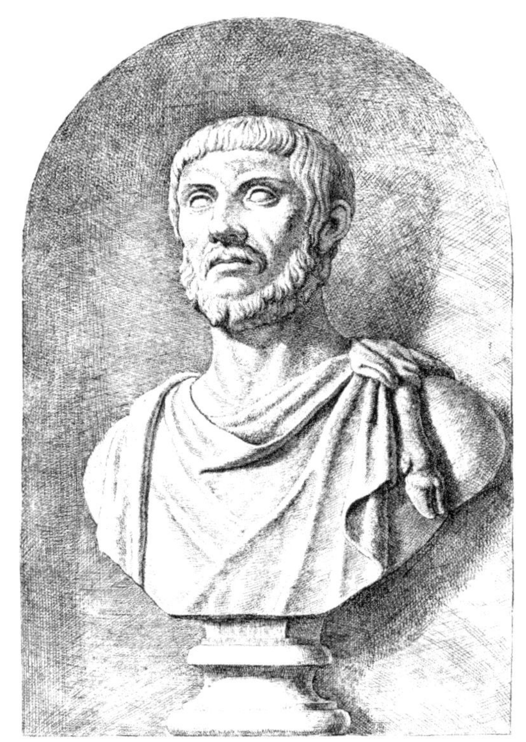

161

162

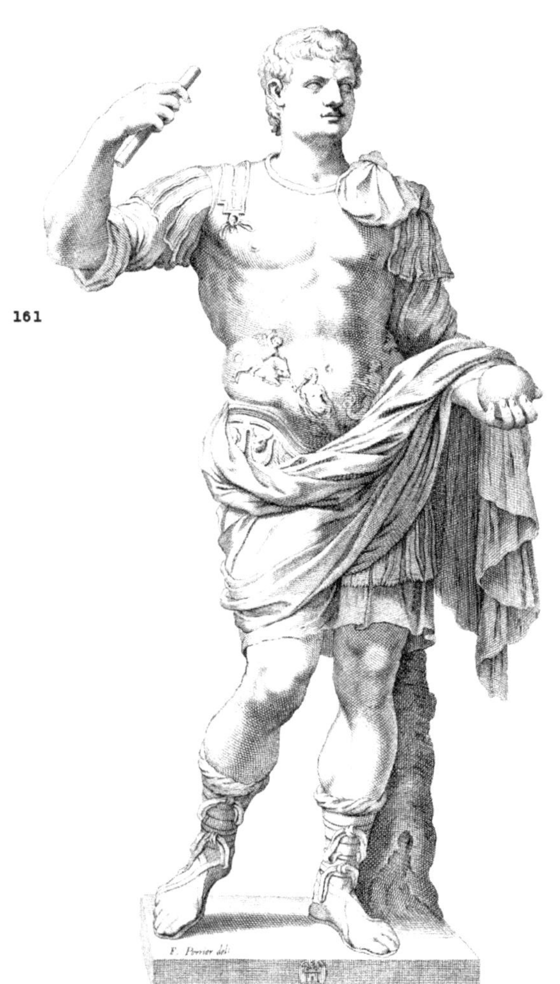

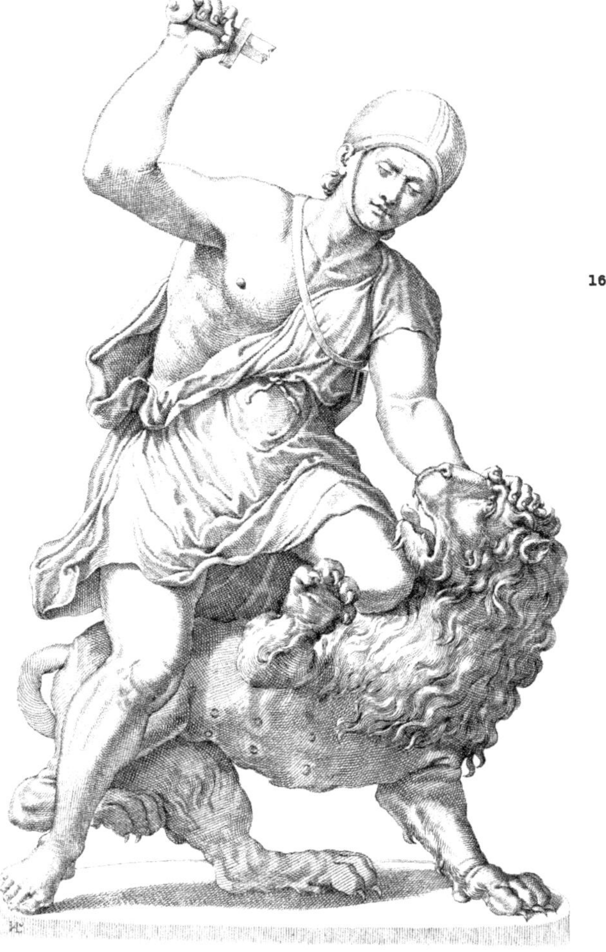

159. Bust of Helena, Hubert Quellinus, 1646 – 1670.

160. Bust of Milenus, Hubert Quellinus, 1646 – 1670.

161. Statue of a Naked Paris, Michel Natalis, after Giovanni Lanfranco, 1640.

162. Statue of a Reclining Gladiator, Giovanni Luigi Valesio, 1636 – 1647.

163

164

165

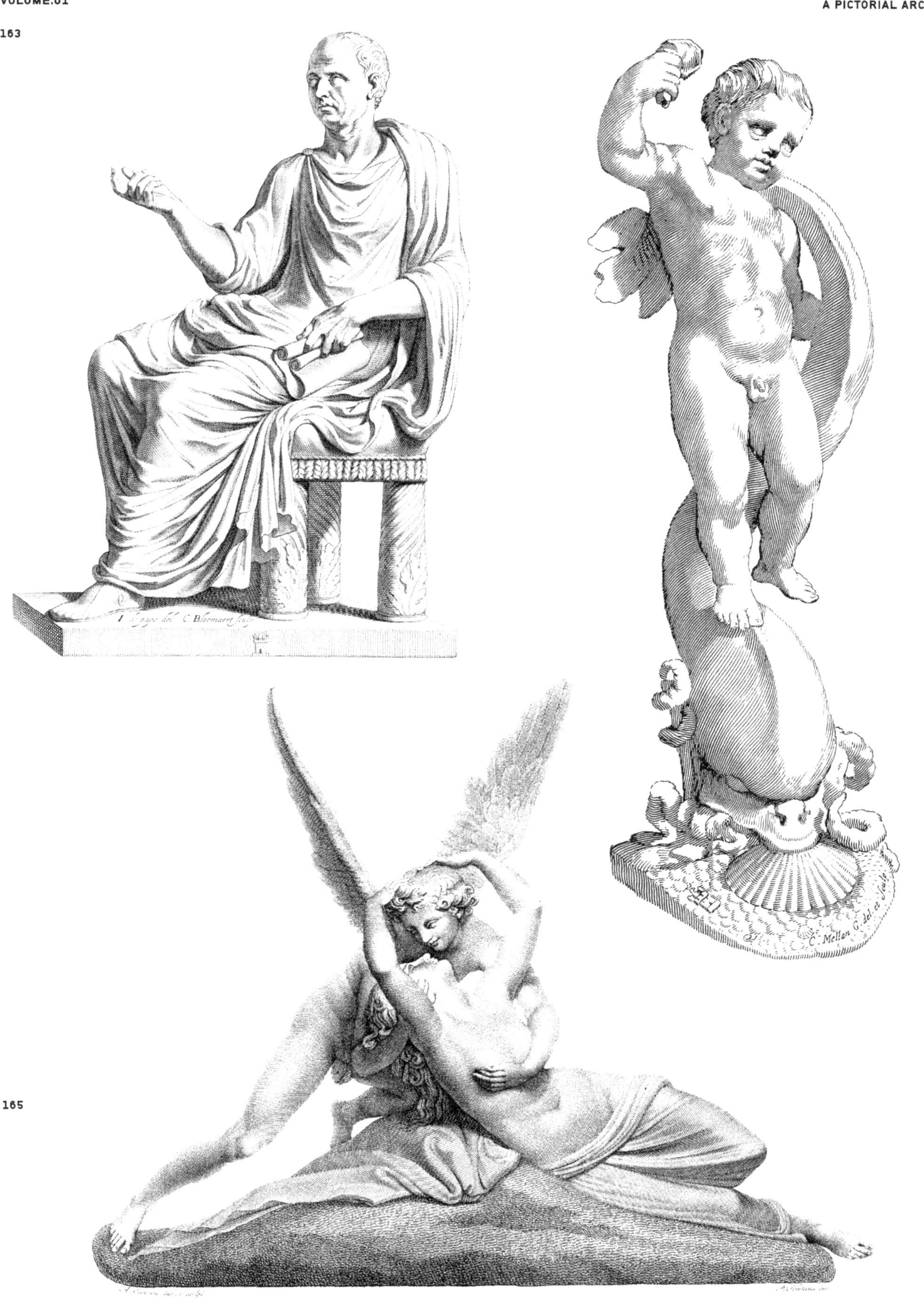

163. Statue of a Seated Consul, Cornelis Bloemaert (ii), after Joos de Pape, 1636 –1647.

164. Statue of a Putto on a Dolphin, Claude Mellan, 1636 – 1647.

165. Amor and Psyche, Pietro Fontana, after Antonio Canova, 1772 – 1837.

166

167

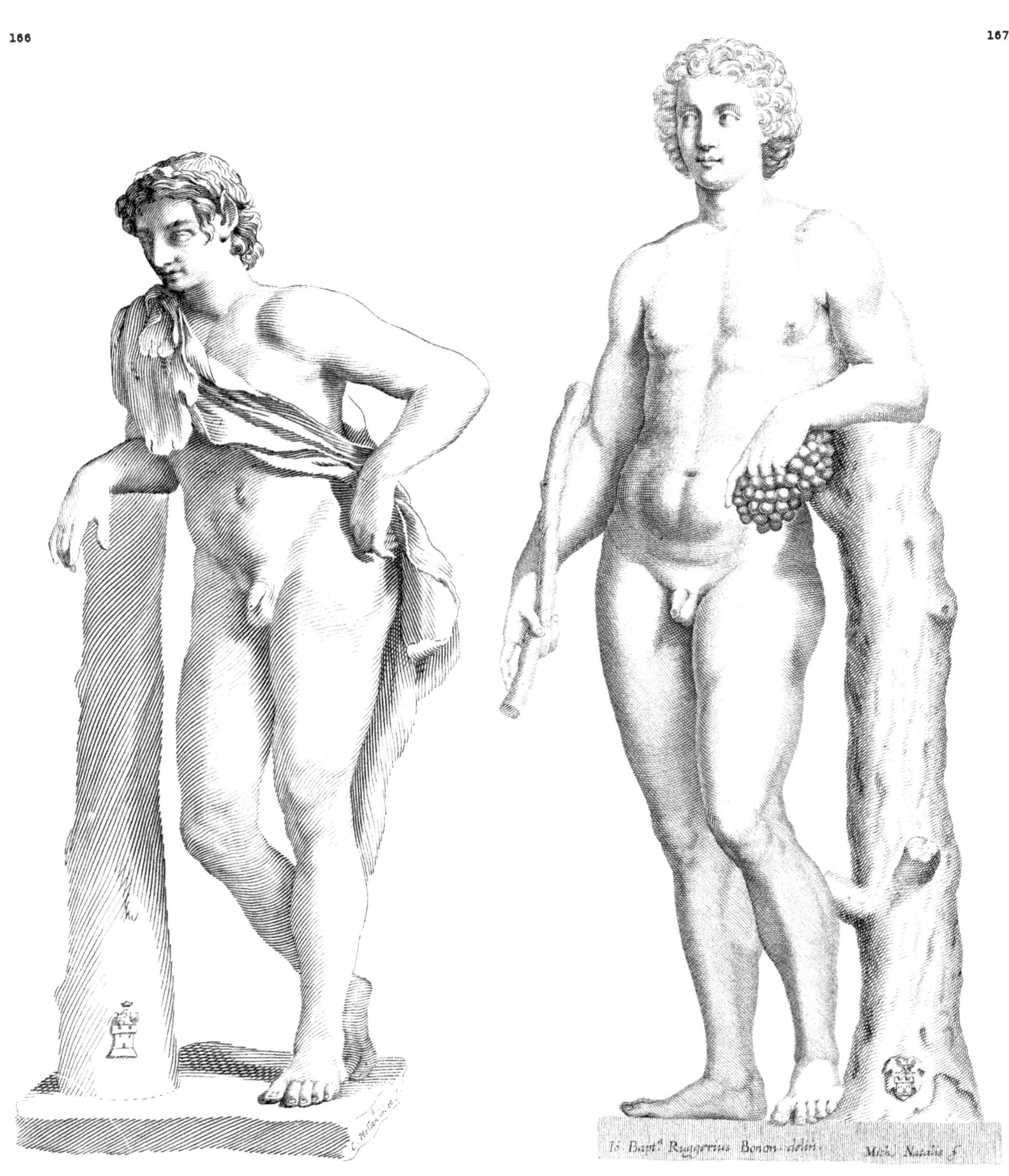

166. Statue of a Faun, Claude Mellan, 1636 – 1647.

167. Statue of a Follower of Bacchus, Michel Natalis, after Giovanni Battista Ruggieri, 1640.

168

169

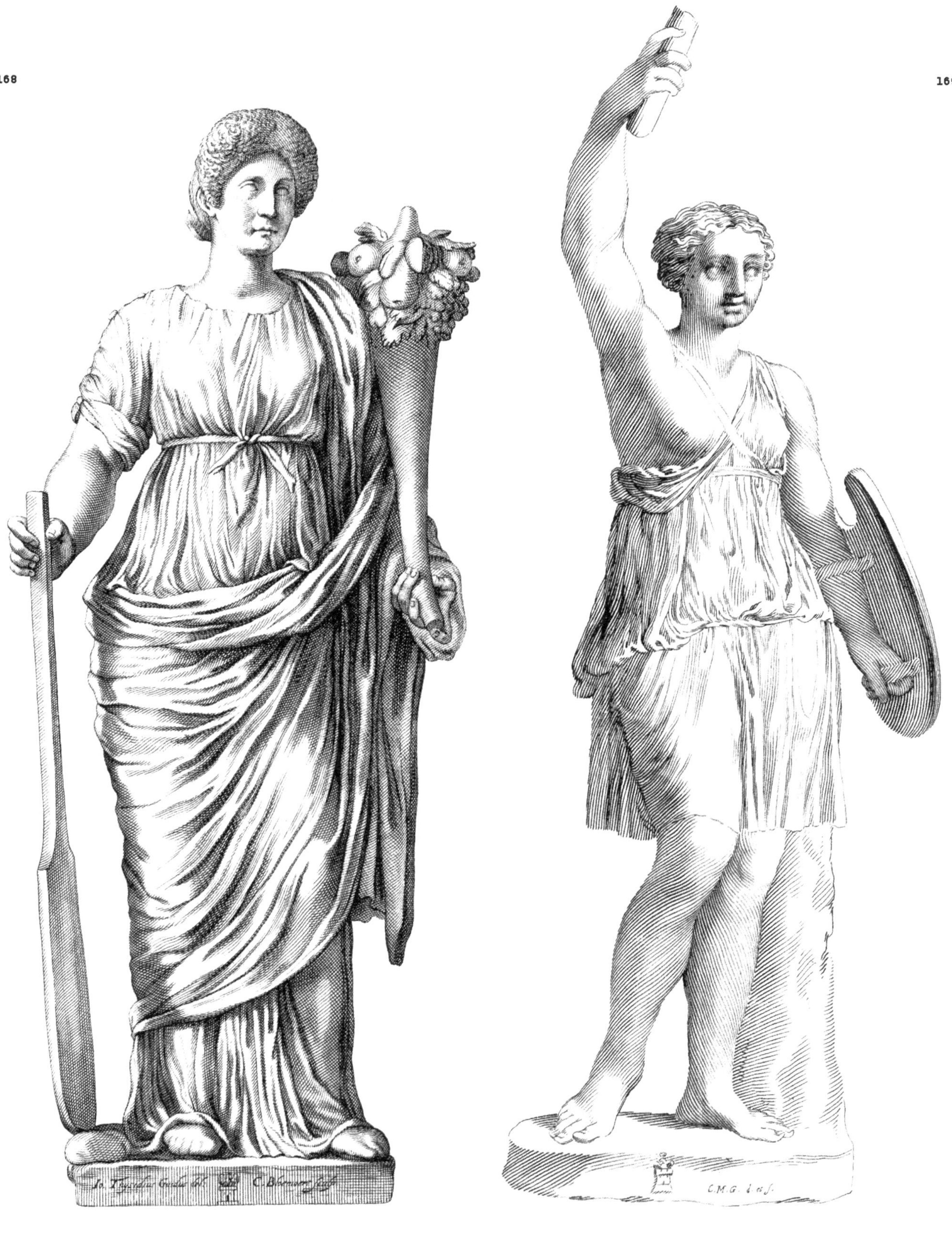

168. Statue of Goddess with Cornucopia, Luca
Ciamberlano, 1636 – 1647.

169. Statue of an Amazon Raising Her Arm,
Claude Mellan, 1636 – 1647.

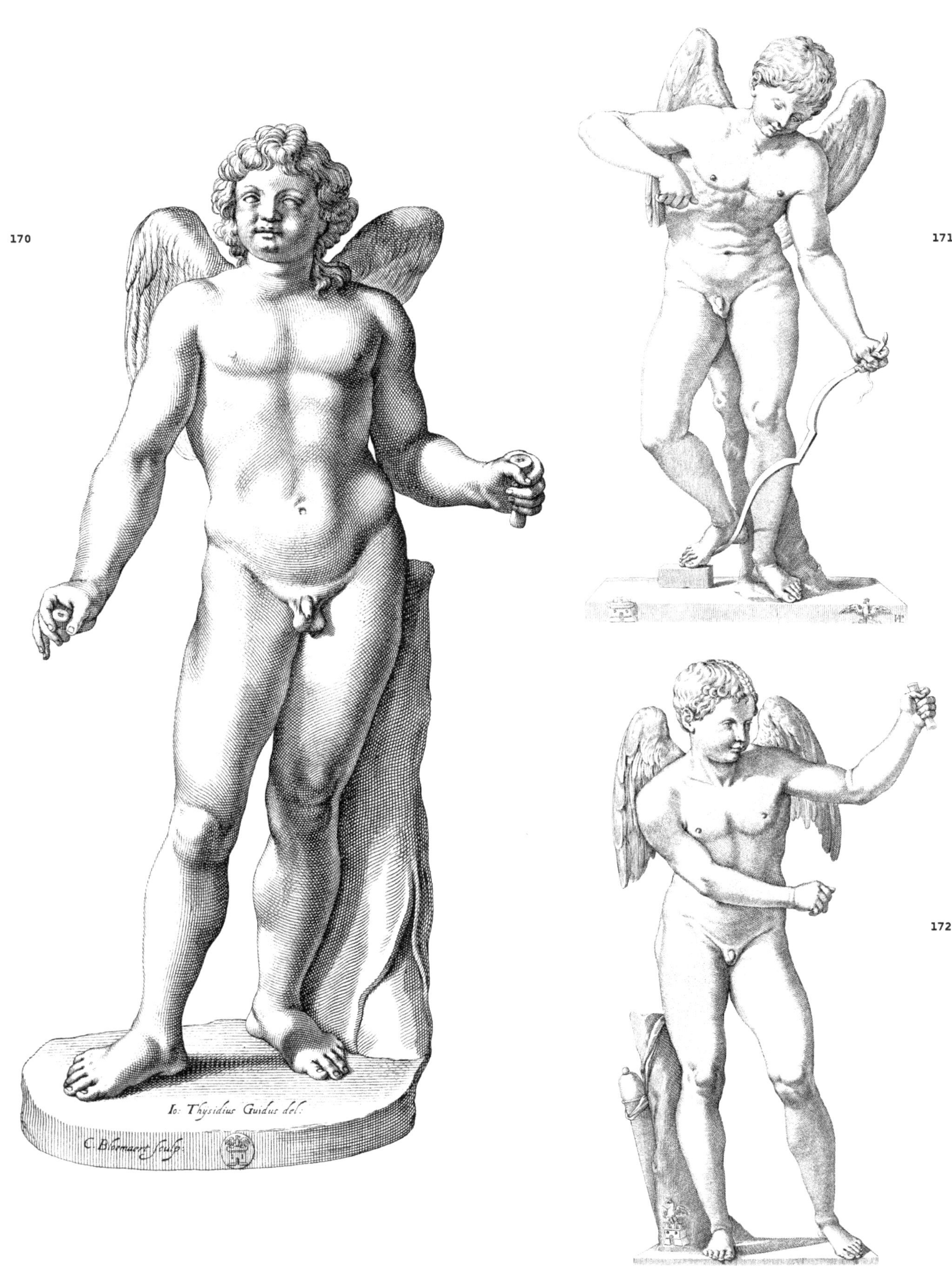

GREEK AND ROMAN SCULPTURE

170. Statue of Amor, Cornelis Bloemaert (II), after Giovanni Citosiblo Guidi, 1636 – 1647.

171. Statue of Amor with a Broken Arch, Giovanni Luigi Valesio, 1636 – 1647.

172. Statue of Amor with his quiver of arrows, Giovanni Luigi Valesio, 1636 – 1647.

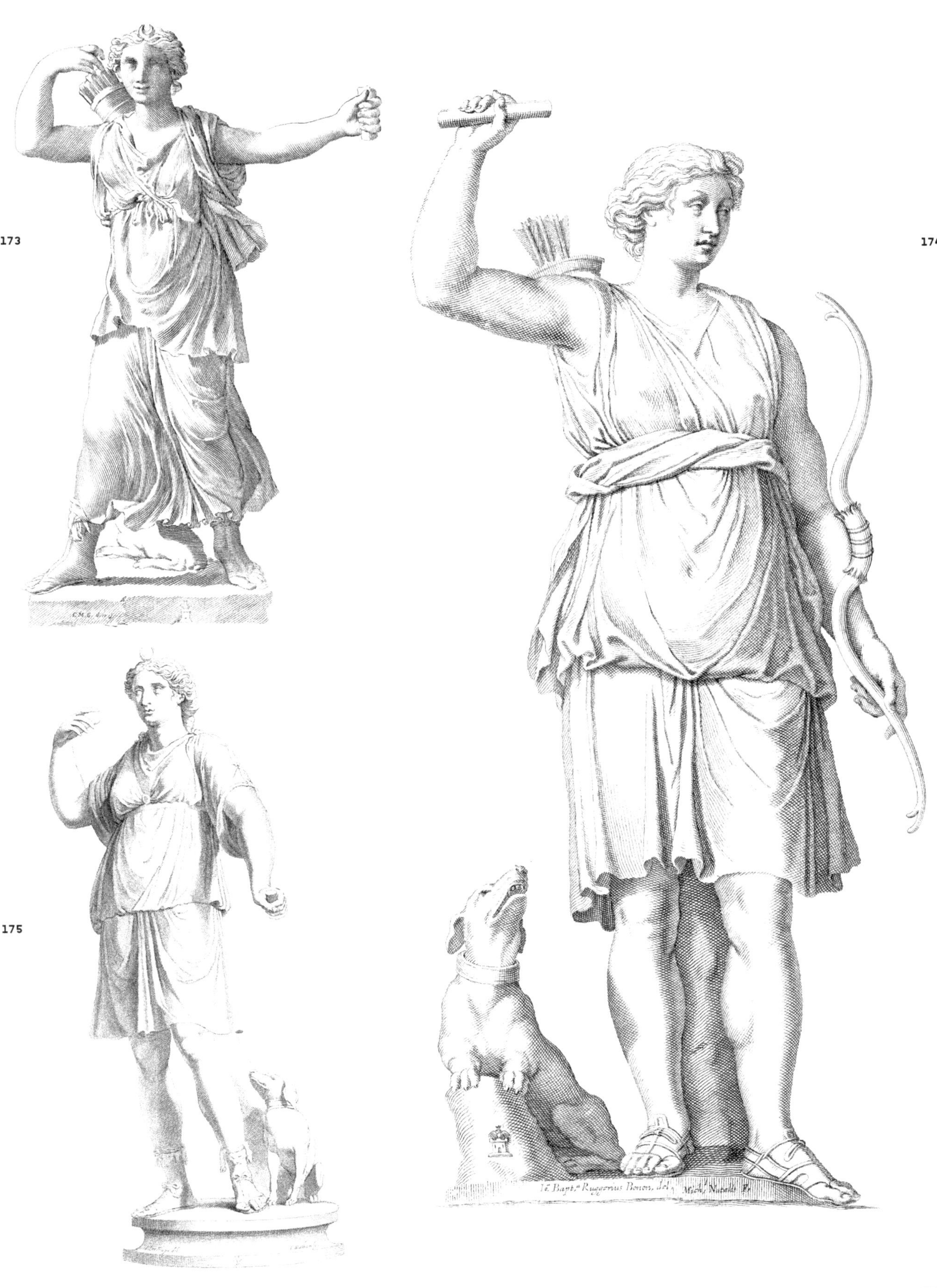

173

174

175

173. Statue of Diana with a Quiver on Her Back, Claude Mellan, 1636 – 1647.

174. Statue of Diana, Michel Natalis, after Giovanni Battista Ruggieri, 1640.

175. Statue of Diana, Theodor Matham, after Joos de Pape, 1640.

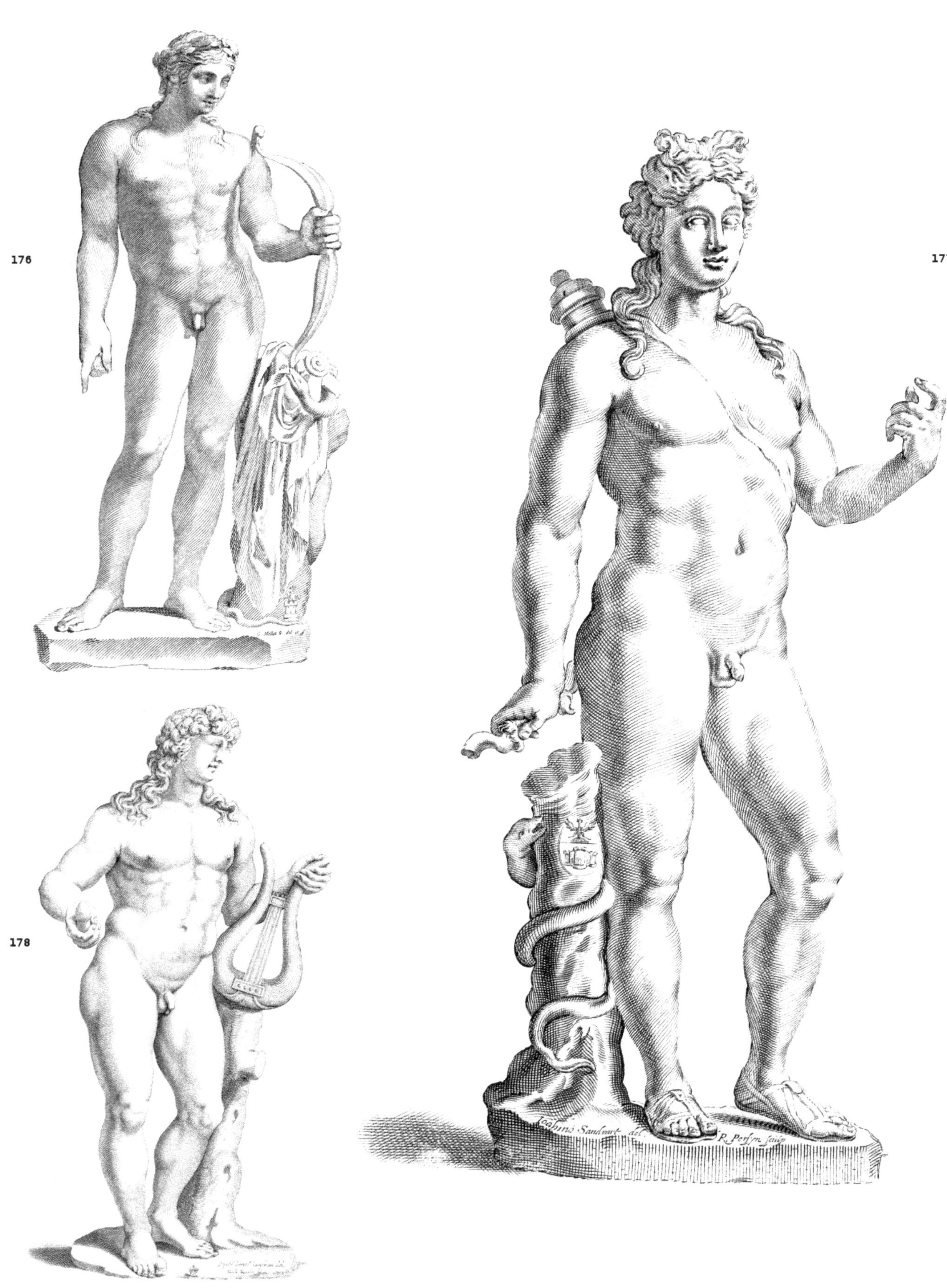

176. Statue of Apollo with Bow in Hand, Claude Mellan, 1636 – 1647.

177. Statue of Apollo, Reinier van Persijn, after Joachim von Sandrart (I), 1640.

178. Statue of Apollo, Michel Natalis, after Giovanni Lanfranco, 1640.

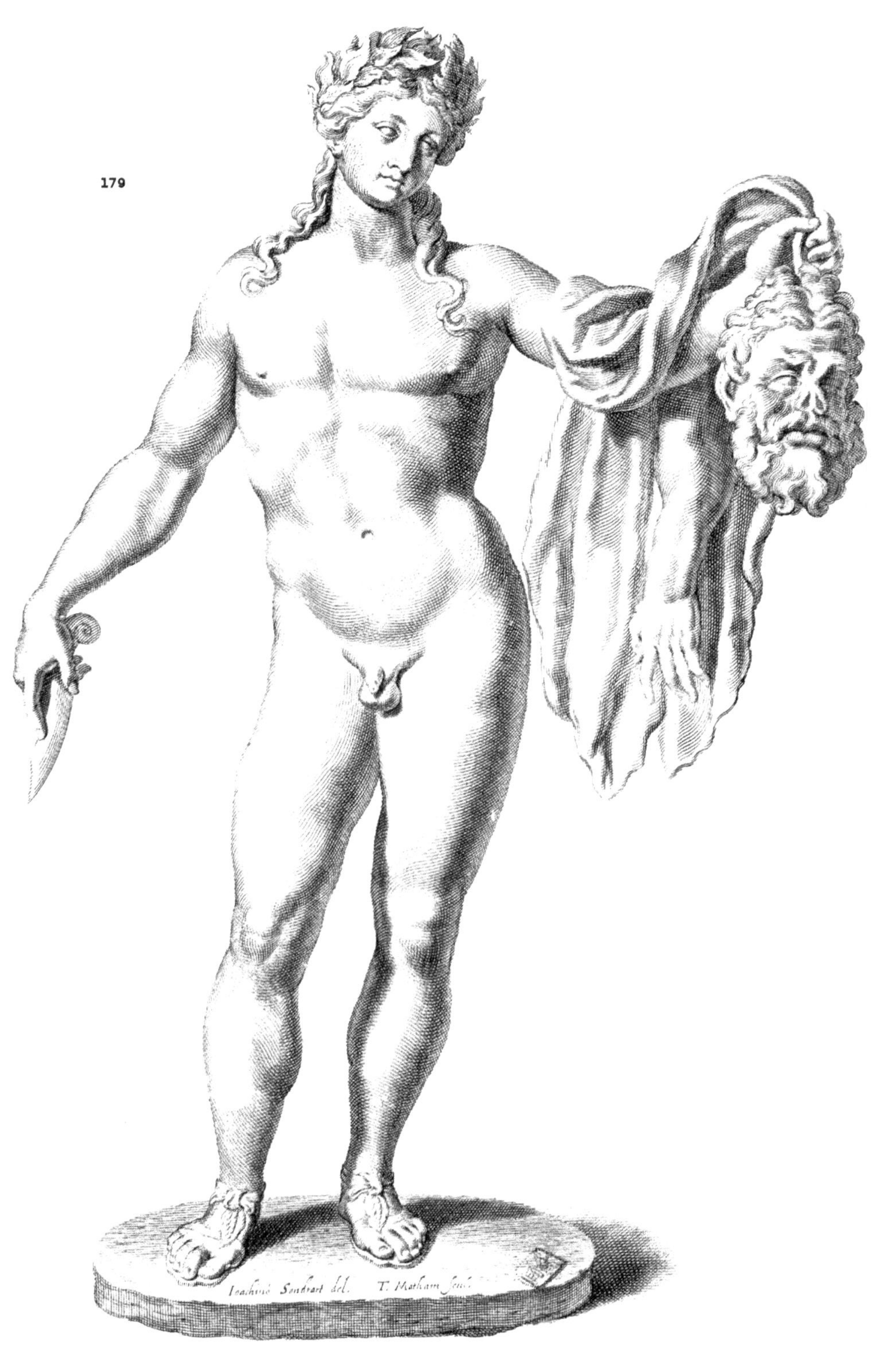

179

179. Statue of Apollo with skin of Marsyas,
Theodor Matham, 1640.

180

181

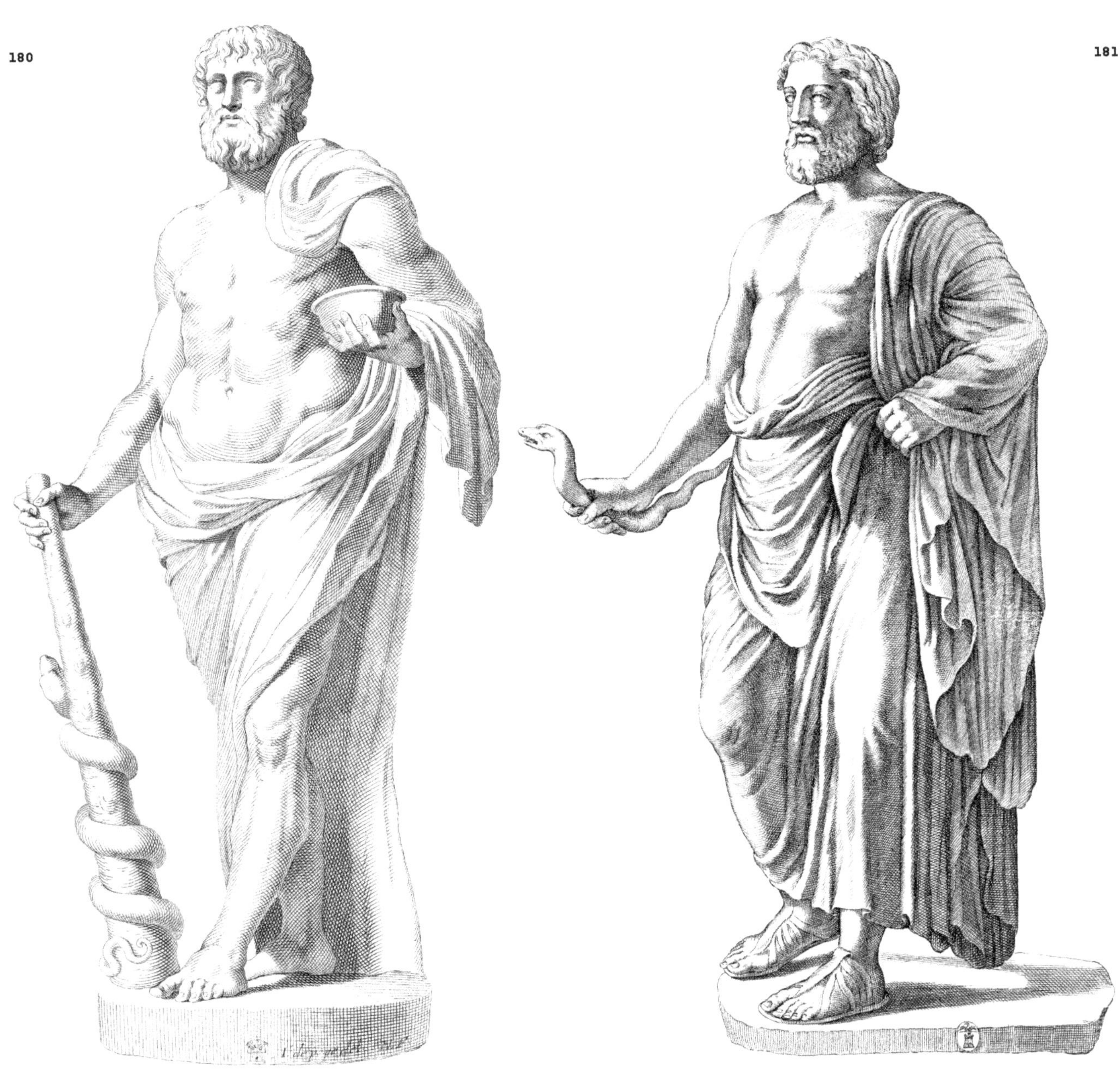

180. Statue of Aesculapius, Michel Natalis, after
Joos de Pape, 1640.

181. Statue of Aesculapius, Luca Ciamberlano,
1636 – 1647.

182

183

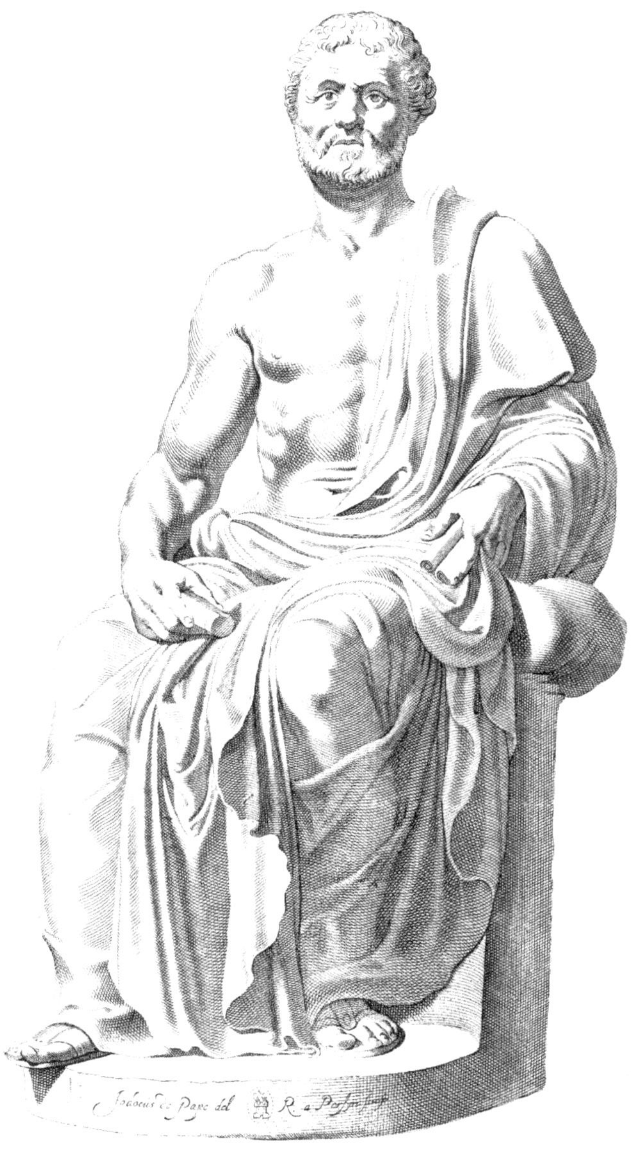

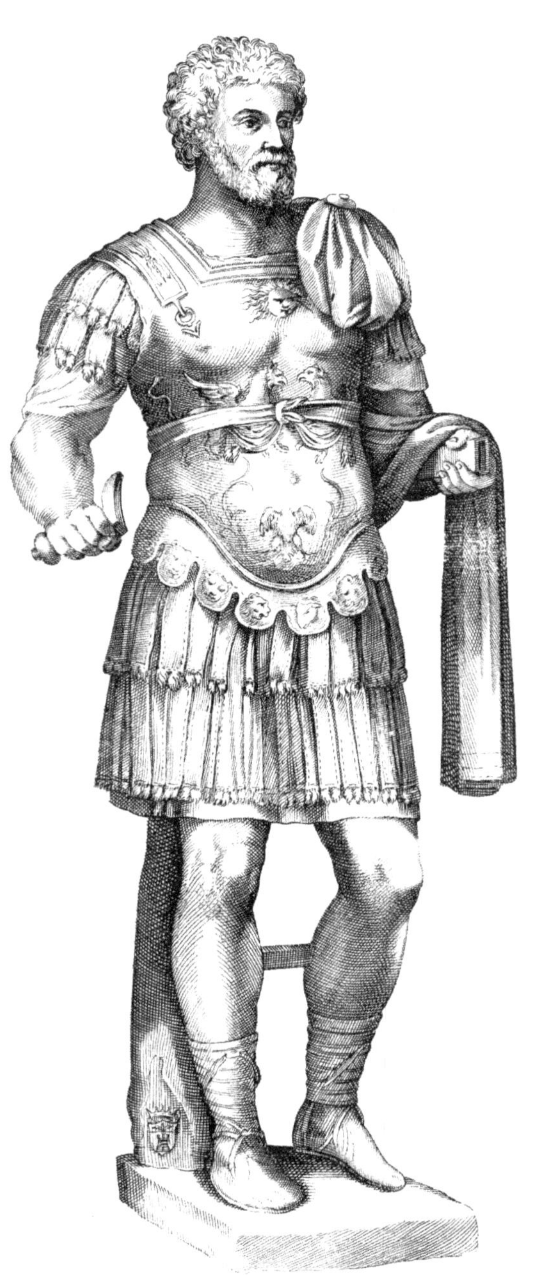

182. Statue of a Seated Man, Reinier van Persijn, after Joos de Pape, 1640.

183. Statue of Marcus Aurelius, Luca Clamberlano, 1636 – 1647.

184

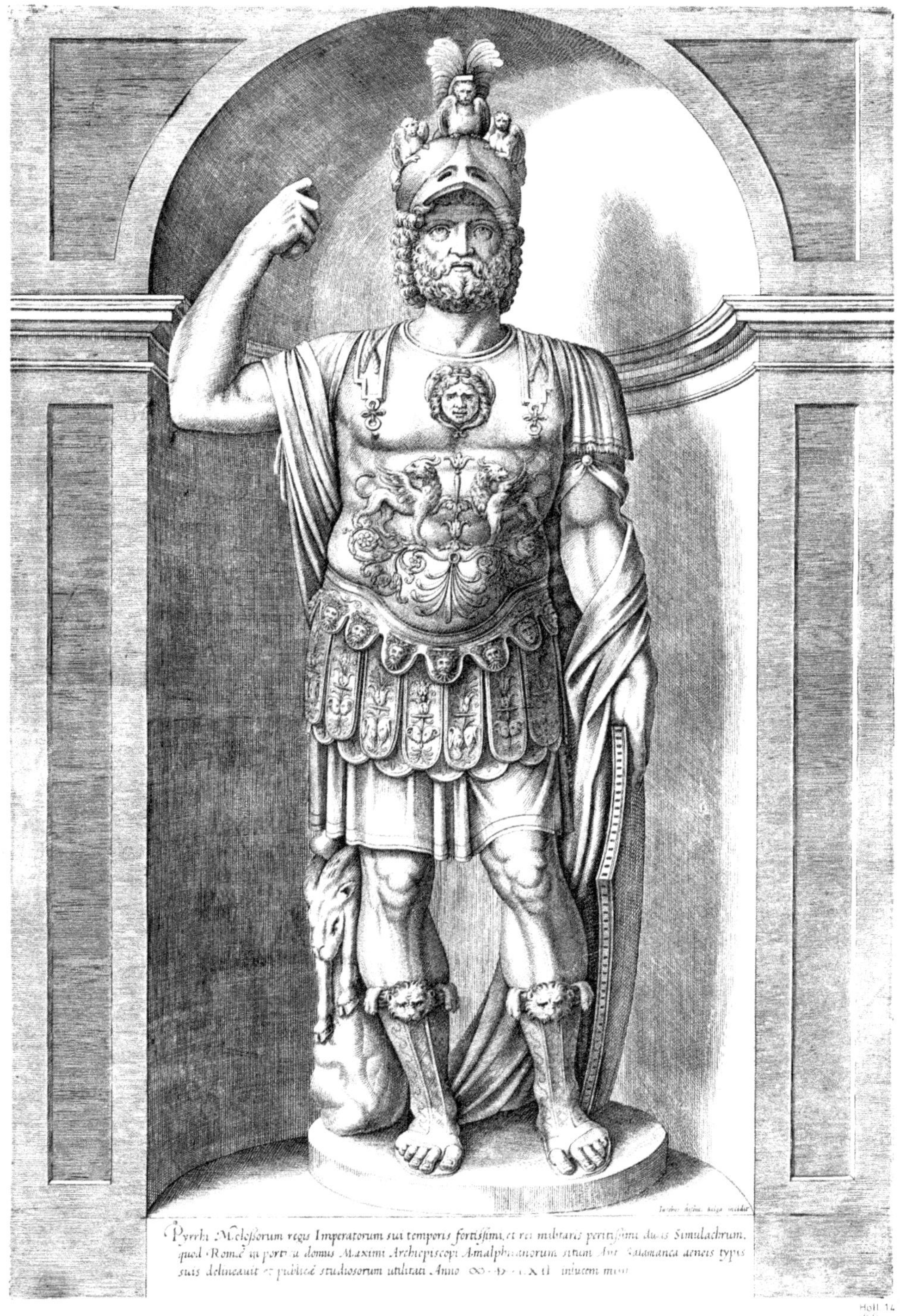

184. Statue of Pyrrhus, Jacob Bos, after
Salamanca, 1562.

185

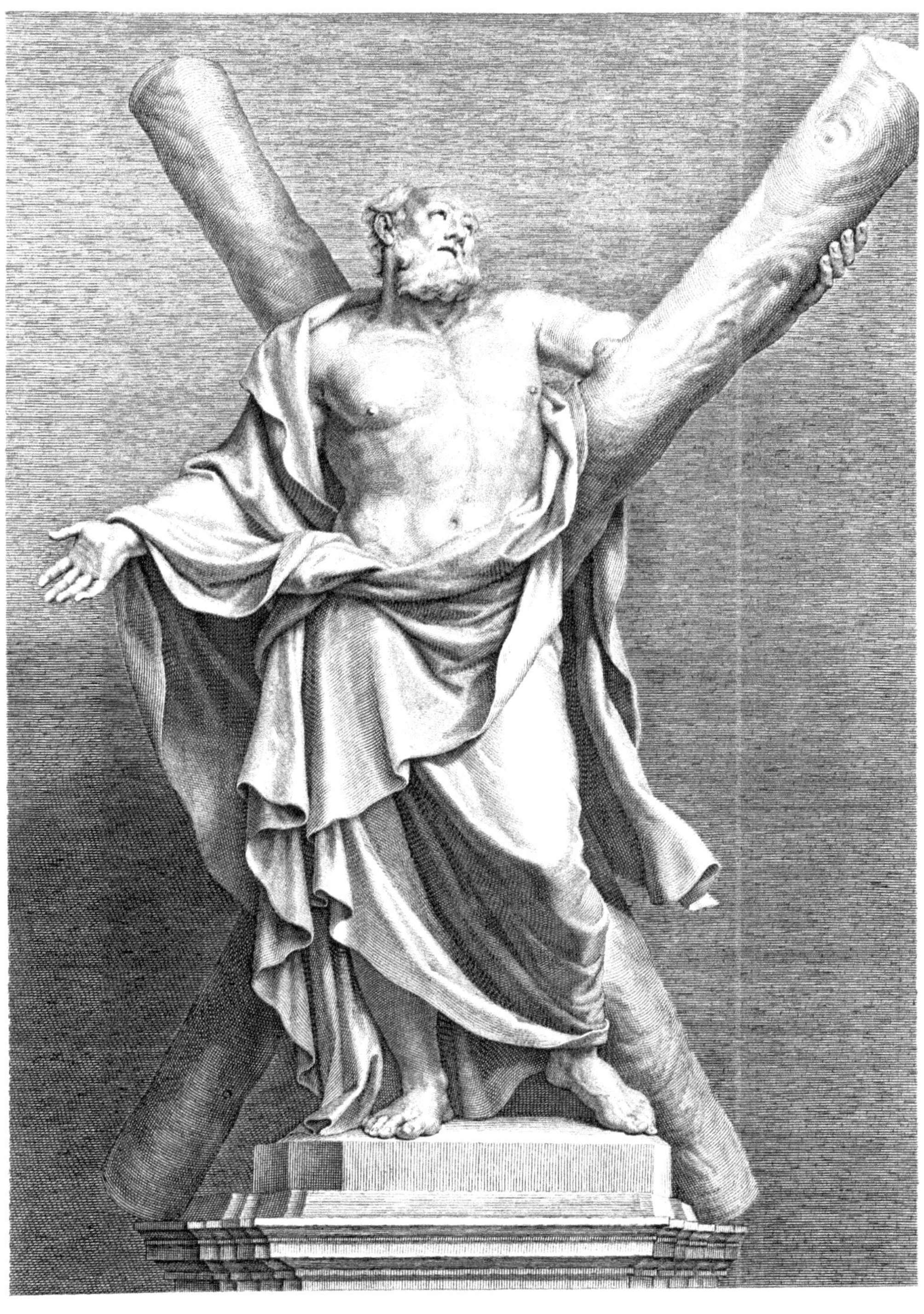

185. Statue of Saint Andrew, Petrus Clouwet,
after Peter van Lint, 1639 – 1670.

186

187

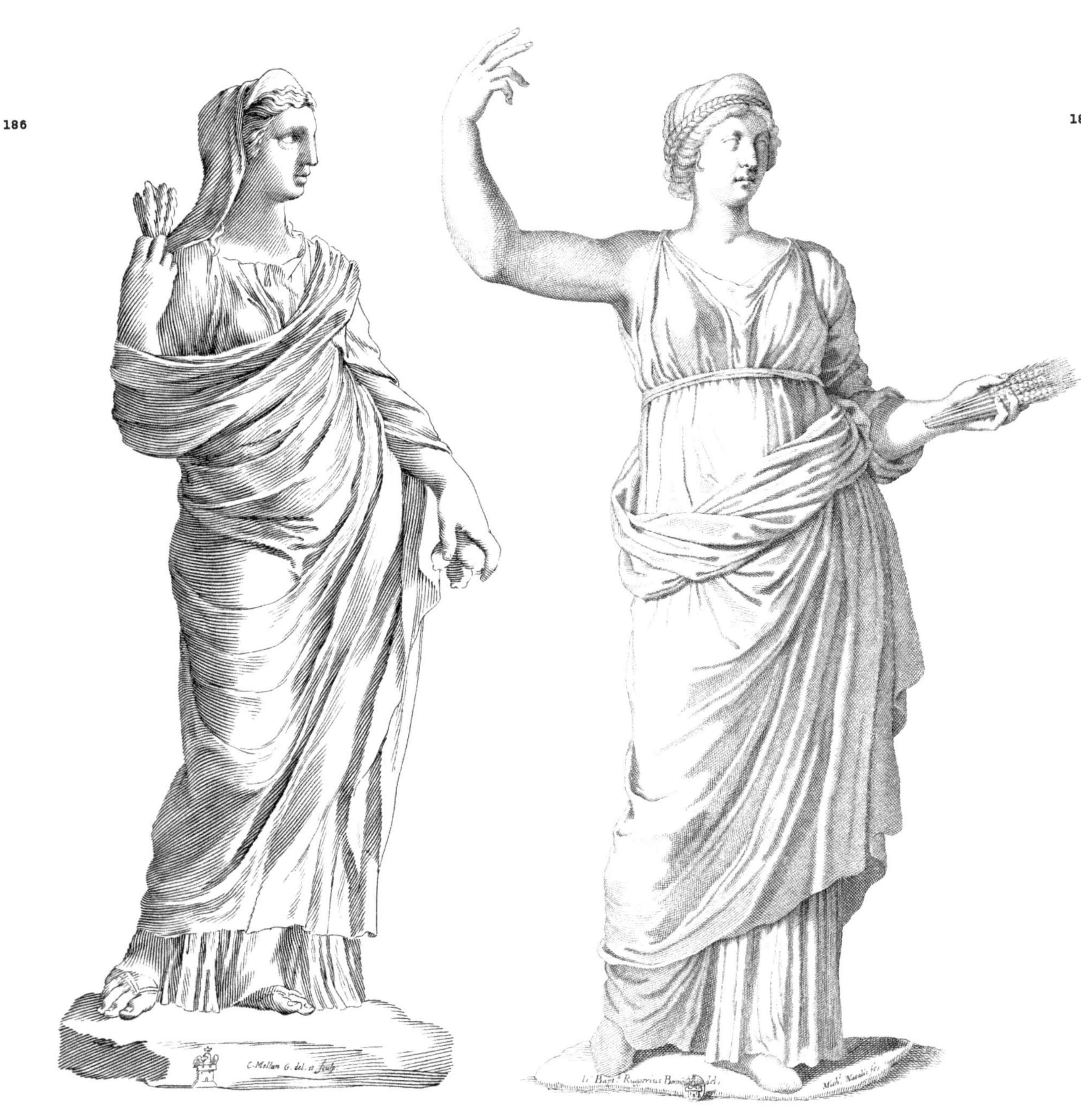

186. Statue of Ceres, Claude Mellan, 1636 –
1647.

187. Statue of Ceres, Michel Natalis, after
Giovanni Battista Ruggieri, 1640.

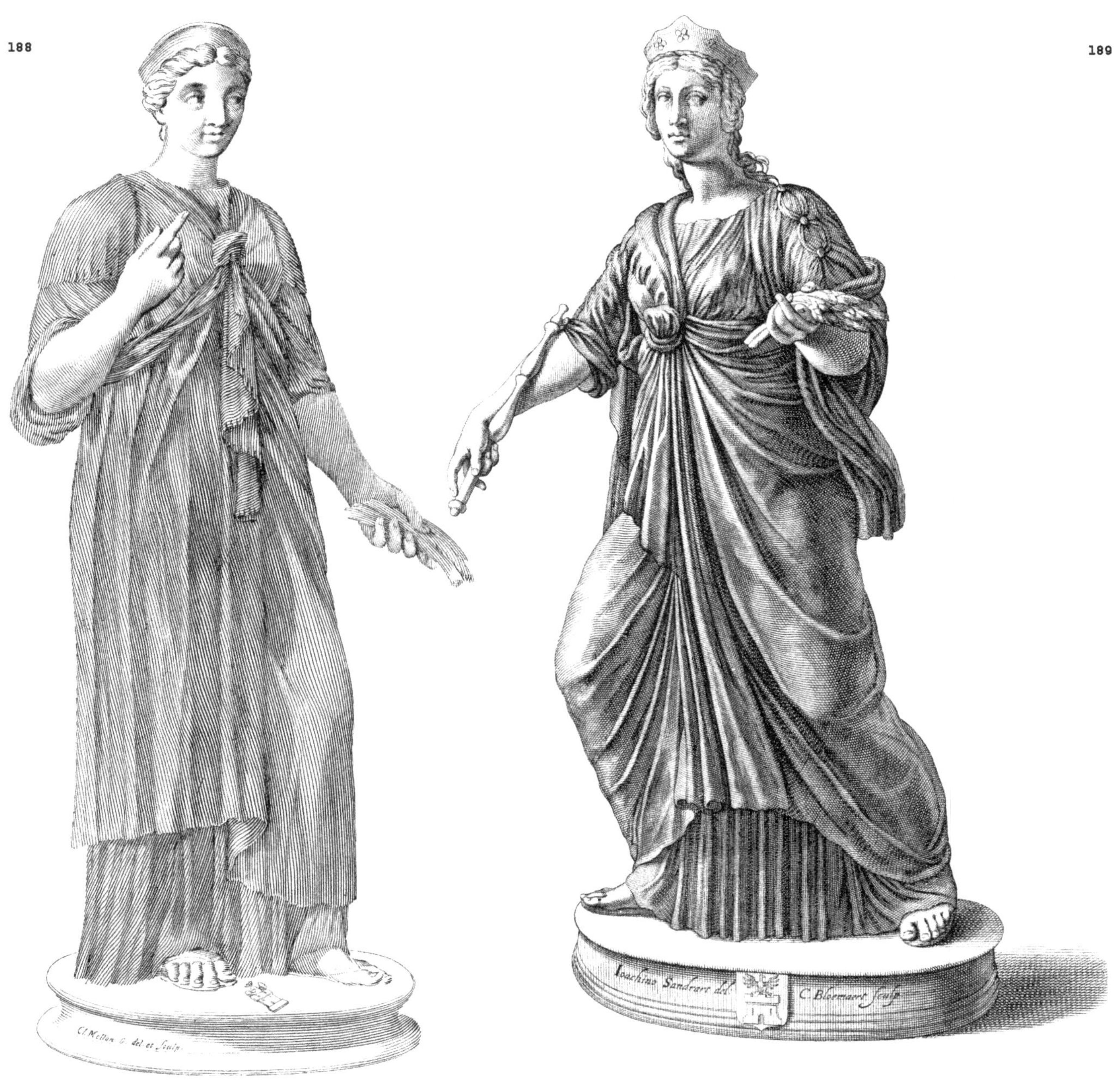

188. Statue of Ceres, Claude Mellan 1636–1647.

189. Statue of Ceres as Queen, Cornelis Bloemaert (II), 1636 – 1647.

190

191

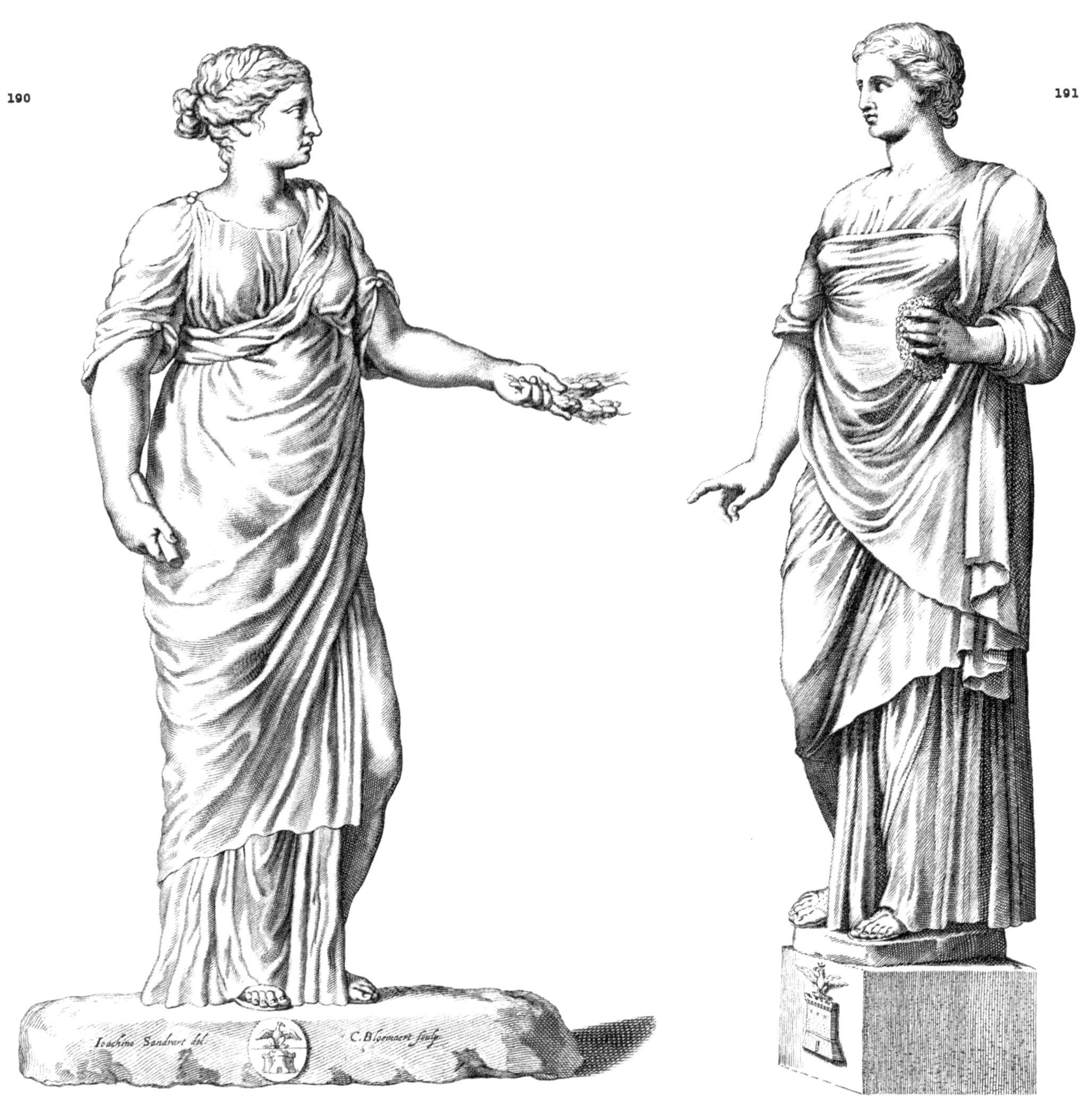

190. Statue of Ceres, Cornelis Bloemaert (II), after
Joachim von Sandrart (I), 1636 – 1647.

191. Statue of Flora with Flowers in Hand, Luca
Ciamberlano, 1636 – 1647.

192

193

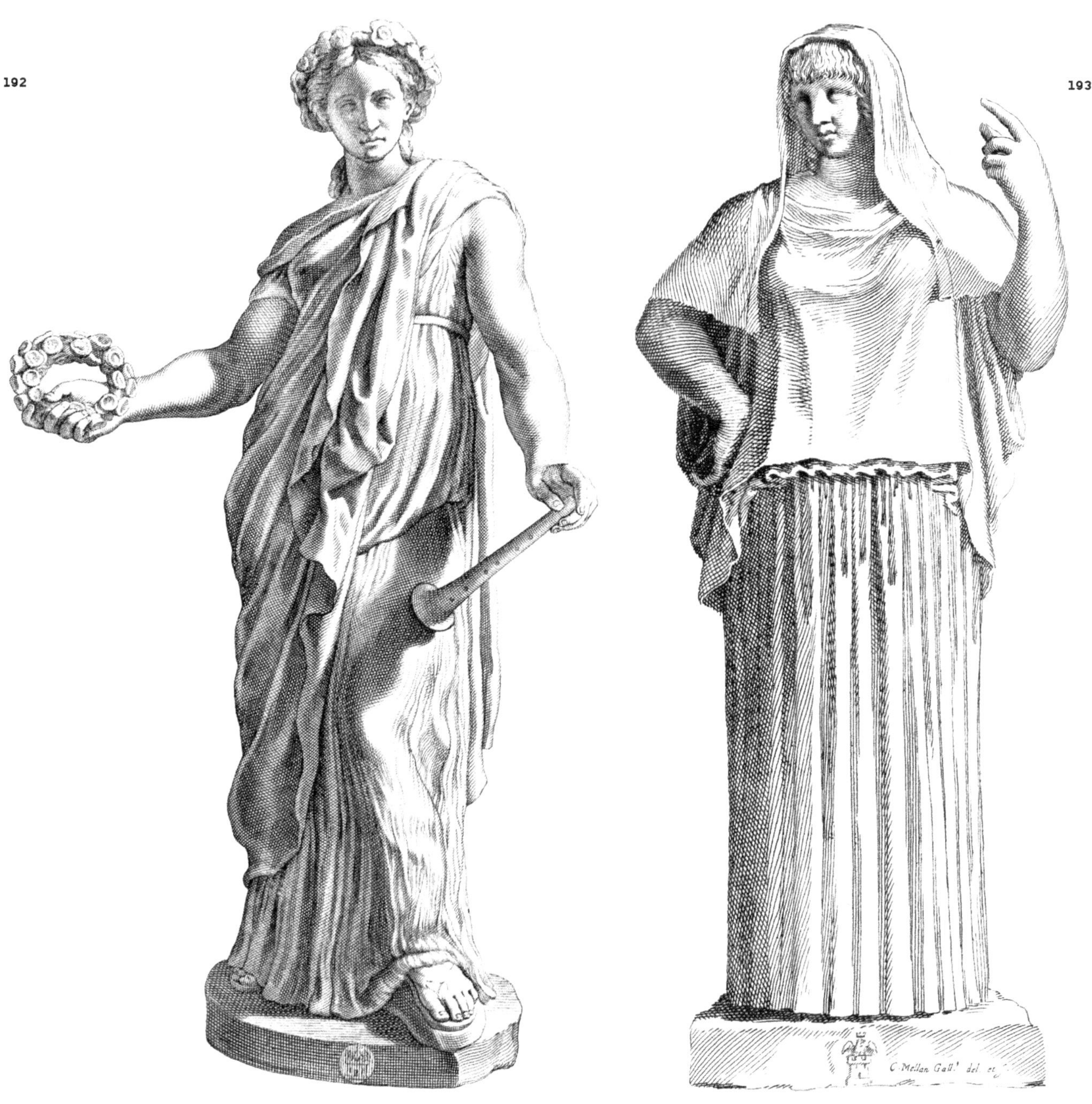

192. Statue of Flora, Cornelis Bloemaert (II), after Giovanni Citosibio Guidi, 1636 – 1647.

193. Statue of Hestia, Claude Mellan, 1636 – 1647.

194

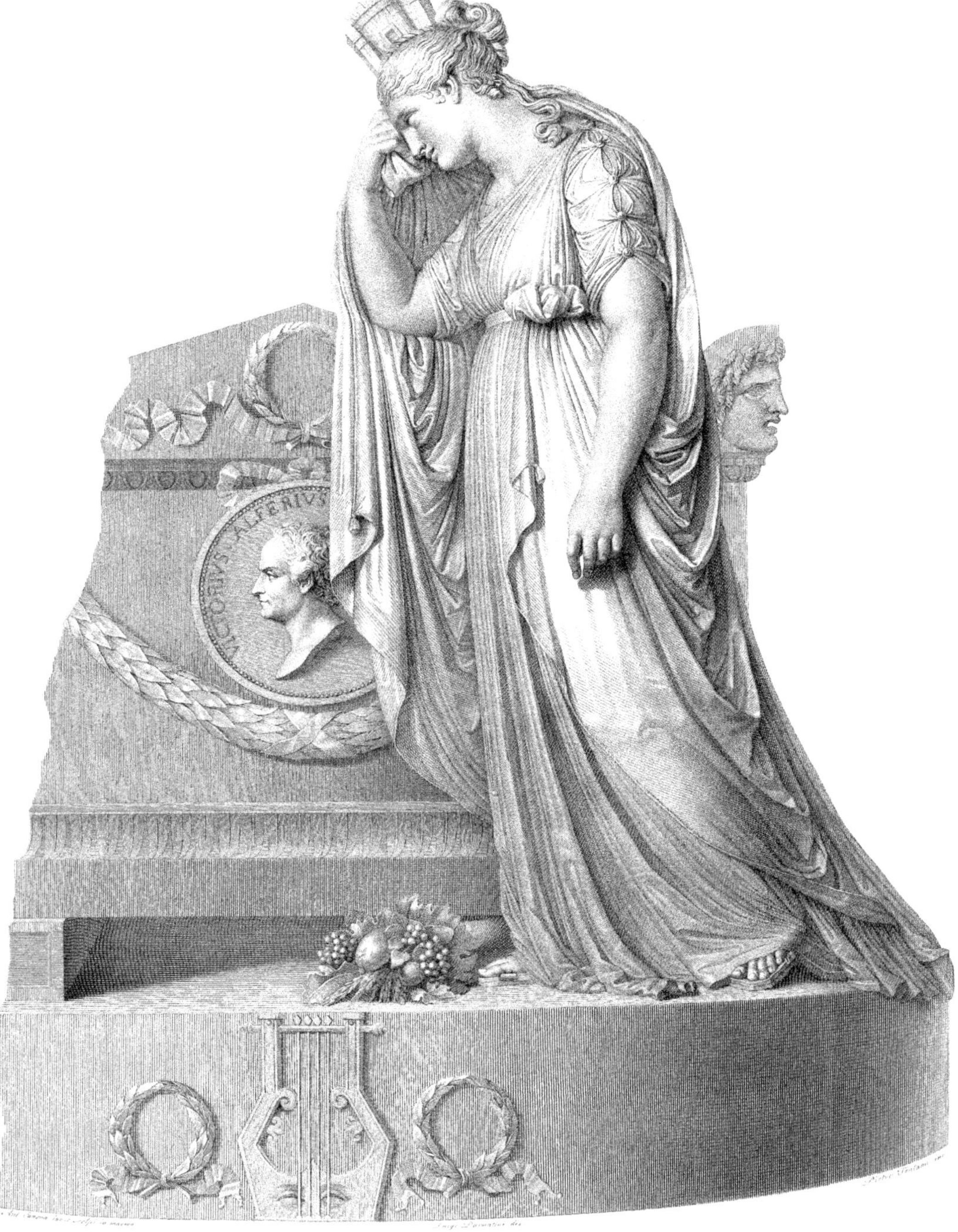

194. Funerary monument of Vittorio Alfieri, Pietro
Fontana, 1772 – 1837.

195

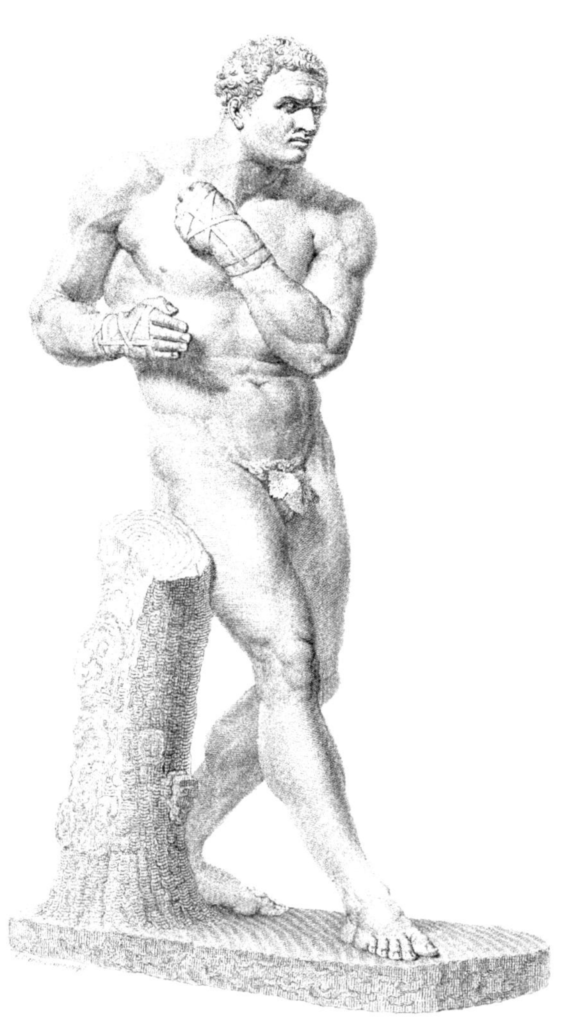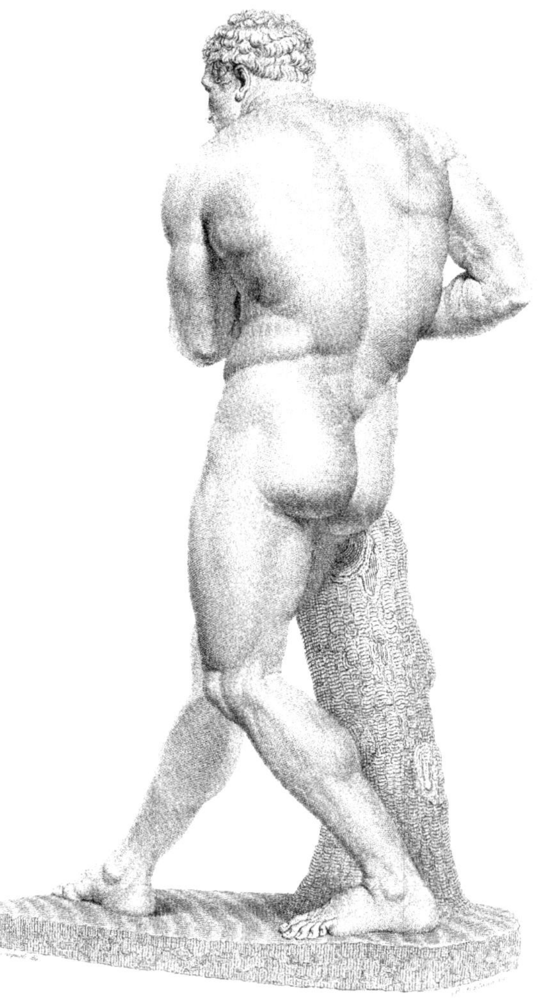

195. Damosseno, Pietro Fontana, after Giovanni
Tognolli, after Antonio Canova, 1772 – 1837.

196

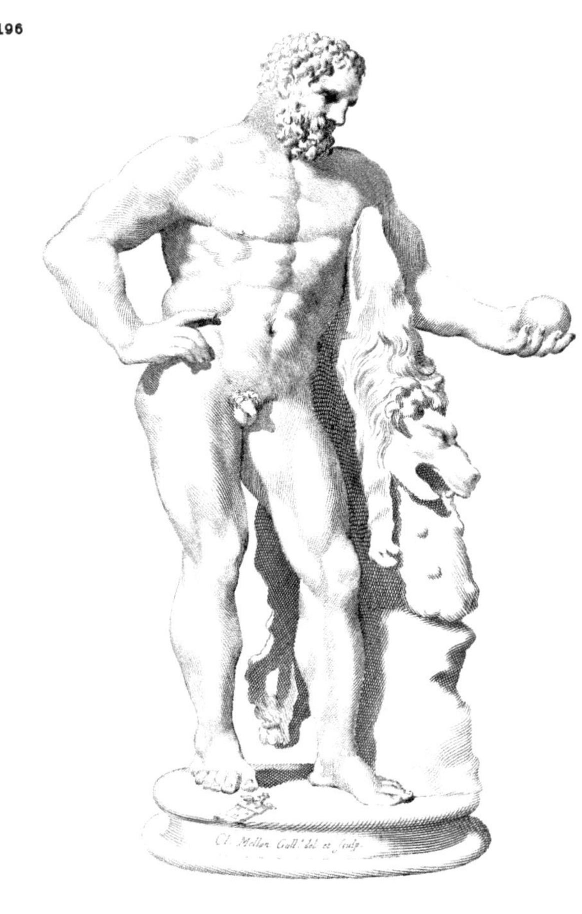

197

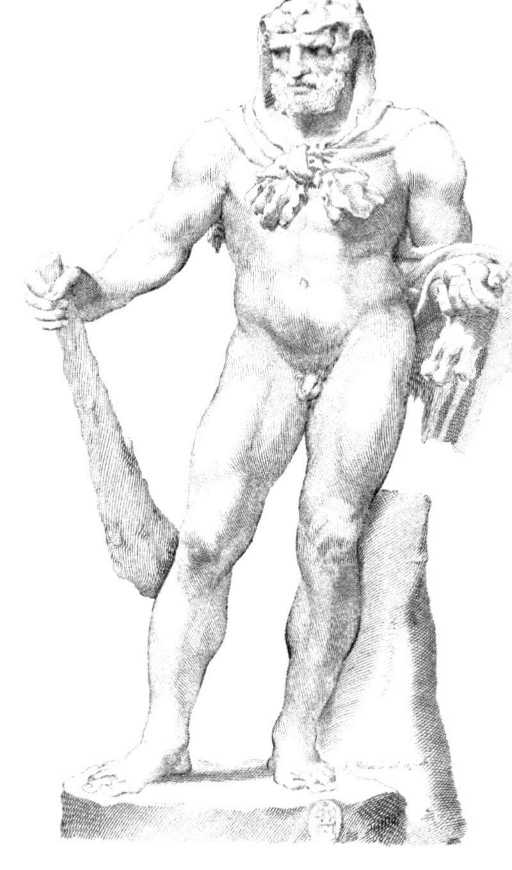

198

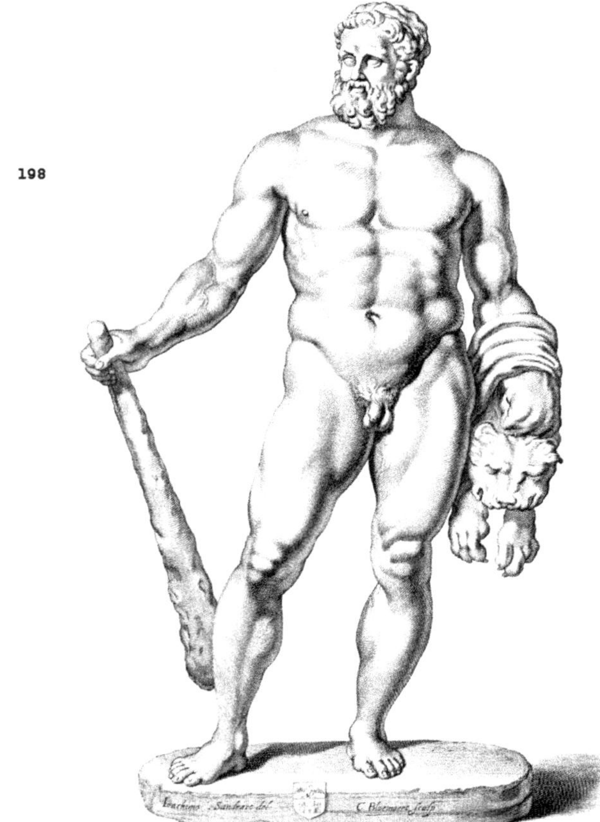

199

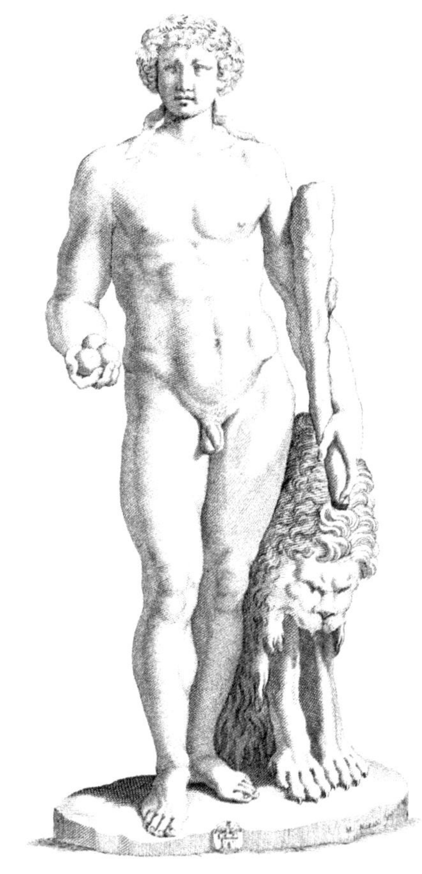

196. Statue of Hercules holding one of the apples of the Hesperides, Claude Mellan, 1636.

197. Statue of Hercules with the Lion's Skin on His Head, Claude Mellan, 1636 – 1647.

198. Statue of Hercules, Cornelis Bloemaert (II), after Joachim von Sandrart (II), 1636 – 1647.

199. Statue of Hercules holding the apples of the Hesperides, Michel Natalis, 1636 –1647.

200

201

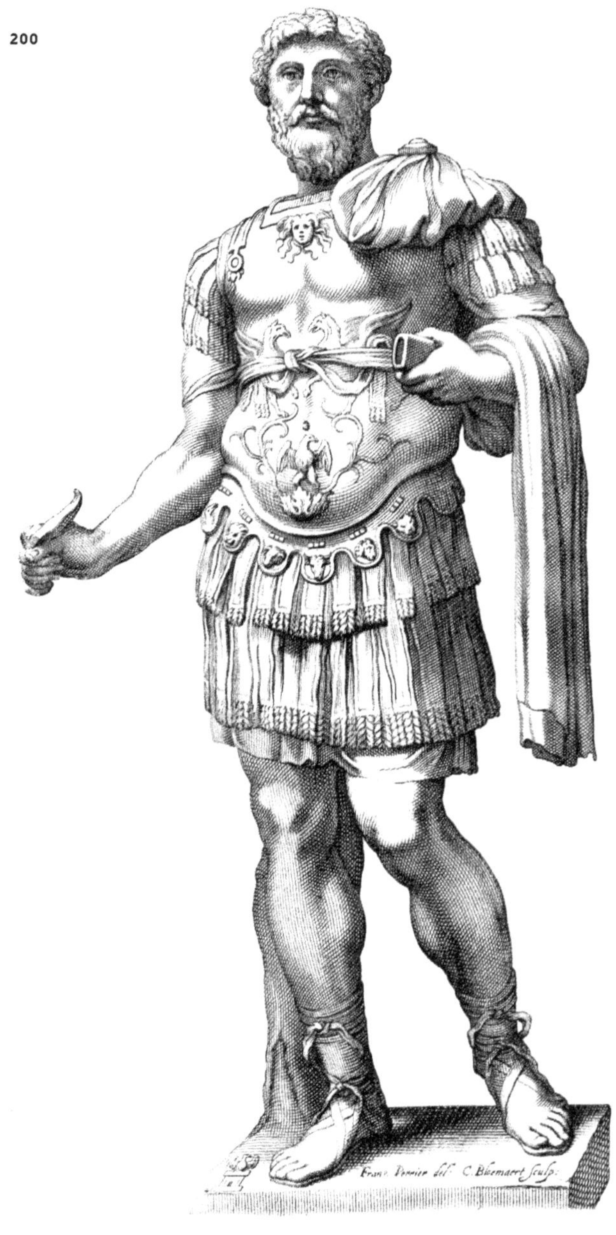

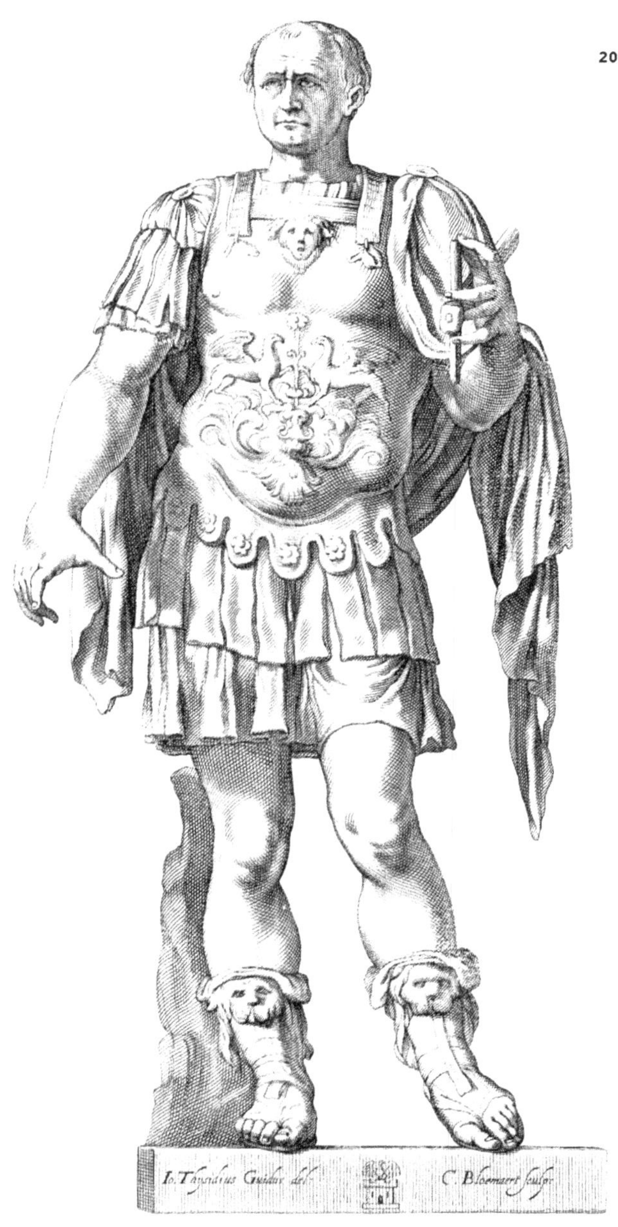

200. Statue of Emperor Marcus Aurelius, Cornelis
Bloemaert (II), 1636 – 1647.

201. Statue of Emperor Vespasian, Cornelis
Bloemaert (II), 1636 – 1647.

202

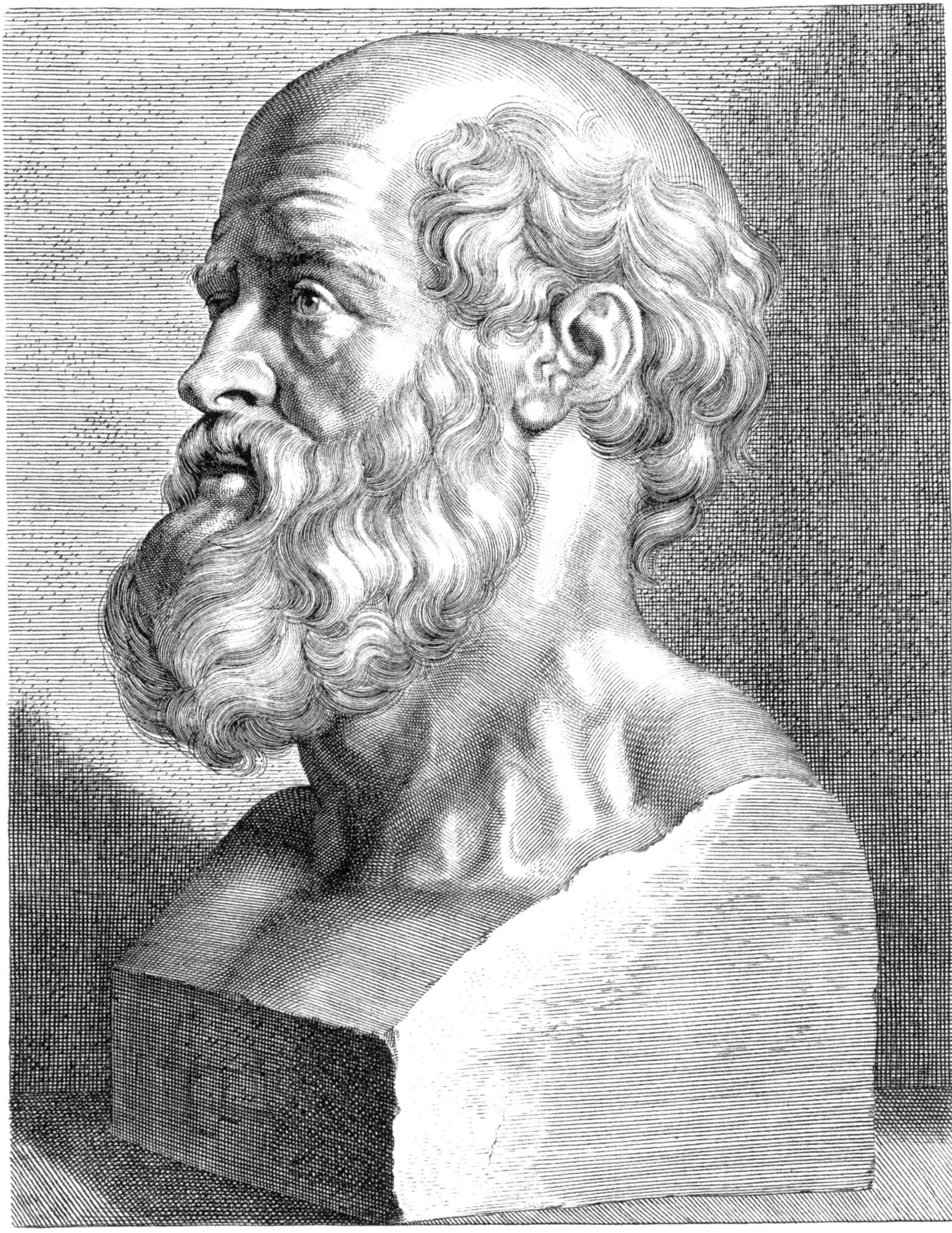

202. Antique bust of Hippocrates, Paulus
Pontius, after Peter Paul Rubens, 1638.

203

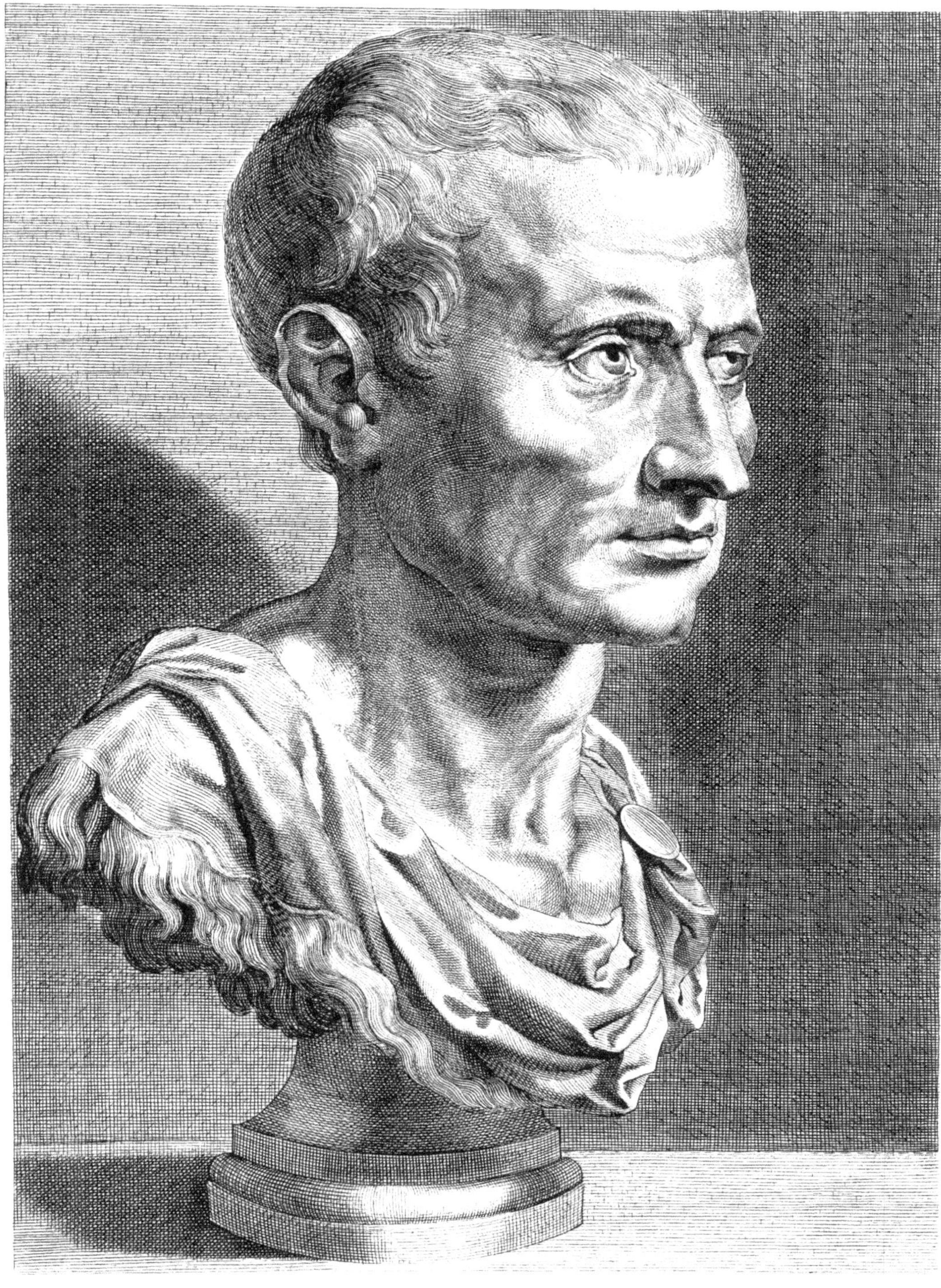

203. Bust of Marcus Tullius Cicero, Hans
Witdoeck, after Peter Paul Rubens, 1638.

204

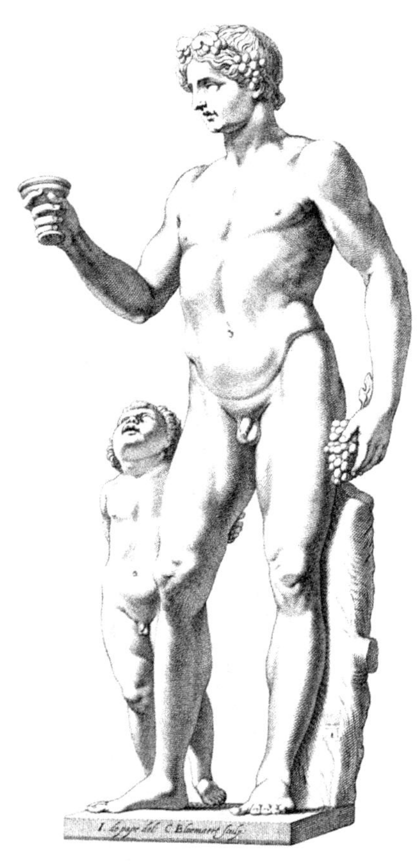

205

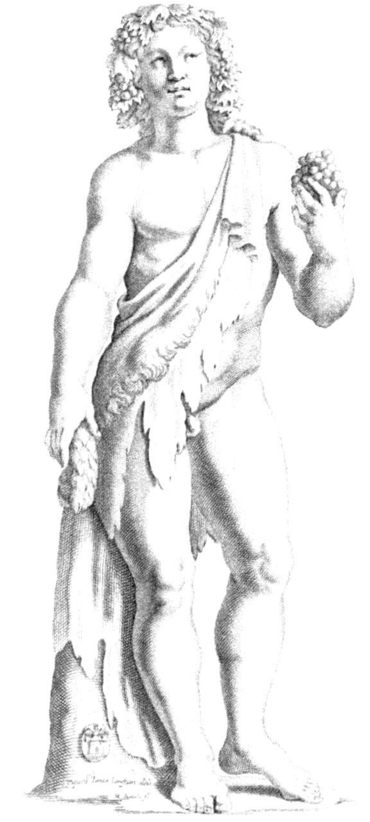

206

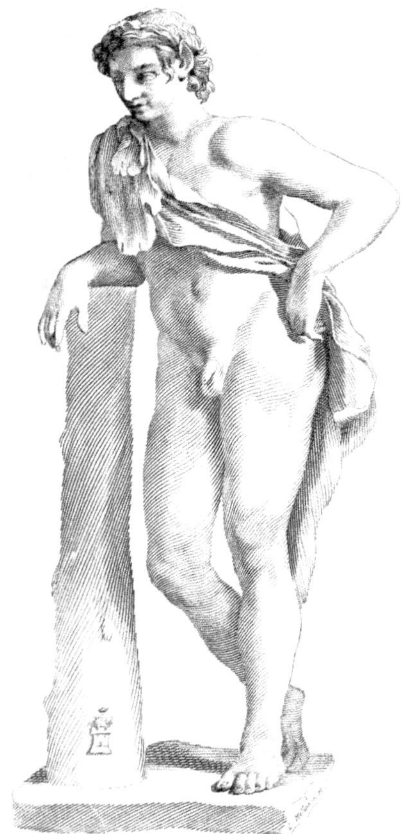

207

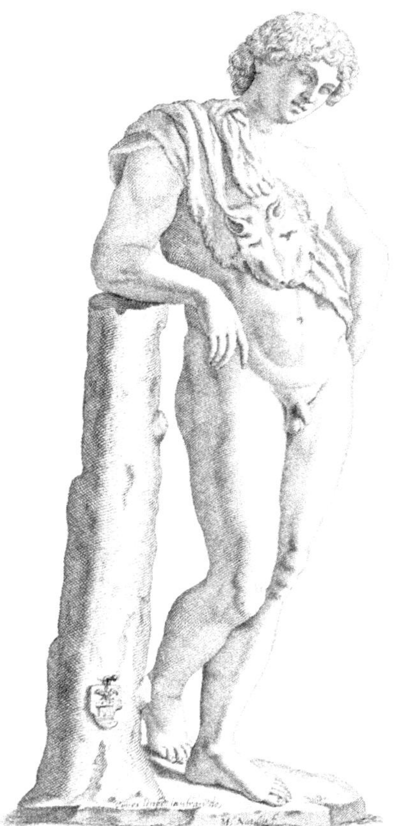

204. Statue of Bacchus with a putto, Cornelis Bloemaert (II), after Joos de Pape, 1636 – 1647.

205. Statue of Bacchus, Michel Natalis, after Giovanni Lanfranco, 1640.

206. Statue of Bacchus with Panther Skin, Michel Natalis, 1636 – 1647.

207. Statue of Bacchus with panther skin, Michel Natalis, after Giovanni Lanfranco, 1640.

208

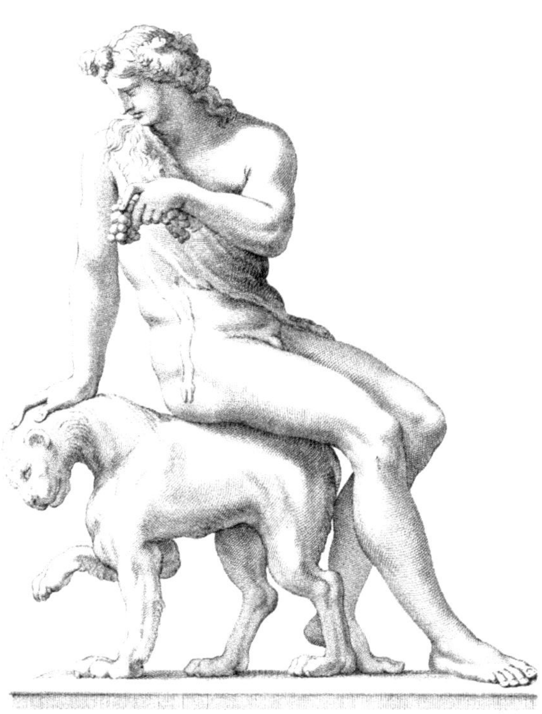

209

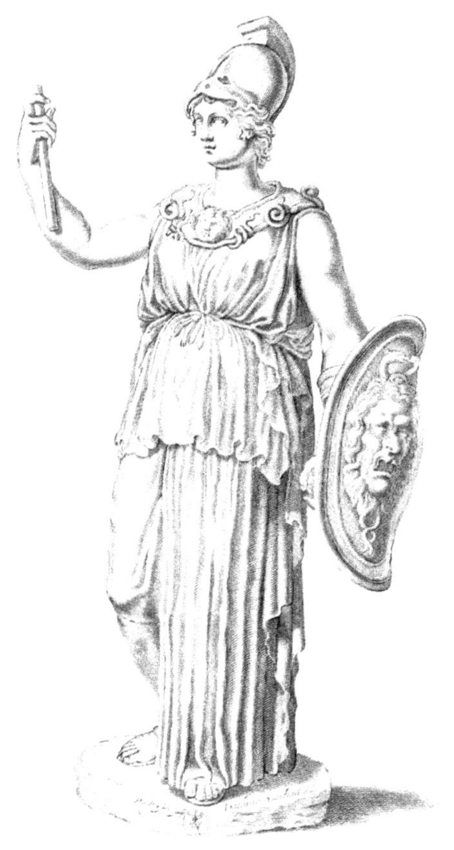

210

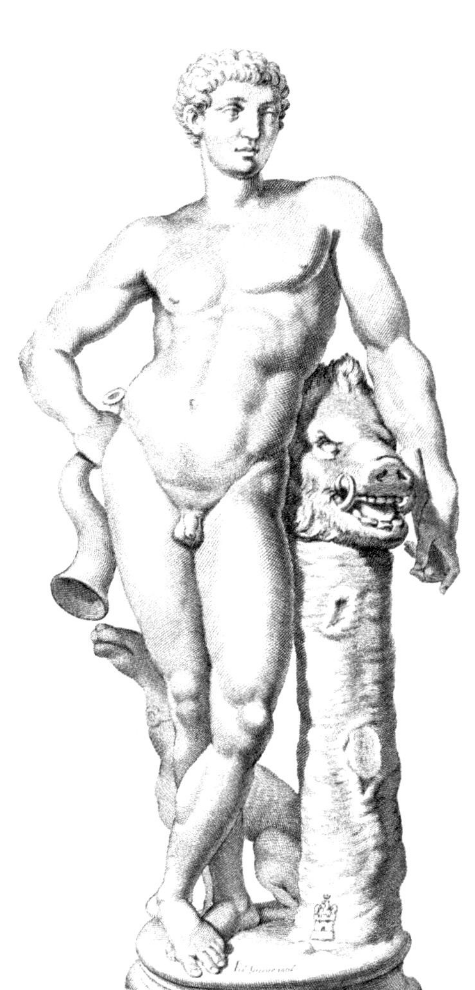

211

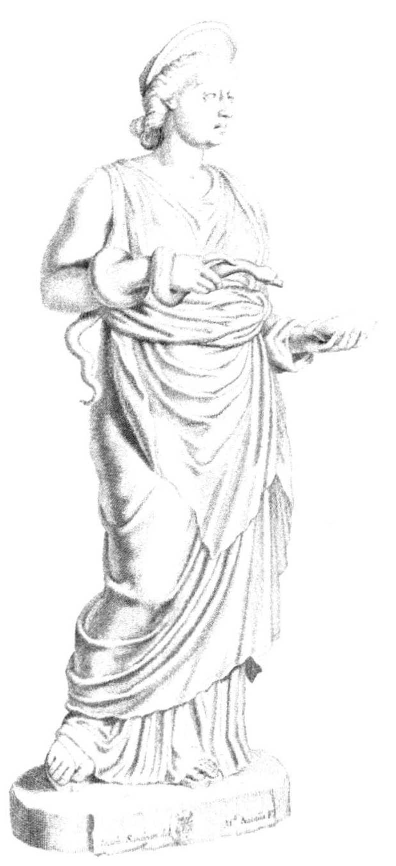

208. Statue of Bacchus on a Tiger, Cornelis
Bloemaert (II), 1636 – 1647.

209. Statue of Hygieia – Michel Natalis, after
Joachim von Sandrart (I), 1640.

210. Statue of Meleager, Johann Friedrich
Greuter, 1636 – 1647.

211. Statue of Hygieia, Michel Natalis, after
Joachim von Sandrart (I), 1640.

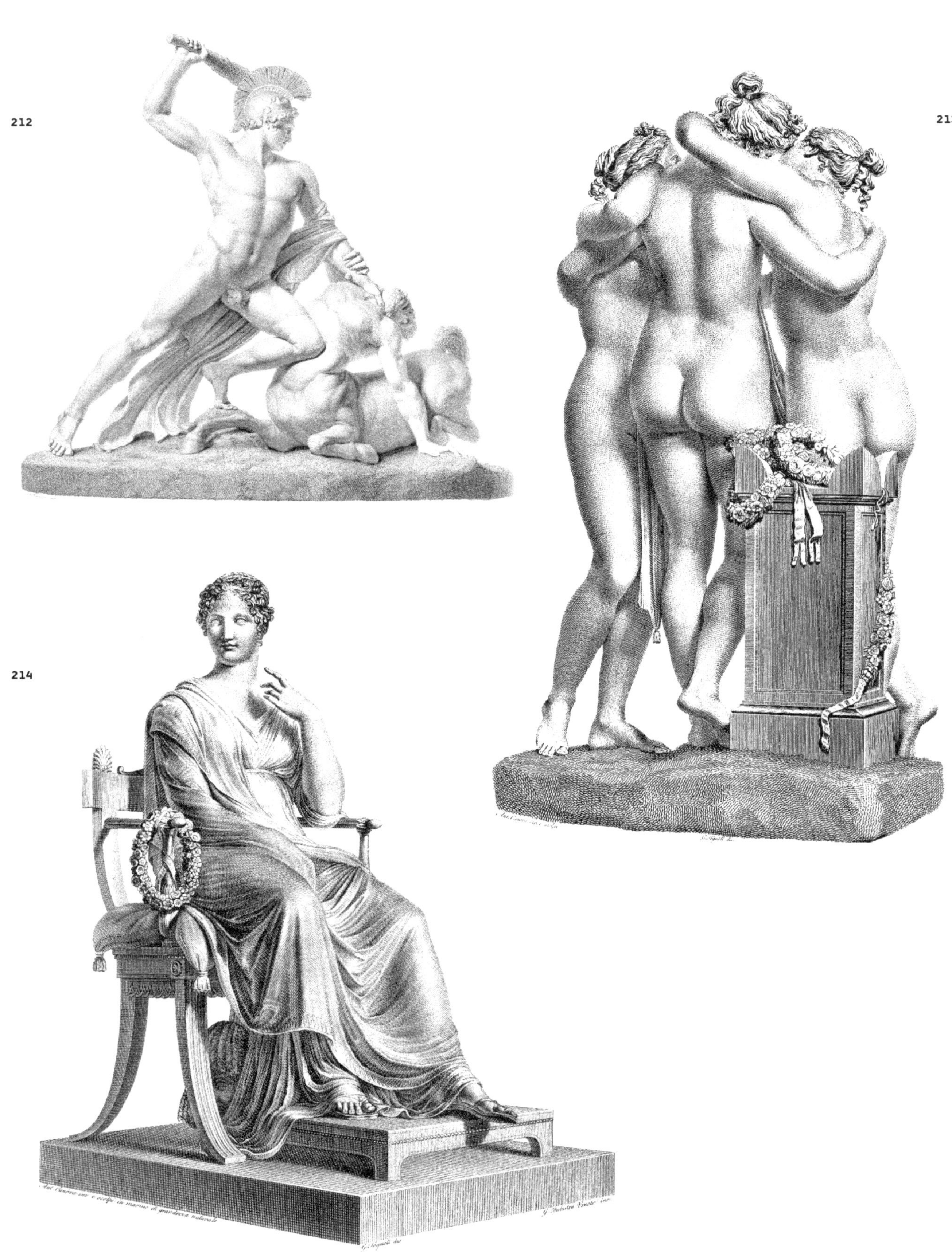

212. Theseus Conquering the Centaur, Pietro Bettelini, 1773 – 1829.

213. The Three Graces, Domenico Marchetti, 1814 – 1815.

214. Polinnia, Giovanni Balestra, after Antonio Canova, after Giovanni Tognolli, 1784 – 1842.

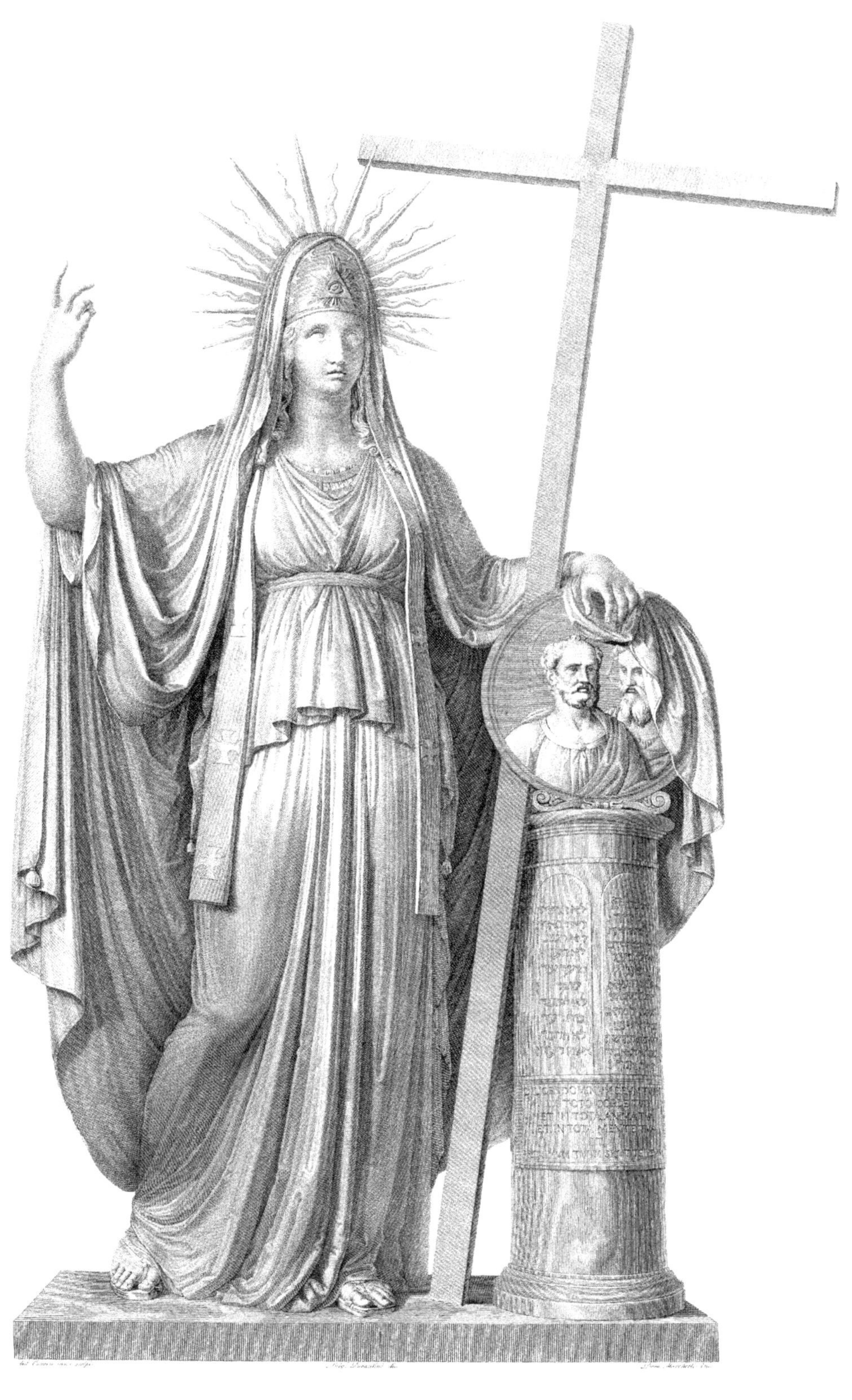

215. The Catholic Faith, Domenico Marchetti,
1790 – 1844.

216

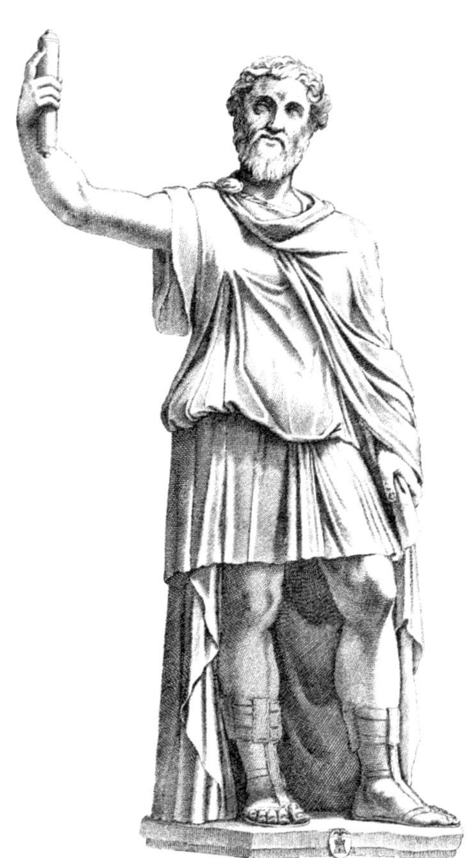

217

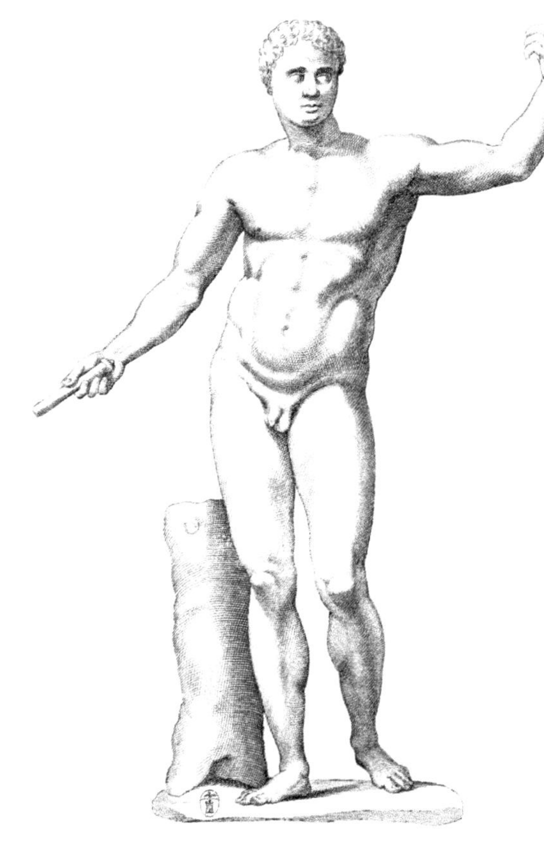

218

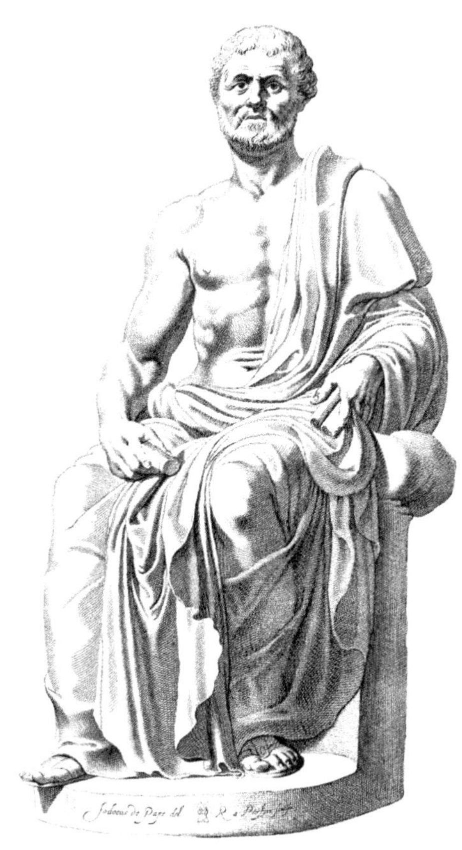

219

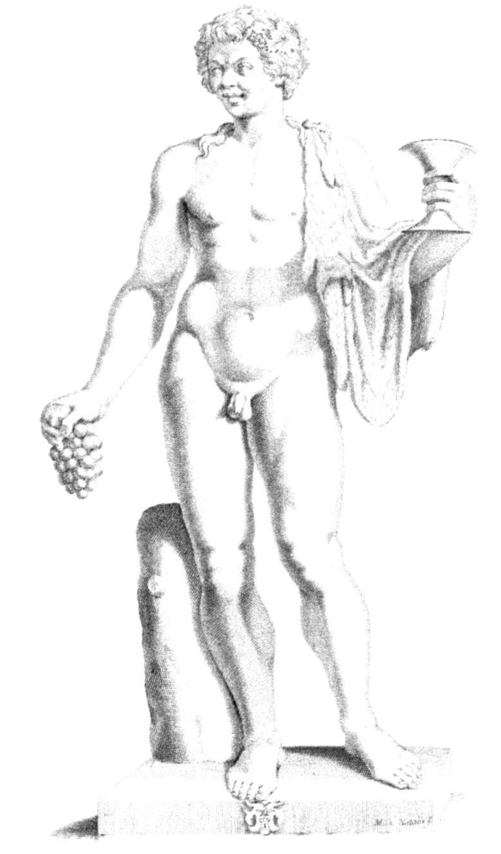

216. Statue of Emperor Septimius Severus, Luca Ciamberlano, 1636 – 1647.

217. Statue of a Naked Gladiator, Luca Ciamberlano, 1636 – 1647.

218. Statue of a Consul Seated on a Cushion, Claude Mellan, 1636 – 1647.

219. Statue of a Satyr, Michel Natalis, 1640.

220

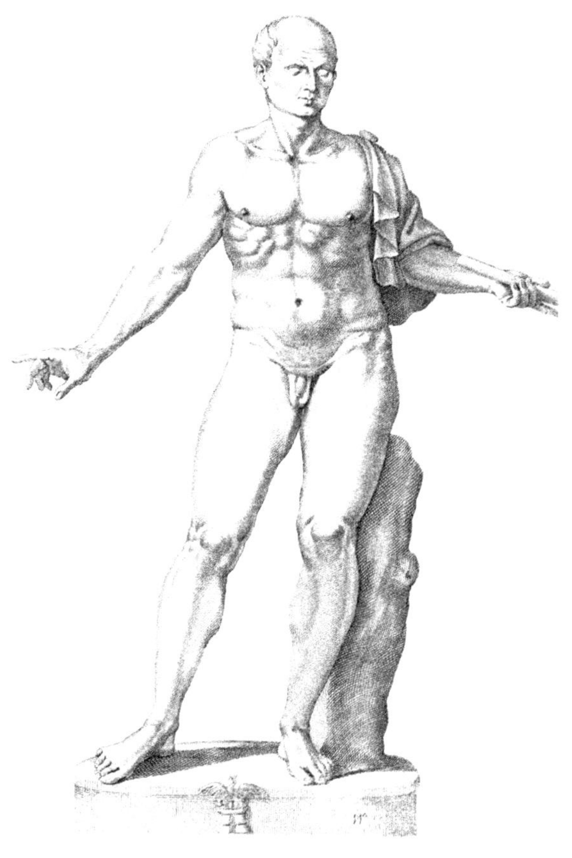

221

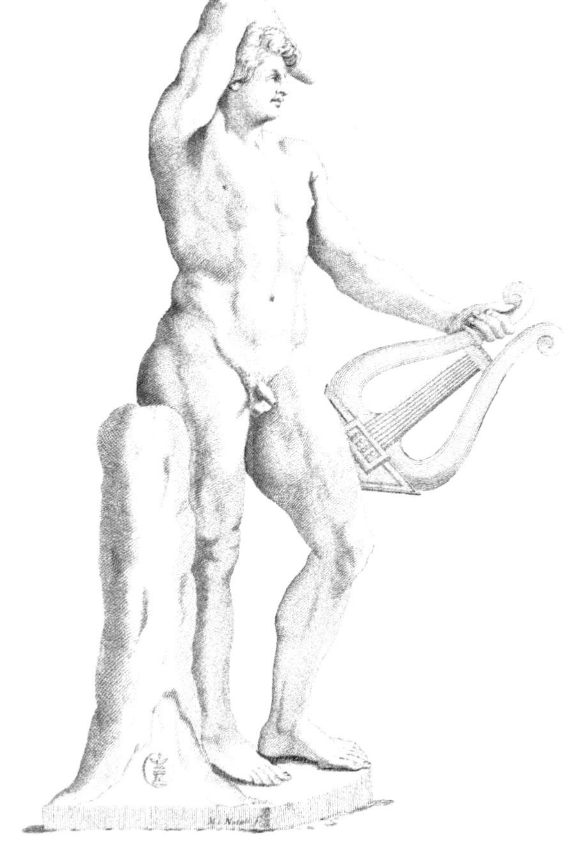

222

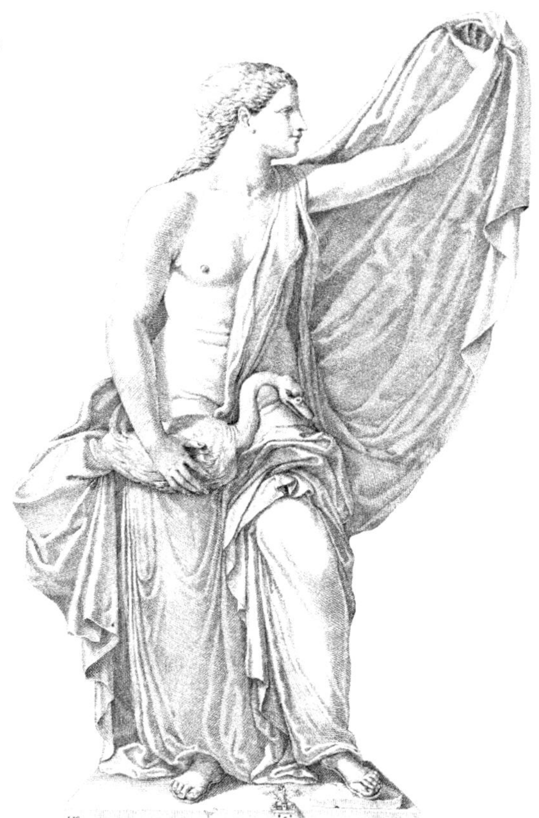

223

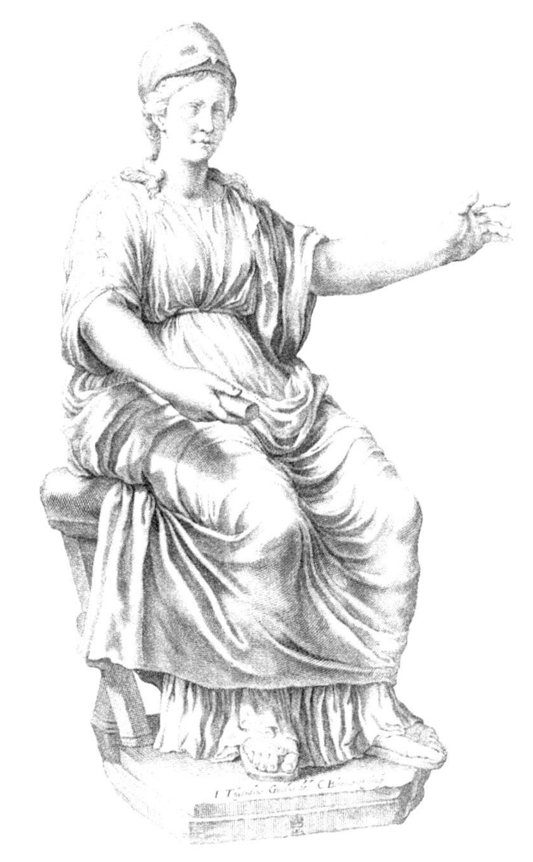

220. Statue of the Naked Julius Caesar, Giovanni Luigi Valesio, 1636 – 1647.

221. Statue of Apollo, Michel Natalis, 1640.

222. Statue of Leda and the Swan, Giovanni Luigi Valesio, 1636.

223. Statue of the Goddess Roma, Cornelis Bloemaert (II), c. 1636.

224

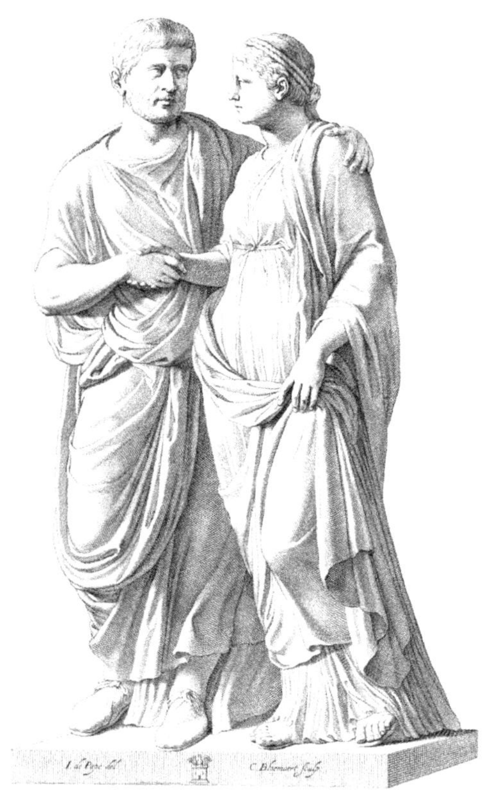

225

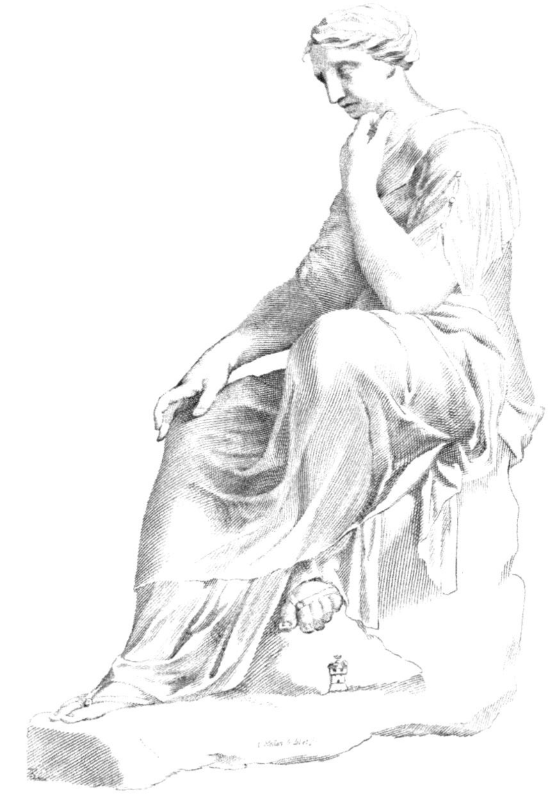

226

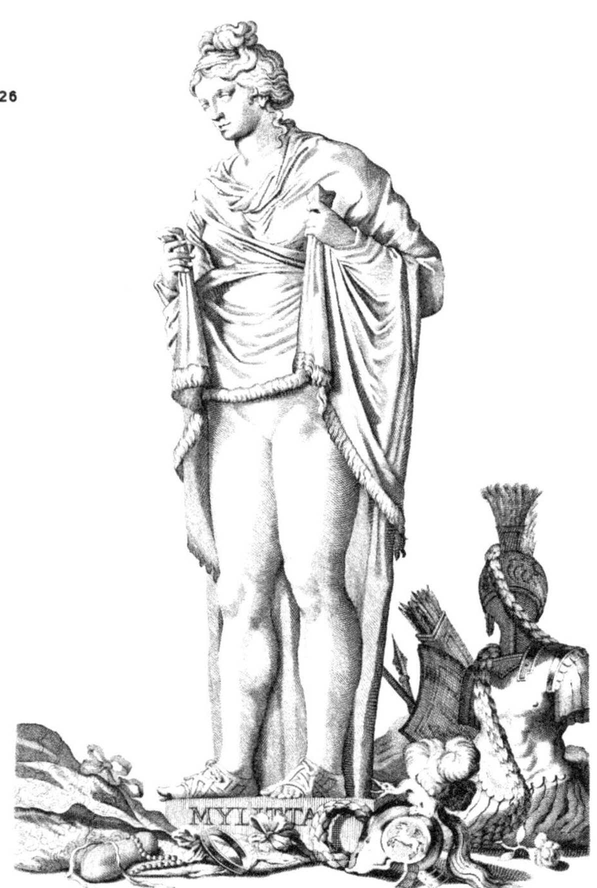

227

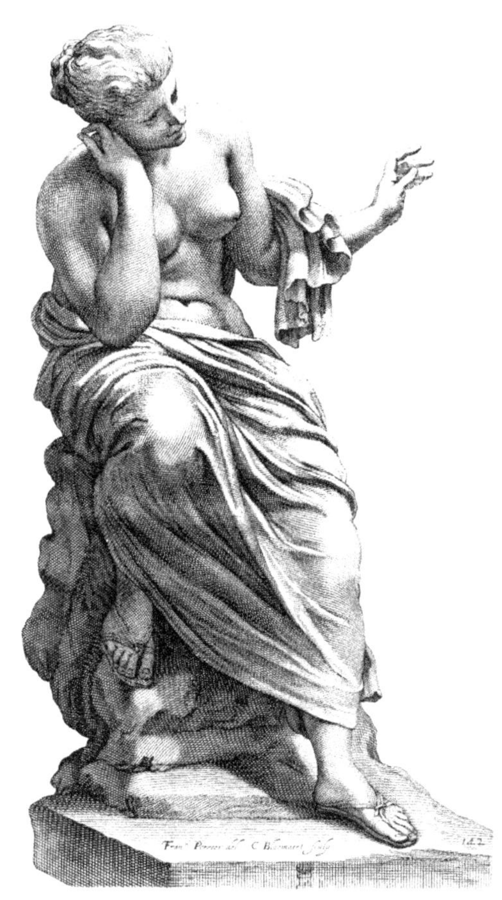

224. Statue of a Man and a Woman Holding
Hands, Cornelis Bloemaert (II), 1636 – 1647.

225. Statue of a Woman Supporting Her Head,
Claude Mellan, 1636 – 1647.

226. Statue of Mylitta, Daniel with the Tokens,
1690.

227. Statue of a seated half–naked woman,
Cornelis Bloemaert (II), 1636 – 1647.

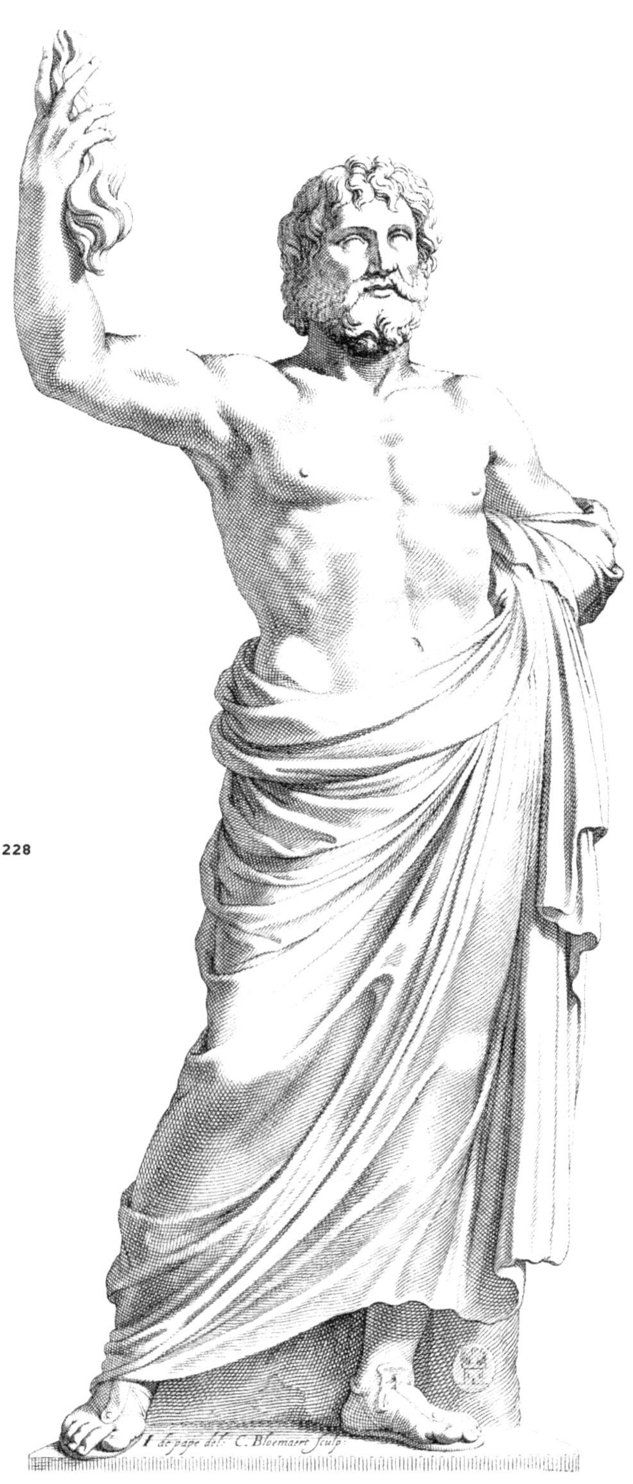

228

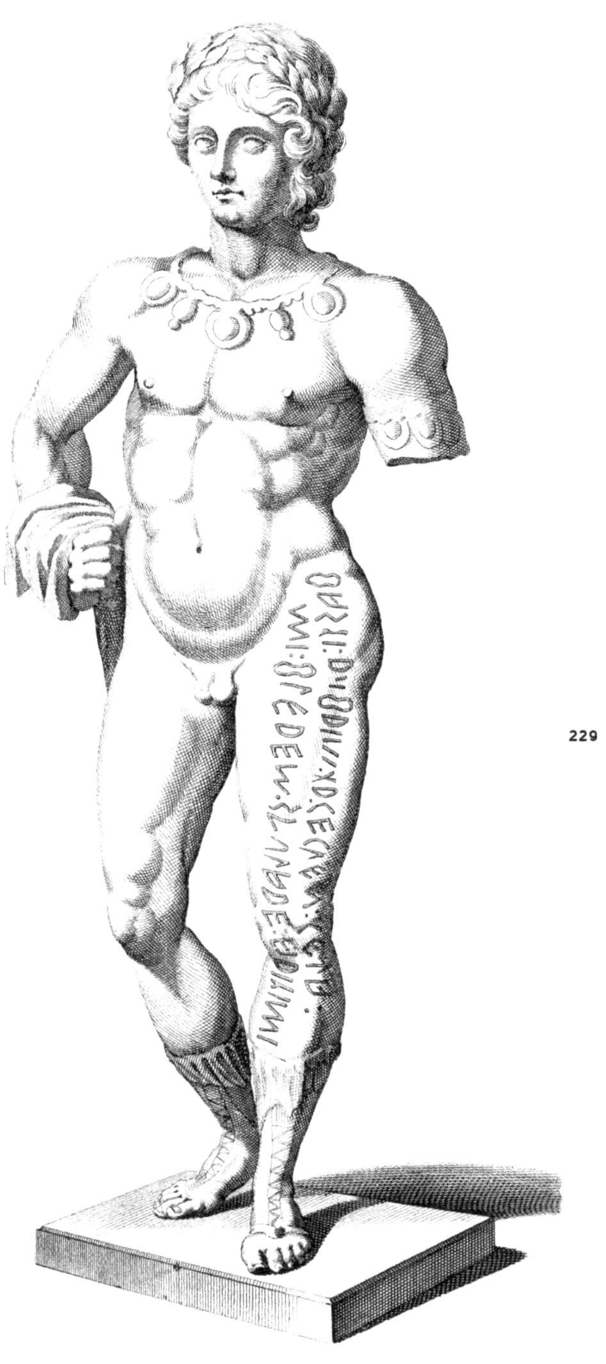

229

228. Statue of Jupiter, Cornelis Bloemaert (II),
after Joos de Pape, 1636 – 1647.

229. Statue of King Herod, Daniel with the
Pennies, after Jacob Neefs, 1690.

230

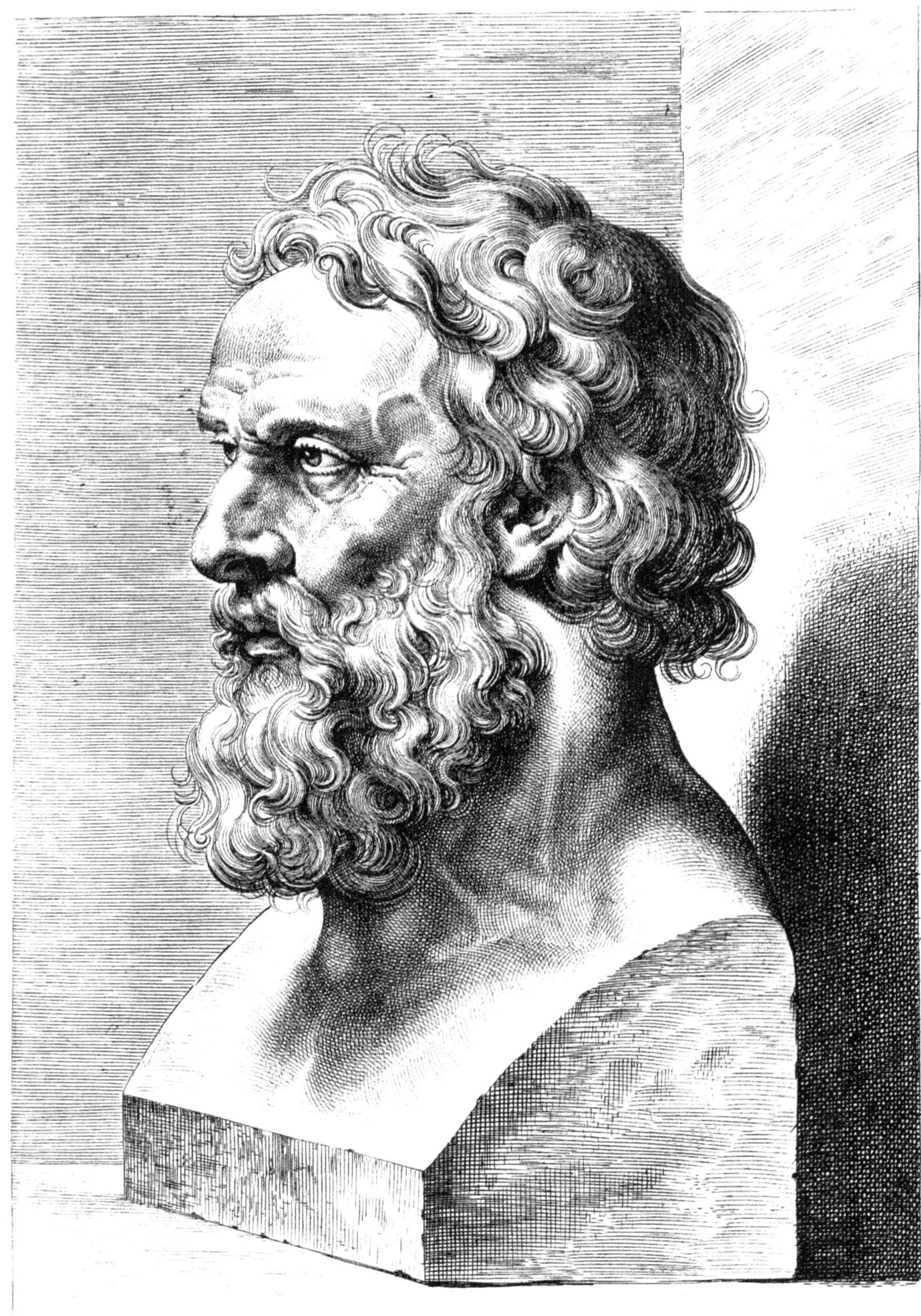

230. Bust of Plato, Lucas Vorsterman (I), after
Peter Paul Rubens, 1630 – 1638.

231

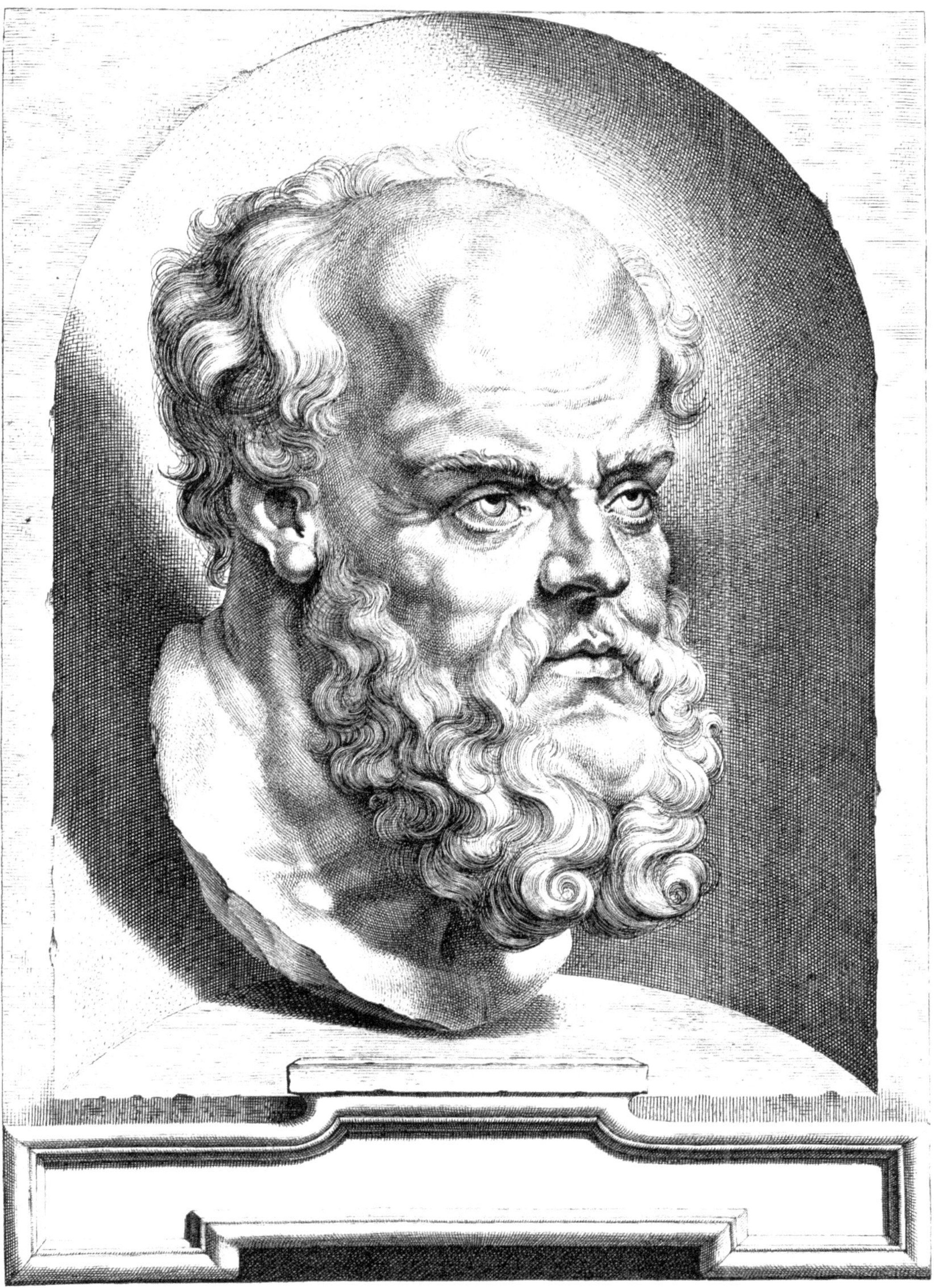

231. Antique bust of Socrates, Paulus Pontius,
after Peter Paul Rubens, 1638.

232

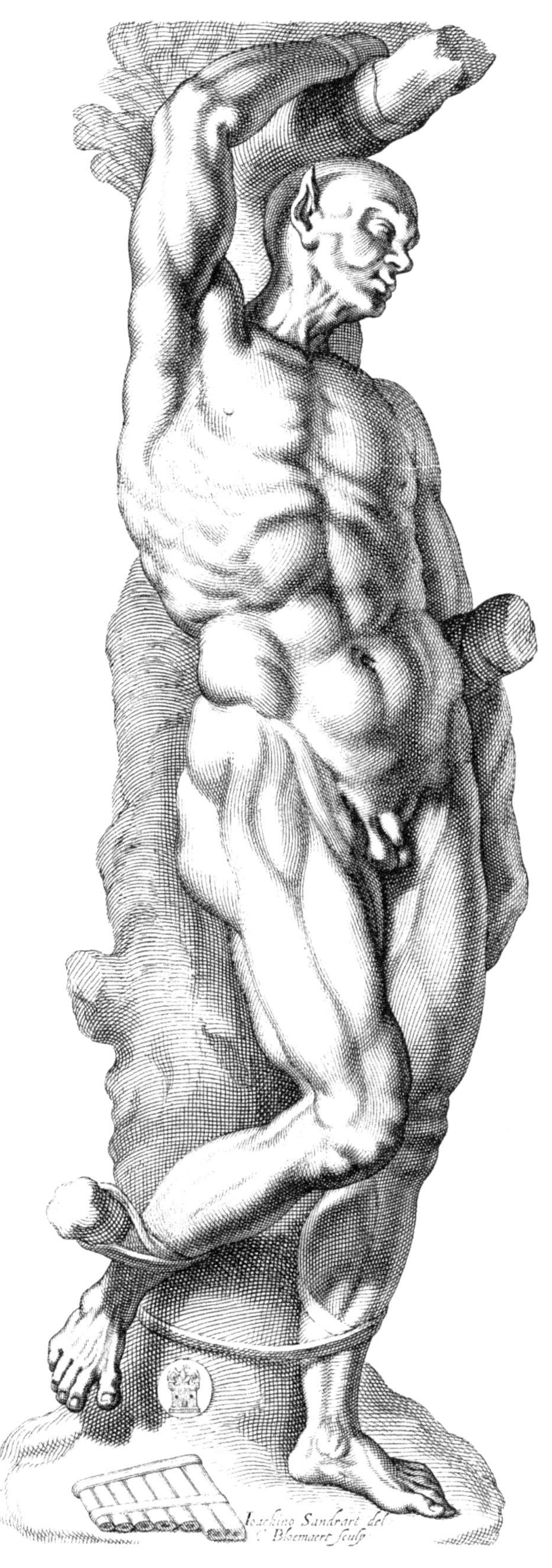

232. Statue of Marsyas, Cornelis Bloemaert (II),
after Joachim von Sandrart (I), 1636 – 1647.

235

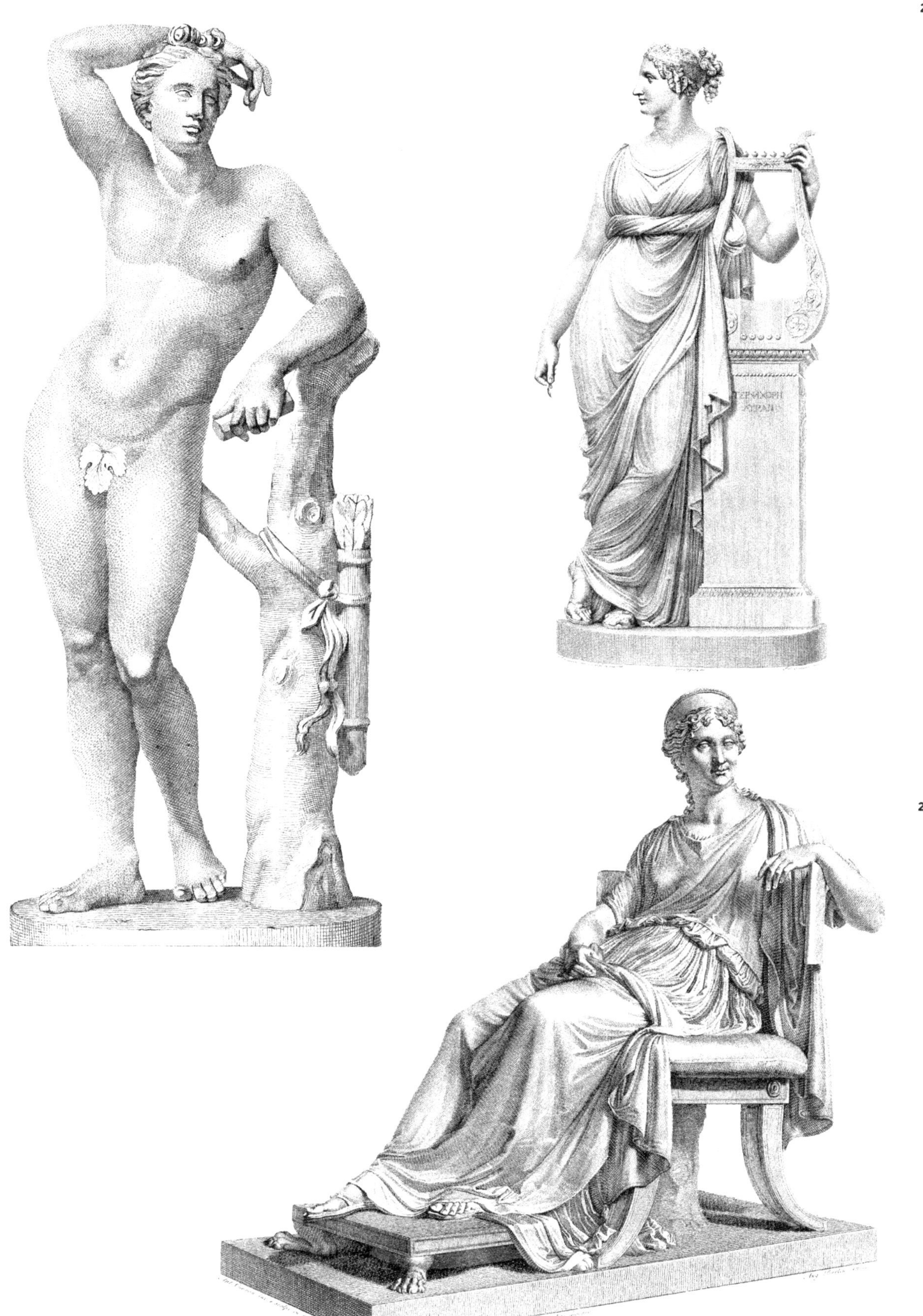

233. Statue of Apollo, Jean Théodore Joseph
Linnig, 1839.

234. Terpsichore, Pietro Fontana, after Antonio
Canova, after Giovanni Tognolli, 1816 – 1837.

235. Statue of Napoleon's Mother, Angelo Bertini,
after Luigi Durantini, 1793 – 1838.

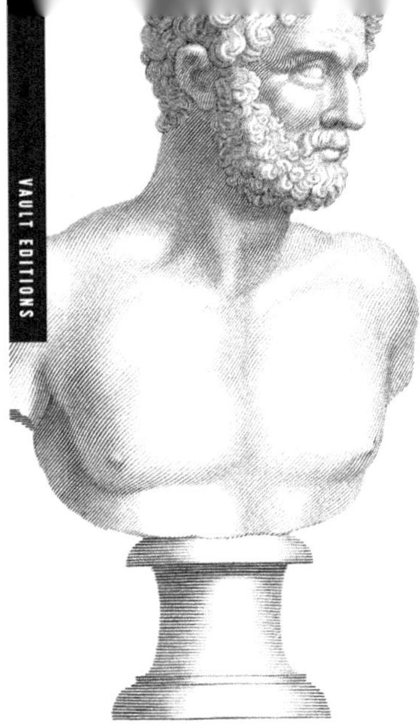

LEARN MORE

At Vault Editions, our mission is to create the world's most diverse and comprehensive collection of image archives available for artists, designers and curious minds. If you have enjoyed this book, you can find more of our titles available at vaulteditions.com.

REVIEW THIS BOOK

As a small, family-owned independent publisher, reviews help spread the word about our work. We would be incredibly grateful if you could leave an honest review of this title wherever you purchased this book.

JOIN OUR COMMUNITY

Are you a creative and curious individual? If so, you will love our community on Instagram. Every day we share bizarre and beautiful artwork ranging from 17th and 18th-century natural history and scientific illustration, to mythical beasts, ornamental designs, anatomical illustration and more. Join our community of 100K+ people today— search @vault_editions on Instagram.

DOWNLOAD YOUR FILES

STEP ONE

Enter the following web address in your web browser on a desktop computer.

www.vaulteditions.com/pages/gars

STEP TWO

Enter the following unique password to access the download page.

gar345837rtsd637215

STEP THREE

Follow the prompts to access your high-resolution files.

TECHNICAL ASSISTANCE

For all technical assistance, please email: info@vaulteditions.com

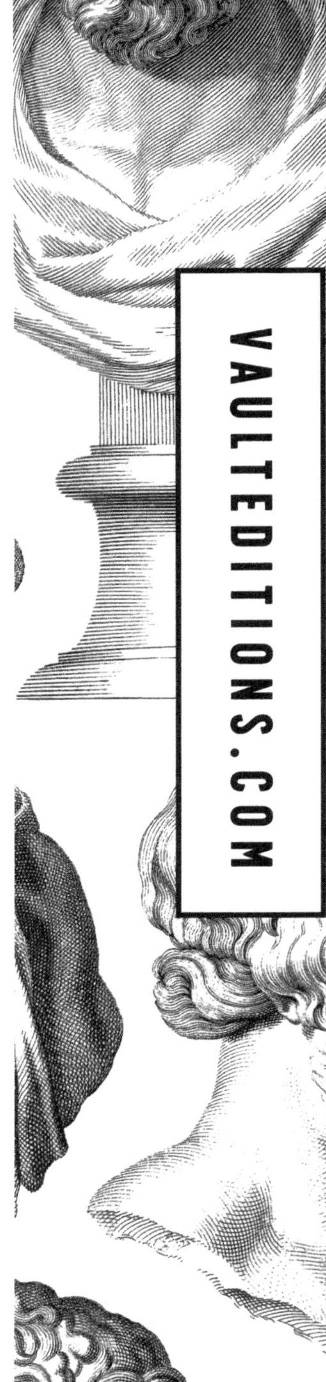

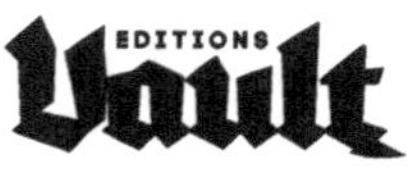

9 781925 968859